LGBT+ Issues in the United States

LGBT+ Issues in the United States

An Anthology

First Edition

Sage Alan Mauldin, M.H.R.

cognella® | ACADEMIC PUBLISHING

Bassim Hamadeh, CEO and Publisher
Angela Schultz, Acquisitions Editor
Michelle Piehl, Senior Project Editor
Alia Bales, Production Editor
Emely Villavicencio, Senior Graphic Designer
Stephanie Kohl, Licensing Coordinator
Natalie Piccotti, Director of Marketing
Kassie Graves, Vice President of Editorial
Jamie Giganti, Director of Academic Publishing

Cover image copyright © 2018 iStockphoto LP/Mixmike.

Printed in the United States of America.

ISBN: 978-1-5165-2554-6 (pbk) / 978-1-5165-2555-3 (br)

cognella® | ACADEMIC PUBLISHING

For the sexual/gender minority—
The best decision you will make in life is deciding to love yourself.

CONTENTS

PREFACE

I wrote and edited this anthology to empower and give voice to the lesbian, gay, bisexual, transgender, queer, intersex, and asexual (LGBTQIA) community—a community that continues to experience multiple forms of oppression and the evils of discrimination.

Despite the social, legal, and political advances that have been made to protect the LGBTQIA community, LGBTQIA people are still not able to live completely free of violence, prejudice, or injustice.

Even now, private organizations, anti-LGBTQIA groups, individuals, and the United States government work both overtly and covertly to strip away the rights of the LGBTQIA community.

However, from the Stonewall uprising at Stonewall Inn in New York's Greenwich Village on January 28, 1969 to the 5–4 US Supreme Court ruling on June 26, 2015 that same-sex couples have the same fundamental right as opposite-sex couples to marry, history teaches us the LGBTQIA community is resilient in times of hardship and will stop at nothing to ensure equality.

———————— ○ ————————

As I researched material for this anthology, I learned LGBTQIA people's personal, lived experiences with oppression and discrimination cannot be understood without also understanding intersectionality theory, the matrix of domination, and queer theory.

Renowned black feminist scholars Kimberlé Crenshaw and Patricia Hill Collins developed intersectionality theory and the matrix of domination, respectively; Queer Theory is heavily influenced by the work of Judith Butler, Eve Kosofsky Sedgwick, and Lauren Berlant.

Kimberlé Crenshaw's intersectionality theory argues people are disadvantaged by multiple sources of discrimination (their sexual orientation, gender identity, sex, race, age, class, national origin, genetic information, religious affiliation, and/or disability); and the marginalized aspects of a person's identity cannot be separated.

Take, for example, a disabled gay male who is black. Not only is he affected by ableism, homophobia, and racism, he is also affected by anti-black, racialized hegemonic masculinity. Here is another example: a female Muslim who is black. Not only do sexism, Islamophobia, and racism affect her, anti-black, anti-Muslim racialized misogyny affect her, as well.

One of the main concepts of Patricia Hill Collins's matrix of domination is a person may be privileged in one aspect of their identity, yet experience discrimination on the basis of other aspects of their identity.

Take, for example, an able-bodied, heterosexual, black male. While he may be privileged for his ability, sexual orientation, and sex, he is discriminated against for his race. Here is another example: a gay, white, Christian male. While he may be privileged for his race, religion, and sex, he is discriminated against for his sexual orientation. This indicates all aspects of a person's identity cannot be looked at as individual markers, but rather as a relationship.

Queer theory, which originates in gay and lesbian studies, among other schools of thought, seeks to challenge the preconceived idea that human nature is unchangeable; and argues sexuality, gender, and the qualities traditionally associated with women and men are not rigid binaries (such as heterosexuality and homosexuality; female and male; or feminine and masculine), but rather spectrums of sexualities, gender identities, and masculinities and femininities.

In addition, queer theory diverges from the biological essentialism of second-wave feminism, which claims sex is fundamental to biology. Borrowing from poststructuralist theories, queer theory argues gender is performative; in other words, gender is governed by society and culture. Examples of how gender is performed could be the way we speak, the way we act or behave, the way we dress, or the way we walk.

Queer theory forces us to think about how important and critical language is. For instance, people use sex and gender interchangeably, but they are quite different. While sex refers to biology, gender is a societal and cultural construct. Also, queer theory helps us deconstruct societal "norms" to which we cling. Not very many people know this, but male and female are merely two genders of at least 25 genders. A few other genders are pangender, androgynous, genderless, agender, intergender, and gender fluid.

I could go on and on about these theories, but I should stop here.

——————————— ○ ———————————

My hope is by reading this anthology you will gain a deeper, richer understanding of the negative effects homophobia, biphobia, and transphobia have on the LGBTQIA community, and how these negative effects, when they are compounded by racism, classism, ableism, or sexism, can (and do) result in the disempowerment and voicelessness of the LGBTQIA community in the United States.

REFERENCE

Zinn B. M., and Eitzen S. D. *In Conflict and Order: Understanding Society*. New York City, NY: Pearson, 1978.

ACKNOWLEDGMENTS

Without the tireless help of the entire team at Cognella Academic Publishing, this timely and important piece of work would have been impossible. I am especially indebted to Michelle Piehl, senior project editor, and Angela Schultz, senior field acquisitions editor, for their guidance and feedback.

I also am indebted to the Department of Human Relations at The University of Oklahoma for supporting my academic goals.

Nobody has been more important to my pursuit of academic excellence than my parents, who are a constant source of motivation, support, and inspiration, and my dearest friends (Scott and Tanner Williams, Sarah Short, and Jade Javellas) who encourage, support, and challenge me to be my best.

GLOSSARY OF TERMS

Human Rights Campaign

Many Americans refrain from talking about sexual orientation and gender expression identity because it feels taboo, or because they're afraid of saying the wrong thing. This glossary was written to help give people the words and meanings to help make conversations easier and more comfortable.

Ally—A person who is not LGBTQ but shows support for LGBTQ people and promotes equality in a variety of ways.

Asexual—The lack of a sexual attraction or desire for other people.

Biphobia—Prejudice, fear or hatred directed toward bisexual people.

Bisexual—A person emotionally, romantically or sexually attracted to more than one sex, gender or gender identity though not necessarily simultaneously, in the same way or to the same degree.

Closeted—Describes an LGBTQ person who has not disclosed their sexual orientation or gender identity.

Coming out—The process in which a person first acknowledges, accepts and appreciates his or her sexual orientation or gender identity and begins to share that with others.

Gay—A person who is emotionally, romantically or sexually attracted to members of the same gender.

Homophobia—The fear and hatred of or discomfort with people who are attracted to members of the same sex.

Lesbian—A woman who is emotionally, romantically or sexually attracted to other women.

LGBTQ—An acronym for "lesbian, gay, bisexual, transgender and queer."

Living openly—A state in which LGBTQ people are comfortably out about their sexual orientation or gender identity—where and when it feels appropriate to them.

Outing—Exposing someone's lesbian, gay, bisexual or transgender identity to others without their permission. Outing someone can have serious repercussions on employment, economic stability, personal safety or religious or family situations.

Queer—A term people often use to express fluid identities and orientations. Often used interchangeably with "LGBTQ."

Questioning—A term used to describe people who are in the process of exploring their sexual orientation or gender identity.

Same-gender loving—A term some prefer to use instead of lesbian, gay or bisexual to express attraction to and love of people of the same gender.

Selections from Human Rights Campaign, "Glossary of Terms," https://www.hrc.org/resources/glossary-of-terms. Copyright © by Human Rights Campaign. Reprinted with permission.

Sexual orientation—An inherent or immutable enduring emotional, romantic or sexual attraction to other people.

Transphobia—The fear and hatred of, or discomfort with, transgender people.

GLOSSARY OF GENDERS

Sex—Someone's assigned gender at birth on the basis of their reproductive functions.

Gender—Someone's perception of having a particular gender that may or may not be male or female.

Cisgender—Someone whose assigned gender at birth aligns with their reproductive functions.

Transgender—Someone whose assigned gender at birth does not align with their reproductive functions.

Transsexual—When someone goes through Gender Reassignment Surgery (GRS) to change the sexual reproductive functions with which they were born to align with their gender identity.

Male to Female—Someone who is assigned male at birth, but identifies as female.

Female to Male—Someone who is assigned female at birth, but identifies as male.

Binary—When male and female are at either end of the gender spectrum.

Nonbinary—When someone's gender identity is not strictly male or female and falls somewhere between male and female on the gender spectrum.

Gender fluid—Someone whose gender identity fluctuates.

Agender—Someone who does not identify with any particular gender.

Bigender—Someone who identifies with two genders (male and female).

Polygender/Multigender—Someone who identifies with three or more genders.

Neutrois—Someone who identifies as genderless, agender, and/or neither male nor female.

Gender apathetic—Someone who does not identify with—or shows no concern for—any particular gender.

Androgyne—A term used to describe someone who identifies as neither male nor female or as a gender that does not fit into the binary gender spectrum.

Intergender—Someone whose gender falls somewhere between male and female on the binary gender spectrum.

Demigender—Someone who feels they are one part a defined gender and other parts an undefined gender (demiboy, demigirl, or demigender).

Greygender—Someone with a weak gender identity.

Aporagender—Someone with a strong gender identity.

Maverique—Someone with a non-binary gender that exists beyond the social or cultural bounds of gender.

Novigender—Someone with a complex gender identity that is impossible to describe in basic terms.

Designated gender—The gender assigned at birth based on someone's sexual reproductive functions.

AFAB—Assigned Female at Birth.

AMAB—Assigned Male at Birth.

Gender presentation—The identity that someone presents as having.

Transitioning—Using medical means to change one's sex.

Fem—Someone with a gender expression that is considered more feminine.

Butch—Someone with a gender expression that is considered more masculine.

Trans Woman—Someone who was assigned a male at birth, but identifies as a woman.

Trans Man—Someone who was assigned a female at birth, but identifies as a man.

Trans Feminine—Someone who identifies as neither a man nor a woman, but identifies as feminine.

Trans Masculine—Someone who identifies as neither a man nor a woman, but identifies as masculine.

Intersex—Someone born with sexual reproductive functions that do not fit the standard definitions of male or female.

Dyadic—Someone who is not intersex.

Intergender—Someone whose gender identity is between male or female, or a combination of both.

Androgynous—someone whose gender identity is partly male and partly female.

Pangender—Someone who identifies with two or more—or all—genders.

PART I

Social Justice

CHAPTER 1

The "Treatment" of Intersex and Transgender Individuals

Eve Shapiro

T he construction of binary genders that correspond to binary sexes is a social endeavor that, while not universal, has dominated North American and European thought since the nineteenth century. Researchers have increasingly documented, however, that this model is inadequate; it does not reflect the diversity of human bodies and lives. The hegemonic sex equals gender paradigm in North American societies asserts that male and female bodies are clearly, dimorphically distinguished by chromosomes (specifically XX for females and XY for males), internal and external biology (the presence of testes or ovaries, penis or vagina), as well as by naturally corresponding secondary sex characteristics (whether breasts or an adam's apple, and the appropriate presence or absence of body hair). In this idealized model all bodies clearly fit into one, and only one, of two possible sex categories in which each individual's genetic information matches his or her genitals and those genitals are the visible key that decodes his or her sex and attendant gender (Kessler and McKenna 1978).

This two sex/two gender paradigm so strongly structures our social scripts and meaning making that even scientists describe male biological attributes and processes as aggressive, violent, and strong and female biological functions as passive, soft, and receptive (Allen 2007). In both medical and lay publications, for example, descriptions of conception typically depict sperm that compete, race, burrow, and hunt while eggs wait patiently to be inseminated. This is held as true even though a more accurate description of biological processes would cast the egg as far more active and the sperm as more receptive (Tomlinson 1995). As Anne Fausto-Sterling, a biologist who has written extensively about the social construction of sex, summarizes, "reading nature is a socio-cultural act" (Fausto-Sterling 2000). The scripts for what "normal" bodies are and the dominant paradigm for sex and gender shape what we see when we look at the human body from a scientific perspective.

Reality is much more complex, however. Fausto-Sterling estimates that between 1 and 2 percent of infants are born intersex, possessing ambiguous genetic and/or physiological sex characteristics, but many of these cases are undiagnosed until something precipitates closer inspection. For example, in 1996, eight female bodied women, classified, raised as, and identifying as women their whole lives, failed the International Olympics Committee's chromosomal testing used to prevent men from competing as women (Fausto-Sterling 2000). This technologically advanced method of verification replaced the "primitive" method of genital inspections for women athletes, which was required until 1968. Instead of clarifying the "real" sex of athletes, however, these "advanced" technological methods only muddied the waters, so much so, in fact, that the International Olympics Committee dropped genetic testing for sex in 2000. Instead it returned to a reliance on lived experience and presentation. In this case, instead of offering clarity into competitors' "true" sex, new technologies highlighted the very instability and constructed nature of sex and gender.

Human bodies are not as clearly distinct in terms of sex or gender as most think. There are more physical and mental similarities than differences between men and women, and the considerable presence of intersex bodies challenge the veracity of a bipolar model of sexed bodies. This variation is viewed as disordered, however, and doctors—and the sciences that underlie their practice—impose a binary imperative on biological variation. Until very recently, the constructed binary was so naturalized that this diversity of sexed bodies was not allowed to exist. Instead, parents of intersex infants were pushed into surgical "correction" of their children's bodies, even when the surgical intervention served no purpose whatsoever outside of the construction of clear bodily distinction between male and female.

We as a society are so invested in this binary sex system, this notion that bodies come in only two forms, male and female, that we surgically alter bodies that do not fit this model simply because they do not fit. Indeed, decisions about whether to make intersex infants male or female have as much to do with social beliefs as any biological truth. Shaped by gendered beliefs (for example men need sexual satisfaction, women do not), infants are much more likely to be "made" female, in part because medical guidelines sway surgeons away from selecting maleness unless the child will have a "large enough" penis. Simultaneously, "feminizing" surgeries often permanently destroy sexual sensation for the girl child (Allen 2007). This profound commitment to a sex/gender paradigm is a clear example of how dominant social paradigms for sex and gender inform technological intervention into and personal experiences of bodies. Only in recent years has activism on the part of intersex individuals (often through advocacy groups like Intersex Society of North America [ISNA]) begun to change the treatment of intersex infants.

ISNA has worked for many years now to educate doctors and parents about intersex conditions and to advocate for delaying surgical or hormonal intervention. Driven by their own experiences of dishonesty on the part of parents and doctors, surgeries that scarred their bodies and removed pleasure (often surgeries on intersex children result in the loss of sexual sensation or function), and gender identities mismatched to their surgically assigned sex, intersex activists have protested, advocated, and fought for new treatment protocols. Most significantly, activists have argued that medically unnecessary treatment should be delayed until intersex children develop their own gendered sense of self and can participate in the decision-making.

And they have been reasonably successful; increasingly hospitals have intersex advocates on call so that when intersex children are born an advocate can come in alongside doctors to offer support and counseling. In the past parents were pushed by doctors to make quick decisions about treatment, often without access to any information about intersexuality in general or their child's condition more specifically. Now, the increased access to information and support has resulted in more parents choosing to delay or refuse surgical intervention. ISNA's work is just a fraction of what must be done to refashion our sex/gender paradigm in line with the diversity of human bodies, however.

Why might we as a society reinforce a two-sex system even though evidence supports a more diverse conceptualization of sex? Answers to this question reveal a lot about the power of sex and gender as a social institution. To begin with, our social order is based around two sexes: marriage laws and norms assume only men and women; buildings are required to have single-sex male and female bathrooms and locker rooms but not private or unisex ones; schools and organizations divide individuals by male/

female; and official forms all offer only two distinct sex-categories. The binary sex/gender paradigm works interactively with other social institutions such as marriage, medicine, education, and sport to structure and direct our society, bodies, and identities. In this binary system, non-conforming bodies must be "disciplined," as Foucault would say, into place by available technologies of power. Although this discipline does not work perfectly, these societal forces are so powerful that diverse bodies are forced to conform, at least on the surface. As a consequence, the social invisibility of intersex contributes to the naturalized belief in a binary gender model.

As social context shifts and communities advocate for change, these same technologies can be used in new and non-normative ways. Groups like ISNA have been increasingly successful in changing how intersex infants are treated at birth, counseling parents to leave them to develop their own gender identities and then decide whether to avail themselves of any available technological interventions later in life. In many cases, intersex individuals are now choosing to leave their bodies as they are, and in the process are manifesting new sexed bodies. Meanwhile, transsexual and gender non-conforming individuals are also using the same technologies to intentionally construct differently gendered and sexed bodies.

In response to changes in societal gender paradigms and scripts, brought on by transgender and intersex activism, medical gate keepers such as psychiatrists and surgeons are slowly relaxing medical barriers to breast and genital (re)construction surgery. These changes are creating a diverse array of gendered and sexed bodies as individuals may solicit some but not all sexed/gendered bodily modifications. For example, an individual may choose to have breast augmentation or reduction ("top" surgery), genital (or "bottom") surgery, hormones, a combination of these biomedical interventions, or none of them.

Based on evidence discussed [...], it will come as little surprise to discover that rates of surgery, hormone use, and cross-gender dress and bodily comportment vary dramatically across racial, economic, geographic, and sexual communities. We can begin to understand why hormone use dominates transsexual treatment in North America, for example (as opposed to primary reliance on hair removal or transplant, social role changes, or dress), by examining dominant paradigms of sex and gender and paying close attention to the central role of hormones in defining sex, the need for distinct physical sex characteristics, and the naturalization of gender (Fausto-Sterling 2000). The United States and Canada have legislated the validity of these types of differences—but not others—by requiring irreversible bodily changes in order to legally change one's gender status on official documents like driver's licenses, birth certificates, and bank records. While the requirements vary by state, those states that do allow changes in legal status tend to require significant bodily transformations as opposed to less invasive ones like a change in personal identity or social role. This is one of many reasons that transgender women and men with class privilege in North America are more able to gain recognition for their chosen identities than poor individuals; the ability to deploy legitimized gender change scripts requires the financial and social capital to afford the required transformations.

The set of surgical procedures aimed at changing an individual's body to match a gender identity have traditionally been called sex-reassignment surgery (and before that sex-change surgery). In recent years, however, as the transgender movement has grown and activists have received more attention, this term has fallen into disfavor by some. Some activists argue that they are not changing their gender or sex, but rather correcting the alignment between their body and their internal sense of self. Many of these individuals have come to use the terminology "gender confirmation surgery" to reflect these beliefs. Similarly, some transgender individuals bristle at the term "gender identity disorder," claiming that their gender—their internal sense of self—has never changed, that only their ability to manifest this self by having their body match it has (Bryant 2008; Waszkiewicz 2006).

As this debate plays out in media and press materials, in transgender activist and organizational statements, and among scholars and medical professionals, it is clear that the debate is really about sex and gender ideologies. These new technologies and attendant new scripts for what gender individuals can be are challenging the gender paradigms utilized to structure the dominant sex/gender system. If power is the ability to have one's own knowledge count as true, then this debate reflects the growing power of transgender individuals and communities to set the terms of their own lives, in the face of hegemonic gender paradigms, and the medical institutions empowered to maintain this system. In response to this diversity it is likely we will see more shifts in hegemonic paradigms and sex/gender scripts.

Debates over sex and gender identity reflect how language and attendant explanations for gender non-conformity change alongside ever-broadening gendered and sexed selves. Shifts in dominant gender and transgender paradigms have allowed for more diverse gender and sex scripts, and in turn individuals have advocated for visibility, support, and somatechnic interventions in line with these scripts. In the past, medical gate keeping was routinely used to police transgender body work by demanding that after gender/sex changes people live in line with hegemonic gender and sexuality scripts. Now, however, increasing numbers of endocrinologists and surgeons are willing to perform surgery or prescribe hormones even when individuals do not match heteronormative identity scripts, something that was highly unlikely only ten years ago. As these doctors allow the expansion of appropriate discourses-in-practice, there is less pressure on individuals to construct their own narratives within prescribed boundaries; at the same time the language of gender itself is broader and more readily available. Whereas most individuals identified as transsexual or transgender in the past, contemporary surveys find a multitude of gender non-conforming identities including genderqueer, bi-gender, and androgene (Beemyn and Rankin 2011).

These differences are also generational, which suggests that younger transgender individuals are constructing identities and coming out with very different gender paradigms, social scripts, and technologies at their disposal. For example, young transgender individuals are significantly more likely to claim a diversity of gender nonconforming identities. As Rey, a young female-to-male transgender college student, commented in a 2008 *New York Times Magazine* article,

> Some transmen want to be seen as men—they want to be accepted as born men . . . I want to be accepted as a transman—my brain is not gendered. There's this crazy binary that's built into all of life, that there are just two genders that are acceptable. I don't want to have to fit into that.

> (Quart 2008: 37)

Moreover, there is a strong correlation between age and when individuals report meeting another transgender person for the first time (and presumably when they came to know about transgenderism and gain exposure to transgender identity and body scripts). In Beemyn and Rankin's National U.S. study, 76 percent of individuals under 22 years old had met another transgender individual by the age of 19, while only 32 percent of individuals had between the ages of 23 and 32, and only 5 percent of people 63 years old and older had. That is, the lower the age-cohort a person is in, the more likely they are to have met a transgender person at a young age. In the same study, Beemyn and Rankin found that 27 percent of individuals age 63 or older were totally closeted about their transgender status, while only 10 percent of individuals 22 or younger were, and only 9 percent of people age 23–32 were. Similarly, 34 percent of individuals age 23–32 described themselves as out to all their friends, while only 17 percent of people 63 and over were (other age groups ranged between 26 percent and 30 percent) (Beemyn and Rankin 2011). These statistics alone do not imply any causality; however, this data suggests that who people think they can be, and how able they are to manifest that identity in their body are changing significantly and these changes have everything to do with shifting gender paradigms and social identity and body scripts (Grossman and D'Augelli 2006).

While there has been positive change, it is important not to romanticize transgender lives or choices without grounding them within the lived reality of transgender people. Rey experienced significant levels of harassment and institutional resistance that caused him to move out of the dormitories at Barnard and even take a leave of absence from college. Rates of violence for transgender youth are significantly higher than for their cisgender peers, as are rates of poverty and homelessness (Namaste 2006; Shilling 2008). Some studies report that 60 percent of transgender youth experience physical violence (Moran and Sharpe 2004). Researchers also find that lack of social support from family, GLBT peers, teachers, and school administrators leads transgender youth to disproportionately high rates of suicidal thoughts, loneliness, and homelessness (Pardo 2008; Pardo and Schantz 2008). Moreover, class and race both affect outcomes for young people and adults, and transgender people of color experience more violence, higher rates of homelessness, and lower social status than their White peers do (Xavier et al. 2005).

Social change continues to be a slow process. Transgender social movements have brought transgender advocacy into the public sphere, and gender scholars across a variety of disciplines have documented the complexity of gender and the inadequacy of binary sex/gender systems. However, hegemonic paradigms and scripts have not yet caught up and gender non-conformity remains pathologized. That said, even though transgender individuals face tremendous discrimination and prejudice, transgender youth are more visible and more accepted now than at any other time in modern Western history (Beemyn and Rankin 2011). As individuals live in more complex bodies and with more diverse gender identities, these paradigms will likely continue to loosen, and social gender scripts will likely expand. The biomedical technologies being used to produce embodied gender differently will slowly shape public knowledge and discourse about gender and gender non-conformity.

REFERENCES

Allen, Caitilyn. 2007. "It's a Boy! Gender Expectations Intrude on the Study of Sex Determination." *DNA and Cell Biology* 26(10): 699–705.

Beemyn, Brett-Genny, and Susan Rankin. 2011. *Understanding Transgender Lives.* New York, NY: Columbia University Press.

Bryant, Karl. 2008. "In Defense of Gay Children? 'Progay' Homophobia and the Production of Homonormativity." *Sexualities* 11(4): 455–75.

Fausto-Sterling, Anne. 2000. *Sexing the Body: Gender Politics and the Construction of Sexuality.* New York, NY: Basic Books.

Grossman, Arnold H., and Anthony R. D'Augelli. 2006. "Transgender Youth: Invisible and Vulnerable." *Journal of Homosexuality* 51(1): 111–28.

Kessler, Suzanne J., and Wendy McKenna. 1978. *Gender: An Ethnomethodological Approach.* Chicago, IL: University of Chicago Press.

Moran, Leslie J., and Andrew Sharpe. 2004. "Violence, Identity and Policing: The Case of Violence against Transgender

People." *Criminal Justice* 1(1): 395–417

Namaste, Viviane K. 2006. "Genderbashing: Sexuality, Gender, and the Regulation of Public Space." Pp. 584–600 in *The Transgender Studies Reader*, eds. Susan Stryker and Stephen Whittle. London: CRC Press.

Pardo, Seth T. 2008. "Growing Up Transgender: Research and Theory." *ACT for (Trans) Youth, Part 1*. New York, NY: Cornell University.

Pardo, Seth T. and Karen Schantz. 2008. "Growing Up Transgender: Safety and Resilience." *ACT for (Trans) Youth, Part 2*. New York, NY: Cornell University.

Quart, Alissa. 2008. "When Girls Will be Boys." *New York Times Magazine*, March 16, pp. 32–37.

Shilling, Chris. 2008. *Changing Bodies: Habit, Crisis and Creativity*. Thousand Oaks, CA: Sage Publications Ltd.

Tomlinson, Barbara. 1995. "Phallic Fables and Spermatic Romance: Disciplinary Crossing and Textual Ridicule." *Configurations* 3(2): 105–34.

Waszkiewicz, Elroi. 2006. "Getting by Gatekeepers: Transmen's Dialectical Negotiations within Psychomedical Institutions." Master's Thesis, Georgia State University, Atlanta, GA.

Xavier, Jessica M., Marilyn Bobbin, Ben Singer, and Earline Budd. 2005. "A Needs Assessment of Transgendered People of Color Living in Washington, DC." pp. 31–47 in *Transgender Health and HIV Prevention: Needs Assessment Studies from Transgender Communities across the United States*, eds. Walter Bockting and Eric Avery. New York, NY: Haworth Medical Press.

———————— o ————————

END OF CHAPTER QUESTIONS

1. Define "sex" and "gender." What is the difference between them?
2. Is genetic testing for sex in the Olympics and other sports competitions necessary?
3. In what ways is the binary gender system challenged by intersex and transgender individuals?

Creating Inclusive Schools for Gay, Bisexual, Lesbian, Transgender, and Queer/ Questioning (GBLTQ) Students

Applying a Social Justice Framework

James Thing and M.C. Kate Esposito

Educators most frequently use the term "inclusion" to refer to a philosophical instantiation of teaching students with disabilities in the same classroom setting and curriculum as their peers who do not have disabilities (Hallahan, Kauffman, & Pullen, 2015). Although the term stems from a specific educational context—that of the education of students with disabilities—it is not outside the larger geopolitical context in which schools operate. For example, Udvari-Solvner (1997) noted that inclusion necessitates a critique of contemporary school cultures that results in the realization of more just, humane, and democratic communities. As part of a larger social justice-based effort aimed at alleviating inequalities within the educational system, and to make the system more responsive to all students, lesbian, gay, bisexual, transgender, and queer/questioning (LGBTQ) activists and allies have for the past three decades advocated for the inclusion of LGBTQ students (e.g., Uribe, 1994). In short, inclusive school environments bring inequities in treatment and opportunity to the forefront so that differences are valued and respected (Udvari-Solvner, 1997). From this perspective, inclusion is concerned with *all* students—especially those who are marginalized (Artiles, Kozleski, Dorn, & Christensen, 2006)—and is situated in a social justice framework (Artiles, Bal, & King Thorius, 2010) that can be applied to any marginalized population within educational settings. For the purpose of this chapter, these authors define social justice within the context of the educational system as a "critique of educational systems in terms of access, power, and privilege based on race, culture, gender, sexual orientation, language, background, ability and/or socioeconomic position" (Brown, 2004, pp. 79–80).

INCLUSION AS A CALL TO INTERROGATE EXISTING EDUCATIONAL REALITIES

One of the most marginalized populations within society and the educational system are students who are lesbian, gay, bisexual, transgendered, or queer/questioning (LGBTQ). Researchers consistently conclude that sexual minority youth (SMY)—those who do not identify as heterosexual—are at increased risk for peer rejection, limited school support, and verbal and physical attacks within school settings (Kosciw, Greytak, Bartkiewicz, Boesen, & Palmer, 2012). Academically, LGBTQ youth are at higher risk for underachievement, absenteeism, diminished educational aspirations, and leaving high school early (Satcher & Schumacker, 2009). It is clear that interrogating the school system with an "inclusionary lens" steeped within a social justice framework is necessary if SMY are to be truly "included" in the educational system and thus have the opportunity to reach their full potential.

As such, this chapter will review the current research specific to academic and social realities for LGBTQ students in secondary academic settings, discuss how the application of a social justice framework will help ensure that schools do not perpetuate the marginalization of SMY, and discuss specific strategies educators can implement to provide inclusive, safe schools for all students. Furthermore, this chapter will add to the extant literature examining strategies for providing inclusive schools to all of our students, especially those who have been historically, systematically, and structurally excluded. Given the paucity of literature specific to the application of a social justice framework to meet the needs of SMY (Hernandez & Fraynd, 2014), this chapter further seeks to provide a framework from which to operate when seeking to mitigate the harsh realities LGBTQ students—youth and young adults—experience in school settings.

Schools as Danger Zones

Secondary schools (middle and high schools) are very often unwelcoming environments for LGBTQ youth (Bidell, 2011; Kosciw et al., 2012; Mahdi, Jevertson, Schrader, Nelson, & Ramos, 2014). Schools have been characterized as "hostile environments for a distressing number of LGBTQ students, the overwhelming majority of whom hear homophobic remarks and experience harassment or assault . . . because of their sexual orientation or gender expression" (Kosciw et al., 2012, p. 5). For example, recent data from the 2011 GLSEN national school climate survey (Kosciw et al., 2012) indicated that 81% of LGBTQ secondary students experienced verbal harassment (e.g., being called names or being threatened), and 38.3% SYM reported physical harassment (e.g., being shoved) in the previous academic year. Verbal and physical bullying of LGBTQ students can cause emotional, psychological, and educational difficulties for victims, bystanders, and the perpetrator (Bidell, 2011). Alarmingly, 18.3% of LGBTQ youth surveyed reported physical assault (e.g., kicked, harmed with a weapon) because of their perceived or actual sexuality. Likewise, students with nonconforming gender expression—those who do meet societal norms for their gender (Roberts, Rosario, Slopen, Calzo, & Austin, 2013)—reported similarly high rates of physical abuse at the hands of their schoolmates. Finally, 63.5 % LGBTQ youth respondents reported that they felt unsafe at school, which led to 31.8 % of these SYM students to skip a day or more of school (Kosciw et al., 2012).

Unfortunately, bullying and harassment do not stop when students leave the school facilities. More than half of students surveyed reported being the victim of electronic harassment or cyberbullying outside of the school setting (Kosciw et al., 2012). Cyberbullying is a significant concern, because, as D'Auria (2014) notes, one act of cyberbullying can quickly escalate when it is sent to thousands of bystanders in cyberspace who join in or forward the harmful information. Because the wounding information is available 24 hours a day, seven days a week "the victim is unable to escape the abuse at home or at school" (p. 19). This sometimes constant harassment as well as the general vulnerability of LGBTQ students in cyberspace can be very detrimental to the health and well-being of SMY (CDC, 2013).

Findings from the Gay, Lesbian and Straight Education Network (GLSEN) national school climate survey are consistently replicated in the extant literature. For example, the CDC (2013) has emphasized that SYM youth are more vulnerable to threats or injuries by a weapon at school than are their heterosexual peers. Furthermore the research has identified many detrimental academic and psychological problems and risk behaviors (e.g., substance abuse) associated with a hostile school climate (D'Auria, 2014; Kosciw et al., 2012; Roberts et al., 2013). The following section will discuss the outcomes in the abovementioned three areas.

Academic Outcomes

The academic outcomes of LGBTQ youth—especially those who are from multicultural, multilinguistic, and economically poor backgrounds—are often vulnerable because considerable cognitive, emotional, and physical resources are spent avoiding victimization within school settings, thus limiting the amount of resources that can be spent on academics and school involvement. Due in large part to being bullied, many LGBTQ students are less attached to schools, as evidenced by several indices, resulting lower academic achievement (i.e., lower grades), truancy, and skipping certain classes (Hillard, Love, Franks, Laris, & Coyle, 2014; Kosciw et al., 2012). Clearly, bullying and harassment put LGBTQ at an academic disadvantage, as their number of hours and sense of safety in school is diminished, which ultimately compromises SMY's opportunities to thrive in school.

Psychological Well-Being and Stress

Research has consistently shown that the psychological well-being of LGBTQ youth can be strained due to social stigma associated with sexuality and gender (CDC, 2013). Social stigma permeates the educational experiences, neighborhood environments, and often familial systems of LGBTQ youth, often leaving them with few sources of social support. As a result, studies consistently show that LGBTQ youth are at greater risk for self-harm, suicidal ideation, depression, and other mental health concerns such as PTSD (see Dragowski, Halkitis, Grossman, & D'Augelli, 2011; Haas et al., 2011) and have higher rates of substance abuse and sexual risk behavior, which often go hand-in-hand (Kecojevic, et al., 2012; Marshal et al., 2008).

As discussed above, LGBTQ youth are victimized in schools by their peers at alarmingly high rates (Kosciw et al., 2012; Toomey, Ryan, Diaz, & Russell, 2011). Further, research shows that families are often unwelcoming to their LGBTQ children and siblings (Švab & Kuhar, 2014). School and family are two vitally critical sources of social support for all youth. Given that many LGBTQ youth are victimized at school and online, and are unable to find the support available to heterosexual youth from their families, their self-esteem and well-being are significantly strained (e.g., Švab & Kuhar, 2014). It is clear that interventions and programs need to be implemented to ensure that schools are safe and provide inclusive environments where SMY can thrive—which should be a birth right.

THE ROLE OF SCHOOL PERSONNEL

Teachers on the Frontlines

The literature concerning school climate suggests that school personnel have a profound effect on the educational climate of a given school. This is especially true with regard to fostering classrooms and schools which accept individual differences among K–12 students and their families. Some 12% of secondary students identify as lesbian, gay, bisexual, transgender, or queer/questioning (Russell, 2006), which, given a typical class size of 30, students, suggests that teachers will have on average three LGBTQ students per class. Sadly, many school personnel have perpetuated and in some cases encouraged unsafe school climates (Kosciw et al., 2012; Milburn & Palladino, 2012). For example, startlingly, more than half of the students' surveyed in the 2011 National School Climate reported hearing homophobic remarks from school faculty and staff (Kosciw et al., 2012). Additionally, students in Hillard and associates' (2014) study reported that teachers took limited actions to educate those students who engaged in harassment. Thus, it is not surprising that most students surveyed in Hillard and associates' study (2014) believed that reporting incidents of victimization would result at best in only minimal intervention by administration (Dykes, 2010; Hillard et al., 2014; Kosciw et al., 2012).

SooHoo (2004) asserts that students glean different lessons from their teachers' (in)actions such that students come to view bullying as acceptable and learn that staying silent in an oppressive situation is appropriate behavior. Teachers' participation in bullying by ignoring it creates hostile environments where all students are adversely affected. Bullies learn that bullying is acceptable. Students learn that bystanderism, the "response of people who observe something that demands intervention on their part, but they choose not to get involved" (SooHoo 2004, p. 200), is acceptable. Finally, targets of bullying suffer the consequences of homophobic bullying that could, if teachers were to work toward creating truly inclusive environments, be avoided or at least diminished. The linchpin role teachers play in reducing bullying (Kosciw et al., 2012) or in perpetuating homophobia (Kosciw et al., 2012; Milburn & Palladino, 2012) for students from marginalized groups—those from sexual minorities and students with disabilities—warrants investigation into the factors that prevent teachers and administrators from intervening (Larrabee & Morehead, 2010).

Teachers may not intentionally perpetuate homophobia in the classroom, however homophobia and heterosexism pervade many classrooms. For example, preservice and in-service teachers report limited knowledge about the academic, psychological, or health risks associated with sexual minority students. Milburn and Palladino (2012) report that teachers (preservice and inservice) "failed to recognize bully-ing as an antecedent for emotional distress and potential health risk behaviors" (p. 97). Larrabee and Morehead (2010) further note that teachers express concern about the appropriateness of LGBTQ issues within the K–12 curriculum. This is troubling because educators' ignorance often results in a "hands-off" approach in confronting issues affecting SMY (Dykes, 2010; Hillard et al., 2014). This hands-off approach may be due to teachers' fear, intimidation, or limited interaction with individuals who are LGBTQ (Larrabee & Morehead, 2010). Studies assessing teacher attitudes indicate that teachers gen-erally have moderate (as opposed to positive or negative) attitudes toward lesbian and gay individuals (Wyatt, Oswalt, White, & Peterson, 2008). These researchers further indicate that teachers held more negative attitudes toward gay males than lesbian females. It is clear that much work remains if teachers are to be prepared to work with and improve the educational setting for SMY (Dykes, 2010; Larrabee & Morehead, 2010; Milburn & Palladino, 2012).

Although teacher education programs address diversity with regard to class, gender, race, and eth-nicity, attention to sexuality and gender[1] expression are considerably absent (Banks, 2014; Dykes, 2010; Larrabee & Morehead, 2010). Athanases and Larrabee (2003) identified several factors impeding the atten-tion given to sexual minority youth within teacher preparation programs; among them are the newness of articulated guidelines to address marginalized youth, limited scope of multicultural agendas which do not adequately address heterosexism, and a limited theoretical base for effectively preparing teachers to advocate for sexual minority youth. Other researchers assert that addressing issues of sexuality within the framework of multicultural classes runs the risk of being additive in nature (Banks, 2014). Additional concerns emerge when including information on SMY is at the discretion of the instructors who may choose to "ignore" this important topic (Wyatt et al., 2008).

Given that queer youth are among the most underserved student populations within our educational system (Kosciw et al., 2012), an ethical imperative and legal precedents exist which necessitates that teacher preparation programs devote the adequate resources and time needed to effectively prepare teachers to not only practice inclusivity but to become advocates for the needs of all marginalized students—including SMY (Bishop & Casida, 2011).

School Health Professionals

School health professionals—social workers, school counselors, school nurses, and other school faculty associated with the healthcare industry—play a central role in providing safe and inclusive educational environments for SMY (Bidell, 2011; Mahdi et al., 2014; Murphy, 2012). School health professionals can educate teachers, staff, administrators, and students about LGBTQ issues and school policy and practices, as well as individual teacher and staff practices that impact the school climate for LGBTQ youth (and ultimately all youth). Further, school health professionals should advocate for equality for all students, including LGBTQ students. Unfortunately, recent research suggests that school health professionals do not feel adequately prepared to address the behavioral health concerns or harassment of LGBTQ students (Bidell, 2011; Mahdi et al., 2014). For example, as Mahdi et al. (2014) found, school counselors and health workers had limited experience discussing at-risk behaviors with LGBTQ students. Further, the majority of respondents in Mahdi's study reported limited or no experience in intervening to address harassment based on actual or perceived sexual identity. It is clear that because of their training, school psychologists and counselors are uniquely positioned to address issues confronting SMY within school settings (Bidell, 2011). As asserted by Griffin and Steen (2011),

> If our educational system intends to fulfill its commitment to serving all students, especially those on the fringes of society, and intends to live up to its promise of providing vital avenues of access and opportunity, school counselors, in conjunction with other important school stakeholders must use their unique educational backgrounds and strategic positioning within schools to make meaningful change in their schools. (p. 75)

School Administrators—School Leaders

As school leaders, principals have tremendous influence on the climate of teaching and learning in their schools (Lynch, 2012). Although the existing literature examining school settings for LGBTQ youth has consistently demonstrated that schools are fraught with bullying, school leaders underestimate the pervasive nature of the problem (Hernandez & Fraynd, 2014; Kosciw et al., 2012). In a national study GLSEN and Harris Interactive (2008) found that the overwhelming majority of principals reported having heard students make sexist or homophobic remarks. Discerning is the fact that most secondary school principals report that male students who do not fit the "typically masculine" image as well as LGBTQ students would feel unsafe at their school (GLSEN & Harris Interactive, 2008).

Central to the role of an effective administrator is the ability to understand school faculty and related personnel's professional development needs. Although research findings consistently demonstrate professional development specific to creating safer environments for LGBTQ youth is critical to the creation of a safe environment, few principles report providing this type of training (GLSEN & Harris Interactive, 2008; Kosciw et al., 2012; Slesaransky-Poe, 2013). For example, although 60% of school principals reported providing professional development for their staff who addressed bullying or harassment, only 5% of those surveyed reported their professional development specifically addressed LGBTQ issues (GLSEN & Harrison Interactive, 2008).

Lynch's (2012) review of the changing responsibilities of school leaders highlights the important roles school leaders play in implementing policies to ensure legal mandates stemming from the state and federal level are met (e.g., No Child Left Behind Act [2001] and IDEIA [2004]). Although principals have a legal obligation to implement antibullying policies, many policies do not specifically address sexual orientation or gender identity (GLSEN & Harris Interactive, 2008; Kosciw et al., 2012) According to Hernandez and Fraynd (2014), "unlike other antidiscrimination measures where school leaders are hyper-vigilant, LGBTQ policies have yet to be implemented" (p. 117). If schools are to meet legal mandates of NCLB and IDEIA, which call for increased student learning outcomes for all students, including those who are LGBTQ, school leaders will need to develop and implement policies specific to this population (GLSEN & Harris Interactive; Kosciw et al., 2012; Pazey & Cole, 2012; Slesaransky-Poe, 2013). From a social justice equity perspective, policies should be implemented not to meet legal mandates but out of an ethical and moral concern for all students. When this is not the case, school districts and school leaders must be held responsible by the court system for their failure to protect SMY students from harassment (Bishop & Casida, 2011). It should be noted that many states have passed legislation specific to LGBTQ youth, which will be addressed in more depth below.

THE INTERSECTIONS OF ETHICAL BEHAVIOR, INCLUSION, AND SOCIAL JUSTICE

Federal law (NCLB, 2001, Safe Schools Provisions) entitles all students to a free, safe, and effective education. If the school system is to fulfill its promise to provide an education to all students, we must create an educational environment that is inclusive to all, including those who have disabilities and those who are LGBTQ, or LGBTQ students with a disability. As evidenced in the extant literature, students with disabilities and students who are gay have been systematically marginalized and excluded (as opposed to included) from an education that meets their unique needs. These current authors profess that inclusion can only occur when the educational program is equitable, that is, tailored to meets a student's specific needs. As asserted by Artiles (2005, as cited in Artiles et al., 2010), an equity-difference socially just approach strives to deliver justice by providing all learners with the same treatment (e.g., a high-quality standards-based education) while recognizing individual differences (e.g., specific learning disabilities) and tailoring education to meet one's need. Further assertion is made that "this approach is ultimately consistent with the justice discourse advanced in the disability social movement" (Artilles et al., 2010, p. 252). In situating LGBTQ students in this social justice narrative, these authors advocate an equity-difference approach, which provides all students with a safe environment and acknowledges the fact that they are part of a marginalized sexual minority group which necessitates that supports are provided to ensure schools are welcoming. Further, we agree with Liassidou's (2013) concern that confronting specific issues in isolation from others (e.g., separately focusing on sexuality or race/ethnicity or class, etc.) is a "futile endeavor" that cannot lead to sustainable systematic change for marginalized groups because such efforts are too narrowly focused. However, we assert that this application of the social justice framework to the improvement of educational realities for LGBTQ youth not only acknowledges that change is possible, but provides a vision for how such change can be accomplished and ultimately how inclusive environments can be constructed. As such, the subsequent sections will address strategies that when implemented will interrogate existing school structures, thus creating inclusive environments.

Support of and Implementation of GSAs

It has been well documented that SMY are frequently physically and verbally victimized at school (Kosciw et al., 2012; Murphy, 2012; Slesaransky-Poe, 2013). Research findings (for complete review, see Toomey et al., 2011) have also consistently demonstrated that one of the most successful strategies—currently available for implementation—to help ensure a safe school climate is the creation of Gay-Straight Alliance clubs (GSAs). GSAs are secondary school student-led groups, held at individuals' school sites, which support and advocate for students who are gay, lesbian, bisexual, transgendered, questioning their sexuality, and/or who have gay family members or are allies (GLSEN, 2007). GSA clubs are open to all students regardless of sexual identity and are intended to improve the school climate for all students through education, support groups, and advocacy (GLSEN, 2007). These clubs seek to (a) provide a supportive and safe space in schools for LGBTQ students, allies, and students who have family members who are gay; (b) educate students about their rights; (c) educate faculty and staff; and (d) foster advocacy and activism (GLSEN 2007; Poteat, Sinclair, DiGiovanni, Koenig, & Russell, 2012). For example, because they are student led (GLSEN, 2007), GSA members can provide support to their peers who may be experiencing difficulties, such as bullying or familial rejection (Poteat et al., 2012). Additionally, they may provide settings for youth to engage in social activities (Poteat et al., 2012) or in advocacy initiatives designed to mitigate inequities at the school or community level (GLSEN, 2007).

The first GSA was formed in 1988 by a straight student who sought to reduce bullying and harassment of LGBTQ students (GLSEN, 2007). Although many schools have attempted to prevent the formation of such groups, they are protected by the Equal Educational Access Act of 1984 (Lambda Legal, 2013). As Murphy (2012) notes, the attempts to stifle or prevent GSA groups from forming is indicative the importance of such organizations. Today GLSEN estimates there are more than 4,000 GSAs across all 50 states and Puerto Rico, Guam, and Washington, DC (GLSEN, 2007) in both middle and secondary settings.

Positive outcomes of GSAs include institutional- and individual-level changes that can become protective factors for LGBTQ youth. Overall, schools with GSAs report a reduction of harassment based upon actual or perceived (homo)sexuality and/or gender expression, as well as a school-wide reduction of homophobic remarks. For individuals, whether LGBTQ or an ally, participation in GSAs potentially precipitates an increased sense of safety, belonging and connectedness, and feelings that the school is less sexually prejudiced, as well as the development of leadership skills, improved grades, and better interpersonal relationships (GLSEN, 2007; Murphy, 2012; Toomy et al., 2011). Support for LGBTQ youth and/or having a GSA in the school is endorsed by several leading professional associations including the American Academy of Pediatrics, the American Association of School Administrators, the American Counseling Association, the American Federation of Teachers, the American School Counselor Association, the National Association of School Nurses, and several other national organizations (Murphy, 2012).

Credentialing Programs Have Obligation to Address LGBTQ Issues

The literature examining the preparation of school personnel demonstrates that teachers (e.g., Larrabee & Morehead, 2010; Wyatt et al., 2008), school health professionals (e.g., Mahdi et al., 2014) and administrators (e.g., Hernandez & Fraynd, 2014) are unprepared to address the unique needs of SMY within the school system. If P–12 schools are to become more inclusive, personnel preparation programs (e.g., policymakers, state and federal legislators, school leadership programs, teacher credentialing programs) must provide a robust curriculum specific to the unique needs of LGBTQ students so that upon graduation, future teachers, health personnel, and administrators are well prepared to meet the needs of LGBTQ students. As Averett and Hedge (2012) so aptly conclude "in an inherently heterosexist society such as the US . . . programs of higher education have a responsibility to educate and prepare their students for nondiscriminatory practice within schools" (p. 547).

The extant literature addressing the preparation of school personnel suggests that one approach to ensuring school personnel are well prepared to actively engage in the work needed to ensure inclusive schools is the application of a social justice framework to existing credentialing programs. For example, as Pazey and Cole (2012) note, "Central to the standards within educational administration is the concept of social justice, which is advanced in the language of inclusion" (p. 253). The infusion of social justice is also evident in school counseling credential programs (Griffin & Steen, 2011) and integral to the preparation of special education teachers because they are trained advocate for students with disabilities (Dykes, 2010). We agree with Bidell (2011), who asserted that counselors who operate from a social justice framework are uniquely prepared to serve as GSA leaders and hope that all school personnel would be prepared to serve not only as GSA leaders, but as advocates for all students, especially those who are marginalized within the current educational system.

The literature has established a clear need for school personnel to be better prepared to meet the needs of SMY. This is particularly true with the development and implementation and institutionalization of inclusive curriculum. For example, as Burdge, Snapp, Laub, Russell, and Moody (2013) note, only recently have states begun to adopt curriculum that is specific to LGBTQ issues. Larrabee and Morehead (2010) suggest credential candidates be provided with many opportunities to discuss and understand inclusive curriculum if they are going to internalize the skills needed to effectively implement inclusive curriculum. These authors agree and suggest that faculty—across all credentialing programs—will need additional training. If issues pertaining to SMY are to be brought to the forefront of credentialing programs, educators must first acknowledge that the need for such an agenda exists. Secondly, future leaders must reflect upon their existing knowledge base with regard to the unique needs specific to GLBTQ in schools and seek to increase such knowledge.

Schoolwide Training Specific to LGBTQ Issues

In order to provide a safe, supportive, and inclusive environment for sexual minority youth, all of the school faculty, staff, administration, and support teams (e.g., school nurses, counselors, and community liaisons) must receive training at the local school or district level. As Slesaransky-Poe (2013) aptly notes, the training must be "inclusive and comprehensive sex, gender and sexuality education (p. 41)" for all adults who work in the school. This training is particularly vital for school personnel who have not received training in their certification programs. Further, schools leaders must actively work to ensure such training is implemented on an ongoing basis (Mahdi et al., 2014).

Development and Implementation of Antidiscrimination Policies

In order to create and ensure an inclusive environment exists for all students, district leaders must implement strong policies specific to the protection of SMY (Bishop & Casida, 2011). As indicated by Kosciw et al.'s (2012) national report on school climate, many schools do not have bullying policies which explicitly address LGBTQ students. Although research suggests a greater number of schools and districts have moved to implementing policies specifically addressing LGBTQ students than in years past (Hillard et al., 2014), many schools have not implemented these vital policies (Kosciw et al., 2012). Research findings further suggest that such policies must be "comprehensive and enumerate the categories of gender identity and expression, sexual orientation and family composition" (Slesaransky-Poe, 2013, p. 43). Once developed and implemented, students and adults must be provided with a comprehensive overview of district and school policies and the protocols thus better ensuring antidiscriminatory policies are adhered to (Flemming, 2012). Schools seeking to implement training that is targeted to the needs of the school should assess school personnel and students annually (Hillard et al., 2014) with respect to their knowledge and abilities to create safe and inclusive environments.

Implementation of Inclusive Curriculum

School climate research suggests that the implementation of inclusive curriculum promotes greater feelings of student safety, health, and well-being (Burdge et al., 2013; Kosciw et al., 2012). Findings further suggest that SMY absenteeism is reduced and academic achievement is increased (Burdge, Sinclair, Laub, & Russell, 2012). Drawing on research findings associated with inclusive curriculum and in efforts to interrogate the harsh realities of schools for LGBTQ youth, the Fair, Accurate, Inclusive, and Respectful Education Act of 2011 (FAIR Act, 2011) was signed into law. This Act requires California's P–12 schools to include age-appropriate, factual information about social movements, current events, and the history of people with disabilities, and LGBTQ individuals in school curriculum. The implementation of the FAIR Act further seeks to ensure that contributions of both men and women, people of color, diverse ethnic communities, and other historically underrepresented groups are represented in the textbooks and curriculum for P–12 students. The Act further prohibits instruction or school-sponsored activities that promote a discriminatory bias based on race or ethnicity, gender, religion, disability, nationality, and sexual orientation, or other characteristics (Penan, 2013). As Burdge, Snapp, Laub, Russell, and Moody (2013) note, a broad approach to the implementation of an LGBTQ inclusive curriculum "likely has the greatest impact on school climate" (p. 5). As such, we encourage school leaders and policymakers across the nation to pass legislation similar to California and to actively seek to implement an inclusive curriculum.

CONCLUSIONS

Schools are in many ways unwelcoming environments for LGBTQ youth. Structurally, LGBTQ youth are excluded with respect to representation in curriculum, unprepared teachers, administrators, and other personnel, and overall heterosexist school climates. Interpersonally, LGBTQ youth often experience verbal and physical harassment from bullies. Structural and interpersonal marginalization manifest simultaneously when school personnel do not intervene to stop bullying of LGBTQ students. The discrimination and marginalization SMY face in school settings can be a barrier to full participation in school activities and success in middle and high schools.

Situating this chapter in a social just framework provides the impetus for change based on ethical and moral obligations that are outside the mandates of the legal system. Research findings from disabilities research, social and behavioral health research, and educational research has provided tangible solutions that when implemented, have the power to dramatically improve the lives of not only LGBTQ youth, but all youth from marginalized backgrounds. It is up to educators themselves and the educational system more broadly to put social justice into practice by fully integrating solutions already available, such as forming and supporting Gay-Straight Alliance clubs on campus, addressing LGBTQ issues in credentialing programs, providing schoolwide training specific to LGBTQ issues, developing and implementing antidiscrimination policies and protocols on how to handle LGBTQ discrimination on campus, and developing inclusive curriculum. These tools can be implemented by policymakers, principals, teachers, and school personnel who should, in the spirit of a social justice of inclusion, seek out new solutions that fit the specific needs of their district, school, and classroom.

Legal protections do exist to protect SYM youth; however, alone, legal mandates are insufficient to bring about the depth of change needed to create environments that foster inclusivity. In addition to legal protections, school personnel are integral to the creation of a truly inclusive school climate since they are on the front lines with students daily. School personnel interact with students throughout the day and are thus in the unique position to model a social justice approach to inclusion. Further, school personnel observing students interacting can intervene when homophobic remarks are made, even if the remarks are not aimed at an LGBTQ student. Finally, school personnel can develop, implement, and support several structural mechanisms (e.g., trainings, inclusive curriculum) designed to educate school personnel and students about the importance of creating inclusive and welcoming environments for all students.

NOTE

1. These authors recognize that these aspects of identity are not mutually exclusive, but rather are intersecting (e.g., Black lesbian).

ACKNOWLEDGMENT

This research has been supported by the Frances McClelland Institute at the University of Arizona and an NIH T32 CA 9492-28 Training Grant

REFERENCES

Artiles, A. J., Bal, A., & King Thorius, K. A. (2010). Back to the future: A critique of response to intervention's social justice views. *Theory Into Practice, 49*, 250–257.

Artiles, A. J., Kozleski, E. B., Dorn, S., & Christenson, C. (2006). Learning in inclusive education research: Re-mediating theory and methods with a transformative agenda. *Review of Research in Education, 30*, 65–108.

Averett, P. E., & Hegde, A. (2012). School social work and early childhood student's attitudes toward gay and lesbian families. *Teaching in Higher Education, 17*(5), 537–549.

Athanases, S. Z., & Larrabee, T. G. (2003). Toward a consistent stance in teaching for equity: Learning to advocate for lesbian- and gay-identified youth. *Teaching and Teacher Education, 19*(2), 237–261.

Banks, J. A. (2014). An introduction to multicultural education (5th ed.). Upper Saddle River, NJ: Pearson.

Bidell, M. P. (2011). School counselors and social justice advocacy for lesbian, gay, bisexual, transgender, and, questioning students. *Journal of School Counseling, 9*(10), 1–22.

Bishop, H. N., & Casida, H. (2011). Preventing bullying and harassment of sexual minority students in schools. *The Clearing House, 84*, 131–138.

Brown, K. M. (2004). Leadership for social justice and equity: Weaving a transformative framework and pedagogy. *Educational Administration Quarterly, 40*, 77–108.

Burdge, H., Sinclair, K., Laub, C., & Russell, S. T. (2012). Research Brief No. 14: Lessons that matter: LGBTQ inclusivity and school safety. *Gay-Straight Alliance Network and California Safe Schools Coalition.* Retrieved September 29, 2014, from https://www.gsanetwork.org/files/aboutus/PSH%20Report%206_2012.pdf

Burdge, H., Snapp, S., Laub, C., Russell, S. T., & Moody, R. (2013). Implementing lessons that matter: The impact of LGBTQ-inclusive curriculum on student safety, well-being, and achievement. *Gay-Straight Alliance Network/ Frances McClelland Institute.* Retrieved September 29, 2014, from http://www.gsanetwork.org/files/aboutus/ImplementingLessons_fullreport.pdf

Centers for Disease Control and Prevention (CDC). (2013). *2012 Division of Adolescent and School Health: Success stories.* Retrieved May 30, 2014, from http://www.cdc.gov/healthyyouth/stories/pdf/ss_booklet_0713.pdf

D'Auria, J. P. (2014). Cyberbullying resources for youth and their families. *Journal of Pediatric Healthcare, 28*(2), 19–22. Dragowski, E. A., Halkitis, P. N., Grossman, A. H., & D'Augelli, A. R. (2011). Sexual orientation victimization and posttraumatic stress symptoms among lesbian, gay, and bisexual youth. *Journal of Gay and Lesbian Social Services, 23*(2), 226–249.

Dykes, F. (2010). Transcending rainbow flags and pride parades: Preparing special education preservice educators to work with gay and lesbian youth. *SRATE Journal, 19*(2), 36–43.

Fair, Accurate, Inclusive, and Respectful (FAIR) Education Act SB 48. (2011) Retrieved September 29, 2014, from http://www.eqca.org/atf/cf/%7B34f258b3-8482-4943-91cb-08c4b0246a88%7D/FAIR%20education%20fact%20sheet%20final.pdf

Flemming, J. (2012, March/April). Bullying and bias: Making schools safe for gay students. *Leadership,* 12–14.

GLSEN. (2007). Research Brief: Gay-straight alliances: Creating safer schools for LGBT students and their allies. *Gay, Lesbian and Straight Education Network.* Retrieved September 16, 2014, from http://glsen.org/sites/default/files/Gay-Straight%20Alliances.pdf

GLSEN & Harris Interactive. (2008). The principal's perspective: School safety, bullying and harassment: A survey of public school principals. New York, NY: GLSEN.

Griffin, D., & Steen, S. (2011). A social justice approach to school counseling. *Journal for Social Action in Counseling and Psychology, 3*(1), 74–85.

Haas, A. P., Eliason, M., Mays, V. M., Mathy, R. M. Cochran, S. D., D'Augelli, A. R., … Clayton, P. J. (2011). Suicide and suicide risk in lesbian, gay, bisexual and transgender populations: Review and recommendations. *Journal of Homosexuality, 58*(1), 10–51.

Hallahan, D. P., Kauffman, J. M., & Pullen, P. C. (2015). *Exceptional learners: An introduction to special education* (13th ed.).

Upper Saddle River, NJ: Pearson.

Hernadez, F., & Fraynd, D. J. (2014). Leadership's role in inclusive LGBTQ-supportive schools. *Theory into Practice, 53*, 115–122.

Hillard, P. L., Love, L., Franks, H. M., Laris, B. A., & Coyle, K. (2014). "They were only joking": Efforts to decrease LGBTQ bullying and harassment in Seattle public schools. *Journal of School Health, 84*(1), 1–9.

Individuals with Disabilities Education Improvement Act (IDEIA) of 2004, P. L.108–446, 20 U.S.C. § 1400 et seq.

Kecojevic, A., Wong, C. F. Schrager, S. M., Silva, K. Bloom, J. J., Iverson, E., & Lankenau, S. E. (2012). Initiation into prescription drug misuse: Differences between lesbian, gay, bisexual, and transgender (LGBT) and heterosexual high-risk young adults in Los Angeles and New York. *Addictive Behaviors, 37*, 1289–1293.

Kosciw, J. G., Greytak, E. A., Bartkiewicz, M. J., Boesen, M. J., & Palmer, N. A. (2012). *The 2011 National School Climate Survey: The experiences of lesbian, gay, bisexual and transgender youth in our nation's schools.* New York, NY: GLSEN.

Lambda Legal. (2013). *Know your rights: Your legal right to form a GSA.* Retrieved September 15, 2014, from http://www.lambdalegal.org/know-your-rights/lgbtq-teens-young-adults/your-legal-right-to-form-a-gsa

Larrabee, T. G., & Morehead, P. (2010). Broadening views of social justice and teacher leadership: Addressing LGB issues in teacher education. *Issues in Teacher Education, 19*(2), 37–52.

Liasidou, A. (2013). Intersectional understandings of disability and implications for a social justice reform agenda in education policy and practice. *Disability & Society, 28*(3), 299–312.

Lynch, J. M. (2012). Responsibilities of today's principal: Implications for principal preparation programs and principal certification policies. *Council on Rural Special Education, 31*(2), 40–47.

Mahdi, I., Jevertson, J., Schrader, R., Nelson, A., & Ramos, M. M. (2014). Survey of New Mexico school health professionals regarding preparedness to support sexual minority students. *Journal of School Health, 84*(1), 18–24.

Marshall, M. P., Friedman, M. S., Stall, R., King, K. M., Miles, J., & Gold, M. A. (2008). Sexual orientation and adolescent substance use: A meta-analysis and methodological review. *Addiction, 103*(4), 546–556.

Milburn, W., & Palladino, J. (2012). Preservice teachers' knowledge, skills, and dispositions of LGBTQ bullying intervention. *The American Association of Behavioral and Social Sciences Journal, 16*, 86–100.

Murphy, H. E. (2012). Improving the lives of students, gay and straight alike: Gay-straight alliances and the role of school psychologists. *Psychology in the Schools, 49*(9), 883–891.

No Child Left Behind (NCLB) Act of 2001. P. L. No. 107–110 § 115, Stat. 1425.

Pazey, B. L., & Cole, H. A. (2012). The role of special education training in the development of socially just leaders: Building an equity consciousness in educational leadership programs. *Educational Administration Quarterly, 49*(2), 243–271.

Penan, H. (2013, June 3). FAIR Education Act. *The Notice.* Retrieved September 29, 2014, from http://thenoticeca.com/2013/06/03/fair-education-act/

Poteat, V. P., Sinclair, K. O., DiGiovanni, C. D., Keonig, B. W., & Russell, S. T. (2012). Gay-straight alliances are associated with student health: A multischool comparison of LGBTQ and heterosexual youth. *Journal of Research on Adolescence, 23*(2), 319–330.

Roberts, A. L., Rosario, M., Slopen, N., Calzo, J. P., & Austin, S. B. (2013). Childhood gender nonconformity, bullying victimization, and depressive symptoms across adolescence and early adulthood: An 11-year longitudinal study. *Journal of the American Academy of Child and Adolescent Psychiatry, 52*(2), 143–152.

Russell, S. T. (2006). Substance use and abuse and mental health among sexual-minoirty youths: Evidence from Add Health. In A. M. Omoto & H. S. Kurtzman (Eds.), *Sexual orientation and mental health: Examining idenity and development in lesbian, gay, and bisexual people* (pp. 13–35). Washington, DC: APA.

Satcher, J., & Schumacker, R. (2009). Predictors of modern homonegativity among professional counselors. *Journal of LGBT Issues in Counseling, 3*(1), 21–36.

Slesaransky-Poe, G. (2013). Adults set the tone for welcoming all students. *Kappan, 94*(5), 40–44.

SooHoo, S. (2004). We change the world by doing nothing. *Teacher Education Quarterly, 31*(1), 199–211.

Švab, A., & Kuhar, R. (2014). The transparent and family closets: Gay men and lesbians and their families of origin. *Journal of GLBT Family Studies, 10*(1/2), 15–35.

Toomey, R. B., Ryan, C., Diaz, R. M., & Russell, S. T. (2011). High school gay-straight alliances (GSAs) and young adult well-being: An examination of GSA presence, participation and perceived effectiveness. *Applied Developmental Science, 15*(4), 175–185.

Udvari-Solner, A. (1997). Inclusive education. In C. A. Grant & G. Ladson-Billings (Eds.), *Dictionary of multicultural education* (pp. 141–144). Phoenix, AZ: Oryxg.

Uribe, V. (1994). Project 10: A school-based outreach to gay and lesbian youth. *High School Journal, 77*, 108–112.

Wyatt, T. J., Oswalt, S. B., White, C., & Peterson, F. L. (2008, Spring). Are tomorrow's teachers ready to deal with diverse students?: Teacher candidates' attitudes toward gay men and lesbians. *Teacher Education Quarterly,* 171–185.

——————————— o ———————————

END OF CHAPTER QUESTIONS

1.   Why is creating inclusive schools for LGBT+ students important?
2.   How are LGBT+ students marginalized in schools?
3.   Which legal protections should be used to protect LGBT+ students in schools?
4.   What can school personnel do to ensure LGBT+ students are protected in schools?

What's Wrong with Trans Rights?

Dean Spade

---

*Rights discourse in liberal capitalist culture casts as private potentially political
contests about distribution of resources and about relevant parties to decision
making. It converts social problems into matters of individualized, dehistoricized
injury and entitlement, into matters in which there is no harm if there is no agent
and no tangibly violated subject.*

—Wendy Brown, *States of Injury*

As the concept of trans rights has gained more currency in the last two decades, a seeming consensus has emerged about which law reforms should be sought to better the lives of trans people.[1] Advocates of trans equality have primarily pursued two law-reform interventions: antidiscrimination laws that list gender identity and/or expression as a category of nondiscrimination, and hate-crime laws that include crimes motivated by the gender identity and/or expression of the victim as triggering the application of a jurisdiction's hate-crime statute. Organizations like the National Gay and Lesbian Task Force (NGLTF) have supported state and local organizations around the country in legislative campaigns to pass such laws. Thirteen states (California, Colorado, Hawaii, Illinois, Iowa, Maine, Minnesota, New Jersey, New Mexico, Oregon, Rhode Island, Vermont, and Washington) and the District of Columbia currently have laws that include gender identity and/or expression as a category of antidiscrimination, and 108 counties and cities have such laws. NGLTF estimates that 39 percent of people in the United States live in a jurisdiction where such laws are on the books.[2] Seven states now have hate-crime laws that include gender identity and/or expression.[3] In 2009, a federal law, the Matthew Shepard and James Byrd, Jr., Hate Crimes Prevention Act, added gender identity and/or expression to federal hate-crime law. An ongoing battle regarding whether and how gender identity and/or expression will be included in the Employment Non-Discrimination Act (ENDA), a federal law that would prohibit discrimination the basis of sexual orientation, continues to be fought between the conservative national gay and lesbian organization, the Human Rights Campaign (HRC), legislators, and a variety of organizations and activists seeking to push an inclusive bill through Congress. Antidiscrimination bills and hate-crime laws have come to define the idea of "trans rights" in the United States and are presently the most visible efforts made by nonprofit organizations and activists working under this rubric.

The logic behind this law-reform strategy is not mysterious. Proponents argue that passing these laws does a number of important things. First, the passage of antidiscrimination laws can create a basis for legal claims against discriminating employers, housing providers, restaurants, hotels, stores, and the like. Trans people's legal claims when facing exclusion in such contexts have often failed in the past, with courts saying that the exclusion is a legitimate preference on the part of the employer, landlord, or business owner.[4] Laws that make gender identity/expression–based exclusion illegal have the potential to influence courts to punish discriminators and to provide certain remedies (e.g., back pay or damages) to injured trans people. There is also a hope that such laws and their enforcement by courts would send a preventative message to potential discriminators, letting them know that such exclusions will not be tolerated; these laws would ultimately increase access to jobs, housing, and other necessities for trans people.

Hate-crime laws are promoted under a related logic. Proponents point out that trans people have a very high murder rate and are subject to a great deal of violence.[5] In many instances, trans people's lives are so devalued by police and prosecutors that trans murders are not investigated or trans people's murderers are given shorter punishments than are typical in murder sentencing. Proponents believe that hate-crime laws will intervene in these situations, making law enforcement take this violence seriously. There is also a symbolic element to the passage of these laws: a statement that trans lives are meaningful, often described by proponents as an assertion that trans people are human. Additionally, proponents of antidiscrimination laws and hate-crime laws argue that the processes of advocating the passage of such laws, including media advocacy representing the lives and concerns of trans people and meetings with legislators to tell them about trans people's experiences, increase positive trans visibility and advance the struggle for trans equality. The data-collection element of hate-crime statutes, through which certain government agencies keep count of crimes that fall into this category, is touted by proponents as a chance to make the quantity and severity of trans people's struggles more visible.

The logic of visibility and inclusion surrounding antidiscrimination and hate-crime law campaigns is very popular, yet there are many troubling limitations to the idea that these two reforms compose a proper approach to problems trans people face in both criminal- and civil-law contexts. One concern is whether these laws actually improve the life chances of those who are purportedly protected by them. Looking at categories of identity that have been included in these kinds of laws over the last several decades indicates that these kinds of reforms have not eliminated bias, exclusion, or marginalization. Discrimination and violence against people of color have persisted despite law changes that declared it illegal. The persistent and growing racial wealth divide in the United States suggests that these law changes have not had their promised effects and that the structure of systemic racism is not addressed by the work of these laws.[6] Similarly, the twenty-year history of the Americans with Disabilities Act (ADA) demonstrates disappointing results. Courts have limited the enforcement potential of this law with narrow interpretations of its impact, and people with disabilities remain economically and politically marginalized by systemic ableism. Similar arguments can be made about the persistence of national origin discrimination, sex discrimination, and other forms of pervasive discrimination despite decades of official prohibitions of such behavior. The persistence of wage gaps, illegal terminations, hostile work environments, hiring/firing disparities, and bias-motivated violence for groups whose struggles have supposedly been addressed by antidiscrimination and hate-crime laws invites caution when assuming the effectiveness of these measures.

Hate-crime laws do not have a deterrent effect. They focus on punishment and cannot be argued to actually prevent bias-motivated violence. In addition to their failure to prevent harm, they must be considered in the context of the failures of our legal system and, specifically, the violence of our criminal punishment system. Antidiscrimination laws are not adequately enforced. Most people who experience discrimination cannot afford to access legal help, so their experiences never make it to court. Additionally, the Supreme Court has severely narrowed the enforceability of these laws over the last thirty years, making it extremely difficult to prove discrimination short of a signed letter from a boss or landlord stating, "I am taking this negative action against you because of your [insert characteristic]." Even in cases that seem as obvious as that, people experiencing discrimination often lose. Proving discriminatory *intent* has become central, making it almost impossible to win these cases when they are brought to court. These laws also have such narrow scopes that they often do not include action taken by some of the most common discriminators against marginalized people: prison guards, welfare bureaucrats, workfare supervisors, immigration officers, child-welfare workers, and others who have significant control over the lives of marginalized people in the United States. In a neoliberal era characterized by abandonment (reduction of social safety nets and infrastructure, especially in poor and people-of-color communities) and imprisonment (increased immigration- and criminal-law enforcement), antidiscrimination laws provide little relief to the most vulnerable people.

In addition to these general problems with law reforms that add gender identity/expression to the list of prohibited characteristics, trans litigants have run into specific challenges when seeking redress from discrimination under these laws. Even in jurisdictions where these laws have been put in place, trans litigants have lost discrimination cases about being denied access to sex-segregated facilities.[7] In the employment context, this often means that even when a worker lives in a jurisdiction where discriminating against trans people is supposedly illegal, denying a trans person access to a restroom that comports with their gender identity at work is not interpreted as a violation of the law. Of course, given the staggering unemployment of trans populations emerging from conditions of homelessness, lack of family support,[8] violence-related trauma, discrimination by potential employers, effects of unmet health needs, and many other factors,[9] even if the legal interpretations of trans people's restroom-access demands were better, they would not scratch the surface of trans poverty.[10] However, these interpretations in employment cases involving restrooms are particularly dangerous, because they can be applied by courts to other high-stakes settings where trans people struggle in systems that rely on sex segregation. Because trans people frequently face violence and discrimination in the context of sex-segregated spaces, such as shelters, prisons, and group homes, and because restroom access is often the most contentious issue between trans workers and their employers, these anti-trans legal interpretations take the teeth out of trans-inclusive laws and are examples of the limitations of seeking equality through courts and legislatures.

Critical race theorists have developed analyses about the limitations of anti-discrimination laws that are useful in understanding the ways these law reforms have and will continue to fail to deliver meaningful change to trans people. Alan Freeman's critique of what he terms the "perpetrator perspective" in discrimination law is particularly helpful in conceptualizing the limits of common trans-rights strategies.[11] Freeman's work looks at laws that prohibit discrimination based on race. He exposes how and why antidiscrimination and hate-crime statutes do not achieve their promises of equality and freedom for people targeted by discrimination and violence. Freeman argues that discrimination law misunderstands how racism works, which makes it fail to effectively address it.

Discrimination law primarily conceptualizes the harm of racism through the perpetrator/victim dyad, imagining that the fundamental scene is that of a perpetrator who irrationally hates people on the basis of their race and fires or denies service to or beats or kills the victim based on that hatred. The law's adoption of this conception of racism does several things that make it ineffective at eradicating racism and help it contribute to obscuring the actual operations of racism. First, it individualizes racism. It says that racism is about bad individuals who intentionally make discriminatory choices and must be punished. In this (mis)understanding, structural or systemic racism is rendered invisible. Through this function, the law can only attend to disparities that come from the behavior of a perpetrator who intentionally considered the category that must not be considered (e.g., race, gender, disability) in the decision he or she was making (e.g., hiring, firing, admission, expulsion). Conditions like living in a district with underfunded schools that "happen to be" 96 percent students of color,[12] having to take an admissions test that has been proven to predict race better than academic success,[13] or experiencing any of a number of disparities in life conditions (access to adequate food, health care, employment, housing, clean air and water) that we know stem from and reflect long-term patterns of exclusion and exploitation cannot be understood as "violations" under the discrimination principle, and thus remedies cannot be won. This narrow reading of what constitutes a violation and can be recognized as discrimination serves to naturalize and affirm the status quo of maldistribution. Antidiscrimination law seeks out aberrant individuals with overtly biased intentions.[14] Meanwhile, all the daily disparities in life chances that shape our world along lines of race, class, indigeneity, disability, national origin, sex, and gender remain untouchable and affirmed as nondiscriminatory or even as fair.

The perpetrator perspective also obscures the historical context of racism. Discrimination is understood as the act of taking into account the identity that discrimination law forbids us to take into account (e.g., race, sex, disability) when making a decision, and it does not regard whether the decision maker is favoring or harming a traditionally excluded group. In this way, the discrimination principle has been used to eviscerate affirmative action and desegregation programs.[15] This erroneously conceptualized "colorblindness" undermines the possibility of remedying the severe racial disparities in the United States that are rooted in slavery, genocide, land theft, internment, and immigration exclusion as well as racially explicit policies that historically and presently exclude people of color from the benefits of wealth-building programs for U.S. citizens, such as Social Security, land grants, and credit and other homeownership support.[16] The conditions that created and continue to reproduce such immense disparities are made invisible by the perpetrator perspective's insistence that any consideration of the prohibited category is equally damaging. This model pretends the playing field is equal, and thus any loss or gain in opportunity based on the category is harmful and creates inequality, again serving to declare the racial status quo neutral. This justification for systemic racism masquerading as a logic of equal opportunity gives rise to the myth of "reverse racism," a concept that misunderstands racism to suggest parallel meanings when white people lose opportunities or access through programs aiming to ameliorate impacts of racism and when people of color lose opportunities due to racism.

Discrimination law's reliance on the perpetrator perspective also creates the false impression that the previously excluded or marginalized group is now equal, that fairness has been imposed, and the legitimacy of the distribution of life chances restored. This declaration of equality and fairness papers over the inequalities and disparities that constitute business as usual and allows them to continue. Narrowing political-resistance strategies to seeking inclusion in antidiscrimination law makes the mistaken assumption that gaining recognition and inclusion in this way will equalize our life chances and allow us to compete in the (assumed fair) system. This often constitutes a forfeiture of other critiques, as if the economic system is fair *but for* the fact that bad discriminators are sometimes allowed to fire trans people for being trans.[17] Constituting the problem of oppression so narrowly that an antidiscrimination law could "solve" it erases the complexity and breadth of the systemic, life-threatening harm that trans resistance seeks to end.

Not surprisingly, the rhetoric accompanying these quests for inclusion often casts "deserving workers"—people whose other characteristics (race, ability, education, class) would have entitled them to a good chance in the workforce were it not for the illegitimate exclusion that happened.[18] Using as examples the least marginalized of the marginalized, so to speak, becomes necessary when issues are framed so narrowly that a person who faces intersecting vectors of harm would be unlikely to benefit from antidiscrimination law. This framing permits—and even necessitates—that efforts for inclusion in the discrimination regime rely on rhetoric that affirms the legitimacy and fairness of the status quo.

The inclusion focus of antidiscrimination law and hate-crime law campaigns relies on a strategy of simile, essentially arguing that "we are just like you; we do not deserve this different treatment because of this one characteristic." To make that argument, advocates cling to the imagined norms of the U.S. social body and choose poster people who are symbolic of U.S. standards of normalcy, whose lives are easily framed by sound bites that resound in shared notions of injustice. "Perfect plaintiffs" for these cases are white people with high-level jobs and lawful immigration status. The thorny issues facing undocumented immigrants; people experiencing simultaneous discrimination through, for example, race, disability and gender identity; or people in low-wage jobs where it is particularly hard to prove discrimination, are not addressed by antidiscrimination law. Laws created from such strategies, not surprisingly, routinely fail to protect people with more complicated relationships to marginality. These people, who face the worst economic vulnerability, are not lifted up as the "deserving workers" that antidiscrimination law advocates rally to protect.

Hate-crime laws are an even more direct example of the limitations of the perpetrator perspective's conception of oppression. Hate-crime laws frame violence in terms of individual wrongdoers. These laws and their advocates portray violence through a lens that oversimplifies its operation and suggests that the criminal-punishment system is the proper way to solve it. The violence targeted by hate-crime laws is that of purportedly aberrant individuals who have committed acts of violence motivated by bias. Hate-crime advocacy advances the fallacy that such violence is especially reprehensible in the eyes of an equality-minded state and thus must be punished with enhanced force. Although it is no doubt true that violence of this kind is frequent and devastating, critics of hate-crime legislation argue that hate-crime laws are not the answer. First, as mentioned above, hate-crime laws have no deterrent effect: People do not read law books before committing acts of violence and then choose against bias-motivated violence because it carries a harsher sentence. Hate-crime laws do not and cannot actually increase the life chances of the people they purportedly protect.

Second, hate-crime laws strengthen and legitimize the criminal-punishment system, a system that targets the very people these laws are supposedly passed to protect. The criminal-punishment system was founded on and constantly reproduces the same biases (racism, sexism, homophobia, transphobia, ableism, xenophobia) that advocates of these laws want to eliminate. This is no small point, given the rapid growth of the U.S. criminal-punishment system in the last few decades and the gender, race, and ability disparities in whom it targets. The United States now imprisons 25 percent of the world's prisoners, although it has only 5 percent of the world's population.[19] Imprisonment in the United

States has quadrupled since the 1980s and continues to increase, despite the fact that violent crime and property crime have declined since the 1990s.[20] The United States has the highest documented rate of imprisonment per capita of any country.[21] A 2008 report declared that the United States now imprisons one in every one hundred adults.[22] Significant racial, gender, ability, and national-origin disparities exist in this imprisonment system. One in nine black men between the ages of twenty and thirty-four are imprisoned. Although men still vastly outnumber women in prisons, the rate of imprisonment for women is growing far faster, largely the result of sentencing changes created as part of the War on Drugs, including the advent of mandatory minimum sentences for drug convictions. An estimated 27 percent of federal prisoners are noncitizens.[23] Although accurate estimates of rates of imprisonment for people with disabilities are difficult to obtain, it is clear that the combination of severe medical neglect of prisoners, deinstitutionalization of people with psychiatric disabilities without the provision of adequate community services, and the role of drug use in self-medicating account for high rates.[24]

In a context of mass imprisonment and rapid prison growth targeting traditionally marginalized groups, what does it mean to use criminal punishment-enhancing laws to purportedly address violence against those groups? This point has been especially forcefully made by critics who note the origins of the contemporary lesbian and gay rights formation in antipolice activism of the 1960s and 1970s and who question how current lesbian and gay rights work has come to be aligned with a neoliberal "law and order" approach.[25] Could the veterans of the Stonewall and Compton's Cafeteria uprisings against police violence have guessed that a few decades later LGBT law reformers would be supporting passage of the Matthew Shepard and James Byrd, Jr., Hate Crimes Prevention Act, a law that provides millions of dollars to enhance police and prosecutorial resources? Could they have imagined that anyone would claim the police as protectors of queer and trans people against violence, while imprisonment and police brutality are skyrocketing? The neoliberal reframing of discrimination and violence that have drastically shifted and undermined strategies of resistance to economic exploitation and state violence produce this narrow law-reform agenda that ignores and colludes in the harm and violence faced every day by queer and trans people struggling against racism, ableism, xenophobia, transphobia, homophobia, and poverty.

These concerns are particularly relevant for trans people given our ongoing struggles with police profiling, harassment, violence, and high rates of youth and adult imprisonment. Trans populations are disproportionately poor because of employment discrimination, family rejection, and difficulty accessing school, medical care, and social services.[26] These factors increase our rate of participation in criminalized work to survive, which, combined with police profiling, produces high levels of criminalization.[27] Trans people in prisons face severe harassment, medical neglect, and violence in both men's and women's facilities. Violence against trans women in men's prisons is consistently reported by prisoners as well as by researchers, and court cases and testimony from advocates and formerly imprisoned people reveals trends of forced prostitution, sexual slavery, sexual assault, and other violence. Trans people, like all people locked up in women's prisons, are targets of gender-based violence, including sexual assault and rape, most frequently at the hands of correctional staff. Prisoners who are perceived as "too masculine" by prison staff at women's facilities are often at significantly increased risk of harassment and enhanced punishment, including psychologically damaging isolation, for alleged violations of rules against homosexual contact. These prisoners also face a greater risk of assault motivated by an adverse reaction to gender nonconformity.[28]

Because the criminal-punishment system itself is a significant source of racialized-gendered violence, increasing its resources and punishment capacity will not reduce violence against trans people. When advocates of hate-crime laws frame the criminal-punishment systems as a solution to the violence trans people face, they participate in the false logic that criminal punishment produces safety, when it is clear that it is actually a site of enormous violence. Criminal punishment cannot be the method we use to stop transphobia when the criminal punishment system is the most significant perpetrator of violence against trans people. Many commentators have used this support of the expansion of punishment regimes through the advent of hate-crime advocacy as an example of cooptation, where resistance struggles that have named certain conditions or types of violence come to be used to prop up the very arrangements that are harming the people who are resisting. A new mandate to punish trans-phobic people is added to the arsenal of justifications for a system that primarily locks up and destroys the lives of poor people, people of color, indigenous people, people with disabilities, and immigrants and that uses gender-based sexual violence as one of its daily tools of discipline against people of all genders.[29]

Much of the thinking behind the need for hate-crime and antidiscrimination legislation, including by advocates who recognize how limited these interventions are as avenues for increasing the life chances of trans people, is about the significance of having our experiences of discrimination and violence named in law. The belief that being named in this way has a benefit for the well-being of trans people has to be reexamined with an understanding that the alleged benefits of such naming provides even greater opportunity for harmful systems to claim fairness and equality while continuing to kill us. Hate-crime and antidiscrimination laws declare that punishment systems and economic arrangements are now non-transphobic, yet these laws not only fail to eradicate transphobia but also strengthen systems that perpetrate it.

This analysis illuminates how law-reform work that merely tinkers with systems to make them look more inclusive while leaving their most violent operations intact must be a concern of many social movements today. For example, prison abolitionists in the United States argue that the project of prison reform, which is usually aimed at reducing certain kinds of violence or unfairness in the prison system, has always functioned to maintain and to expand imprisonment.[30] Prison-reform efforts aimed at a reducing a variety of harms, such as gender and sexual violence, medical neglect and abuse, and overcrowding, to name but a few, have often been made by well-meaning people who wanted to address the horrors of prison life. But these reform efforts have been incorporated into the project of prison expansion, mobilized as rationales for building and filling more and more prisons. Abolitionists caution that a system designed from its inception as a technology of racialized control through exile and punishment will use any rationale necessary to achieve that purpose.

A recent example of particular interest to feminism and trans politics is the 2003 National Prison Rape Elimination Act (NPREA). Although it was passed in the name of preventing sexual assault, the NPREA has been used to further enforce and to increase penalties against prisoners for consensual sexual activity, including such activities as handholding. Abolitionist activists doing prisoner support work have pointed out that because some of the main tools the NPREA uses are punishment tools, those tools have become just another part of the arsenal used by punishment systems to increase sentences, to target prisoners of color and queer and trans prisoners, and to expand imprisonment. It is unclear whether the new rules have reduced sexual violence, but it *is* clear that they have increased punishment.[31] Activists considering using law reform as a tool, then, have to be extraordinarily vigilant to determine whether they are actually strengthening and expanding various systems' capacities to harm or whether our work is part of dismantling those capacities.[32]

In prison- and immigration-reform contexts, trans activists are raising concerns about the danger of dividing affected populations by mobilizing ideas about who constitutes a "deserving" or "undeserving" subject. Campaigns that focus on immigrants portrayed as "hard working" (racist, antipoor code for those who do not need support like public benefits or housing) and "law abiding" (not caught up in the criminal punishment system) or that frame immigration issues in terms of family unity relying on heteropatriarchal constructs, further stigmatize those who do not fit the "deserving" frame and create policies that only benefit a narrow swath of affected people. Similarly, campaigns about imprisonment that only focus on people convicted of nonviolent crimes, "political" prisoners, or people exonerated by the introduction of new evidence, risk refining the system in ways that justify and legitimize the bulk of its continued operation by eliminating its most obvious contradictions. Three concerns about law-reform projects permeate many sites of resistance. First, these projects change only what the law says about what a system is doing but not its actual impact. Second, they refine a system in ways that help it continue to target the most-vulnerable people while only partially or temporarily removing a few of the less vulnerable from its path. And finally, law-reform projects often provide rationales and justifications for the expansion of harmful systems.

Freeman's critique of the perpetrator perspective helps us understand how a discrimination-focused law-reform strategy that aims to prohibit the consideration of certain categories of identity in the context of certain decisions (who to hire, fire, evict, house, or assault) misconceives how the violences of racism, ableism, xenophobia, transphobia, sexism, and homophobia operate. Freeman's work shows how discrimination law fails to remedy the harms it claims to attend to and actually can empower systems that maldistribute life chances. Reconceptualizing the theory of power and struggle that underlies such law reforms allows us to turn our attention to other systems in law that produce structured insecurity and shortened life spans for trans people and consider alternative avenues of intervention.

Examining the operation of legal systems that administer life chances at the population level, such as welfare systems, punishment systems, health-care systems, and immigration systems, can expose how law operates to sort people into subpopulations facing different exposures to security and insecurity. Looking at sites of the legal administration of societal norms, we can see how certain populations come to have such pervasive experiences with both abandonment and imprisonment. From that vantage point, we can strategize about how to use legal reform tools as part of a broader strategy to dismantle capitalism's murderous structures while we build alternative methods of meeting human needs and organizing political participation. Because of the obvious failures of the most-popular contemporary law-reform strategies to address harms trans people are facing, trans experience can offer a location from which to consider the broader questions of the neoliberal cooptation of social movements through law reform and the institutionalization of resistance and from which to reframe the problems of violence and poverty that impact marginalized populations in ways that give us new inroads to intervention.

If we shift our framework from trans rights to critical trans resistance, we find ourselves with new analysis of the harms that people who defy gender norms face and new ideas for how we might dismantle systems that produce and enforce gender norms. Such a shift means that we move from demands for recognition and inclusion in law to demands for material changes to our lives. We recognize formal legal equality as a window dressing for harmful and violent political and economic arrangements (settler colonialism, white supremacy, capitalism, heteropatriarchy), and we come to understand that what we want and need will never be won through a legal system founded in and dedicated to preserving racialized-gendered property statuses. Our social movement strategies, then, become centered in mobilization, and our targets become the sites of violence we see producing trans death.

The demands for wealth redistribution, prison abolition, and an end to immigration enforcement that are emerging from trans communities suggest a critical trans politics guided by the urgent circumstances we face and a desire to center those living under the most severe forms of coercive violence as a guide for prioritization. The social-movement infrastructure we need to win these demands is far more participatory, democratic, and decentralized than what has emerged in law reform-centered rights-seeking formations. The loud concerns raised within social movements in the last decade about the roles nonprofitization and professionalization have played in containing and undermining transformative social change are useful to trans politics: We perceive the current push to institutionalize our work in those same hierarchical, elitist, undemocratic, and unaccountable forms to support the same narrow status-quo affirming agenda.[33] Across the United States, local communities are proposing and creating different tools, forms, and agendas to address these concerns and to innovate infrastructure for trans resistance. This resistance refuses to make itself legible in a neoliberal framework; to articulate demands for rights that reproduce racist, ableist, antipoor, xenophobic frameworks of deservingness and undeservingness; to sell off transformative goals for funding opportunities; or to endorse violent institutions for a chance at being nominally invited to be part of them. Co-developing this critical trans politics requires all of us to tap our creativity, imagination, bravery, compassion, humility, self-reflection, patience, generosity, and perseverance as we seek change deep enough to dismantle the violences that are foundational to our current conditions.

NOTES

1. This text of this chapter is excerpted from my book *Normal Life: Administrative Violence, Critical Trans Politics and the Limits of Law* (Brooklyn, NY: South End Press, 2011).

2. National Gay and Lesbian Task Force, "Jurisdictions with Explicitly Transgender-Inclusive Non-Discrimination Laws," (2008), http://thetaskforce.org/downloads/reports/fact_sheets/all_jurisdictions_w_pop_8_08.pdf (accessed November 27, 2010).

3. National Center for Transgender Equality, "Hate Crimes," 2008, www.nctequality.org/Hate_Crimes.asp.2008 (accessed January 4, 2009).

4. See *Ulane v. Eastern Airlines*, 742 F.2d 1081 (7th Cir. 1984), where the Seventh Circuit Court of Appeals found that a transwoman who was dismissed from her job as an airline pilot was not protected under the sex-discrimination clause of Title VII of the Civil Rights Act of 1964, holding that "Title VII does not protect transsexuals"; and *Oiler v. Winn Dixie, Louisiana Inc.,* No.Civ.A. 00-3114, 2002 WL 31098541 (E.D.La. Sept. 16, 2002), where the U.S. District Court for the Eastern District of Louisiana found that a man who was fired from his job for occasionally cross-dressing outside work was not protected under Title VII sex discrimination, even though his behavior had nothing to do with his job performance.

5. Rebecca L. Stotzer, "Gender Identity and Hate Crimes: Violence against Transgender People in Los Angeles County," *Sexuality Research and Social Policy: Journal of NSRC* 5, no. 1 (March 2008), http://nsrc.

sfsu.edu/sexuality_research_social_policy.

6. Angela P. Harris, "From Stonewall to the Suburbs? Toward a Political Economy of Sexuality," *William and Mary Bill of Rights Journal* 14, no. 4 (April 2006): 1539–1582.

7. See *Goins v. West Group*, 619 N.W.2d 424 (Minn. App. Ct. 2000), where the Minnesota Supreme Court held that employers may restrict restroom and locker-room access based on birth sex; and *Hispanic Aids Forum v. Estate of Bruno*, 16 Misc.3d 960, 839 N.Y.S.2d 691 (N.Y. Sup., 2007), where a New York Supreme Court judge ruled in favor of a nonprofit organization that was facing eviction based on its failure to comply with a landlord's demands that it disclose the birth sex of its clients, holding that the physical anatomy of trans people is not relevant to gender identity. In *Ettsity v. Utah Transit Authority*, 502 F.3d 1215 (10th Cir. 2007), the Tenth Circuit held that a trans woman bus driver who was fired because she used women's restrooms as needed at various stops on her bus route was not protected by Title VII's prohibition against sex discrimination and gender stereotyping.

8. A recent survey of 6,450 transgender and gender-nonconforming people in the United States found that 57 percent had experienced significant family rejection. Jamie M. Grant, Lisa A. Mottet, and Justin Tanis, *Injustice at Every Turn: A Report of the National Transgender Discrimination Survey*, Executive Summary (Washington, DC: National Gay and Lesbian Task Force and National Center for Transgender Equality, 2011), www.thetaskforce.org/downloads/reports/reports/ntds_summary.pdf.

9. The same study found that 19 percent of transgender and gender-nonconforming people had been refused medical treatment due to their gender, 28 percent had postponed medical care when they were sick or injured due to discrimination, and 48 percent had postponed care when they were sick or injured because they could not afford it. The study also found that respondents reported a rate of HIV infection more than four times the national average, with rates higher among trans people of color. Grant, Mottet, and Tanis, *Injustice at Every Turn*.

10. The study also confirmed that trans people live in extreme poverty. Respondents were nearly four times more likely to have a household income of less than $10,000 per year compared to the general population. Grant, Mottet, and Tanis, *Injustice at Every Turn*.

11. Alan David Freeman, "Legitimizing Racial Discrimination through Anti-discrimination Law: A Critical Review of Supreme Court Doctrine," in *Critical Race Studies: The Key Writings That Formed the Movement*, ed. Kimberlé Crenshaw, Neil Gotanda, Garry Peller, and Kendall Thomas (New York: New Press, 1996), 29–45.

12. See *San Antonio Independent School District v. Rodriguez*, 411 U.S. 1 (1973), where the U.S. Supreme Court held that the severe imbalance in a school district's funding of its primary and secondary schools based on the income levels of the residents of each district is not an unconstitutional violation of Equal Protection rights under the Fourteenth Amendment.

13. David M. White, "The Requirement of Race-Conscious Evaluation of LSAT Scores for Equitable Law School Admission," *Berkeley La Raza Law Journal* 12, no. 2 (Fall 2001): 399; Susan Sturm and Lani Guinier, "The Future of Affirmative Action: Reclaiming the Innovative Ideal," *California Law Review* 84, no. 4 (July 1996): 953.

14. Freeman, "Legitimizing Racial Discrimination through Anti-discrimination Law."

15. *Milliken*, 418 U.S. 717; 87 *Parents Involved in Community Schools*, 551 U.S. 701.

16. Mazher Ali, Jeanette Huezo, Brian Miller, Wanjiku Mwangi, and Mike Prokosch, *State of the Dream 2011: Austerity for Whom?* (Boston: United for a Fair Economy, 2011), www.faireconomy.org/files/

State_of_the_Dream_2011.pdf.

17. Dan Irving, "Normalized Transgressions: Legitimizing the Transsexual Body as Productive," *Radical History Review*, no. 100 (Winter 2008): 38–59.

18. Ibid. Several significant famous trans discrimination cases follow this pattern, with media and advocates portraying the assimilable characteristics of the trans person to emphasize his or her deserving nature. One example is the highly publicized case of Diane Schroer, who won a lawsuit after she lost a job at the Library of Congress when disclosed her trans identity. *Time* magazine described her as

> an ex-Special Forces colonel . . . Schroer was a dream candidate, a guy out of a Tom Clancy novel: he had jumped from airplanes, undergone grueling combat training in extreme heat and cold, commanded hundreds of soldiers, helped run Haiti during the U.S. intervention in the '90s—and, since 9/11, he had been intimately involved in secret counterterrorism planning at the highest levels of the Pentagon. He had been selected to organize and run a new, classified antiterror organization, and in that position he had routinely briefed Defense Secretary Donald Rumsfeld. He had also briefed Vice President Cheney more than once. Schroer had been an action hero, but he also had the contacts and intellectual dexterity to make him an ideal congressional analyst.

> Schroer's public persona as a patriot and terrorist-fighter was used by advocates to promote the idea of her deservingness in ways that those concerned about the racist, anti-immigrant, imperialist War on Terror might take issue with. Critics have similarly pointed out dynamics of deservingness that determine which queer and trans murder victims become icons in the battle for hate-crime legislation. White victims tend to be publicly remembered (e.g., Harvey Milk, Brandon Teena, Matthew Shepard), their lives memorialized in films and movies (*Milk, Boys Don't Cry, Larabee*), and laws named after them (Matthew Shepard Local Law Enforcement Enhancement Act). The names of these white victims and the struggles for healing and justice on the part of their friends and family are in greater circulation than victims of color through media and nonprofit channels, even though people of color lose their lives at higher rates. Sanesha Stewart, Amanda Milan, Marsha P. Johnson, Duanna Johnson, Ruby Ordeñana are just a few of the trans women of color whose murders have been mourned by local communities but mostly ignored by media, large nonprofits, and lawmakers.

19. Roy Walmsley, *World Prison Population List*, 7th ed. (London, UK: International Centre for Prison Studies, 2005).

20. U.S. Department of Justice, "Key Crime and Justice Facts at a Glance," 2009, www.ojp.usdoj.gov/bjs/glance.htm.

21. Walmsley, *World Prison Population List*.

22. The PEW Center on the States, *One in 100: Behind Bars in America 2008,* 2008, www.pewcenteronthestates.org/uploadedFiles/8015PCTS_Prison08_FINAL_2-1-1_FOR WEB.pdf.

23. Government Accounting Office, "Information on Criminal Aliens Incarcerated in Federal and State Prisons and Local Jails," Congressional briefing, March 25, 2005, http://gao.gov/new.items/d05337r.pdf.

24. Lauraet Magnani and Harmon L. Wray, *Beyond Prisons: A New Interfaith Paradigm for Our Failed Prison*

System, A Report by the American Friends Service Committee, Criminal Justice Task Force (Minneapolis, Minnesota: Fortress Press, 2006).

25. Anna M. Agathangelou, D. Morgan Bassichis, and Tamara L. Spira, "Intimate Investments: Homonormativity, Global Lockdown, and the Seductions of Empire," *Radical History Review,* no. 100 (Winter 2008): 120–143; Morgan Bassichis, Alex Lee, and Dean Spade, "Building an Abolitionist Trans Movement with Everything We've Got," in *Captive Genders: Transembodiment and the Prison Industrial Complex,* ed. Nat Smith and Eric A. Stanley (Oakland, CA: AK Press, 2011); Magnani and Wray, *Beyond Prisons;* Kristina Wertz and Masen Davis, "When Laws Are Not Enough: A Study of the Economic Health of Transgender People and the Need for a Multidisciplinary Approach to Economic Justice," *Seattle Journal of Social Justice* 8, no. 2 (Spring–Summer 2010): 467–489.

26. Dean Spade, "Documenting Gender," *Hastings Law Journal* 59, no. 4 (2008): 731; Chris Daley and Shannon Minter, *Trans Realities: A Legal Needs Assessment of San Francisco's Transgender Communities* (San Francisco: Transgender Law Center, 2003).

27. Joey L. Mogul, Andrea J. Ritchie, and Kay Whitlock, *Queer (In)Justice* (Boston: Beacon Press, 2011).

28. D. Morgan Bassichis, *"It's War in Here": A Report on the Treatment of Transgender and Intersex People in New York State Men's Prisons* (New York: Sylvia Rivera Law Project, 2007), http://srlp.org/files/warinhere.pdf; Alexander L. Lee, *Gendered Crime and Punishment: Strategies to Protect Transgender, Gender Variant and Intersex People in America's Prisons* (pts 1 and 2), Gender Identity Center *Trans in Prison Journal* (Summer 2004), Gender Identity Center *Trans in Prison Journal* (Fall 2004) (old issues of the journal can be requested through the Gender Identity Center of Colorado, Gender Identity Center Trans in Prison, and an earlier version of this paper is available at www.justdetention.org/pdf/nowheretogobutout.pdf); Christopher D. Man and John P. Cronan, "Forecasting Sexual Abuse in Prison: The Prison Subculture of Masculinity as a Backdrop for 'Deliberate Indifference,'" *Journal of Criminal Law and Criminology* 92, no. 1 (2001): 127; Alex Coolman, Lamar Glover, and Kara Gotsch, *Still in Danger: The Ongoing Threat of Sexual Violence against Transgender Prisoners* (Los Angeles: Stop Prisoner Rape and the ACLU National Prison Project, 2005), www.justdetention.org/pdf/stillindanger.pdf; Janet Baus and Dan Hunt, *Cruel and Unusual* (New York: Reid Productions, 2006).

29. Bassichis, Lee, and Spade, "Building an Abolitionist Trans Movement with Everything We've Got"; Agathangelou, Bassichis, and Spira, "Intimate Investments"; Dean Spade and Craig Willse, "Confronting the Limits of Gay Hate Crimes Activism: A Radical Critique," *Chicano-Latino Law Review* 21, no. 2 (Spring 2000): 38; Sarah Lamble, "Retelling Racialized Violence, Remaking White Innocence: The Politics of Interlocking Oppressions in Transgender Day of Remembrance," *Sexuality Research and Social Policy: Journal of NSRC* 5, no. 1 (March 2008): 24–42.

30. Angela Y. Davis, *Are Prisons Obsolete?* (New York: Seven Stories Press, 2003).

31. Gabriel Arkles's scholarship has explored how rules that purport to protect prisoners from sexual violence are frequently used to punish consensual sexual or friendship relationships, to prohibit masturbation, and to target queer and gender-nonconforming prisoners. The existence of such rules can also increase risks of sexual behavior and create opportunities for blackmail and abuse by corrections officers. See letter from Chase Strangio and Z. Gabriel Arkles to Attorney General Holder, May 10, 2010, page 9, http://srlp.org/files/SRLP%20PREA%20comment%20Docket%20no%20OAG-131.pdf; Gabriel Arkles, *Transgender Communities and the Prison Industrial Complex,* lecture at Northeastern

University School of Law, February 2010. Arkles offers as an example of this type of problematic policymaking Idaho's Prison Rape Elimination Provision (Control No. 325.02.01.001, 2004, www.idoc.idaho. gov/policy/int3250201001.pdf), which includes a prohibition on "male" prisoners having a "feminine or effeminate hairstyle." E-mail from Gabriel Arkles, February 21, 2011 (on file with the author).

32. Further controversy has emerged around the NPREA since the Department of Justice proposed national standards "for the detection, prevention, reduction, and punishment of prison rape, as mandated by" the NPREA, which exclude immigration facilities. See National Juvenile Defender Center and the Equity Project, Transgender Law Center, Lambda Legal Education and Defense Fund, National Center for Lesbian Rights, American Civil Liberties Union, Sylvia Rivera Law Project, National Center for Transgender Equality, "Protecting Lesbian, Gay, Bisexual, Transgender, Intersex, and Gender Nonconforming people from Sexual Abuse and Harassment in Correctional Settings," Comments Submitted in Response to Docket No. OAG-131; AG Order No. 3244-2011 National Standards to Prevent, Detect, and Respond to Prison Rape April 4, 2011, 47–48 (on file with the author); Human Rights Watch, ACLU Washington Legislative Office, Immigration Equality, Just Detention International, National Immigrant Justice Center, National Immigration Forum, Physicians for Human Rights, Prison Fellowship, Southern Center for Human Rights, Texas Civil Rights Project, Women's Refugee Commission, "US: Immigration Facilities Should Apply Prison Rape Elimination Act Protections: Letter to U.S. President Barack Obama," February 15, 2011, www.hrw.org/es/news/2011/02/15/ us-immigration-facilities-should-apply-prison-rape-elimination-act-protections.

33. See INCITE! Women of Color against Violence, ed., *The Revolution Will Not Be Funded: Beyond the Nonprofit Industrial Complex* (Cambridge, MA: South End Press, 2007); Dean Spade and Rickke Mananzala, "The Non-profit Industrial Complex and Trans Resistance," *Sexuality Research and Social Policy: Journal of NSRC* 5, no. 1 (March 2008): 53–71.

———————————— ○ ————————————

END OF CHAPTER QUESTIONS

1. What law reforms should be sought to protect transgender rights?
2. What is "critical trans resistance"? How can it be used to dismantle the legal system, which continues to produce and enforce gender "norms"?
3. What measures can be taken to eliminate transphobia in the legal system?
4. List four things of which transgender people are targets in prisons?

CHAPTER 4

Addressing Homophobia and Heterosexism

Cedric Herring and Loren Henderson

Popular images of lesbian, gay, bisexual, and transgendered (LGBT) people suggest that they are better off economically and occupationally than their heterosexual counterparts. Media representations of LGBT affluence often conceal the possibility of workplace discrimination against these groups. At the same time, scholarly research suggests that LGBT people suffer a discrimination penalty in terms of wages and occupational prestige. This is due to the fact that American society is stratified based on sexuality.

Although sexuality is usually a less obvious characteristic of individuals than their race or gender, it does become salient within institutional settings, especially when those holding power within the workplace categorize employees' sexuality or rely on perceptions of employee sexuality to make discriminatory distinctions. So, even when gay, lesbian, or bisexual employees choose not to disclose their identities to coworkers or employers, others still may speculate about their identities "given military discharge records, arrests and/or convictions, marital status, residential neighborhood, or silences in conversations and gossip."[1]

Over the past two decades, the number of companies addressing sexual orientation as part of their valuing diversity initiatives has increased fairly rapidly. As of 2010, 87 percent of the *Fortune* 500 companies had implemented non-discrimination policies that include sexual orientation, and 46 percent had policies that include gender identity.[2] But as of 2012, there is no federal law that consistently protects LGBT individuals from employment discrimination. It remains legal in 29 states to discriminate based on sexual orientation, and in 35 states to do so based on transgender identity or expression. As a result, LGBT people face discrimination in employment, including being fired, being denied promotions, and experiencing harassment on the job. Hard-working lesbian, gay, bisexual, and transgender Americans have lost their livelihoods simply because of who they are. And millions more go to work every day facing that threat. The purpose of this chapter is to investigate stratification patterns in the economic sphere that are based on sexual orientation and to identify organizational best practices designed to create more inclusive, equitable, and productive workplaces for LGBT employees.

SEXUAL ORIENTATION AND IDENTITY

How large is the LGBT population in the United States? Understanding the size of the LGBT population is an important step in attempting to inform diversity research, public policy, and research topics. But knowing the answer to this question is not as easy or straightforward as we would like. For example, according to Gary Gates, an estimated 19 million Americans (8.2 percent) report that they have engaged in same-sex sexual behavior.[3] More than 25 million Americans acknowledge at least some same-sex sexual attraction. Still, less than 4 percent of adults in the United States identify as lesbian, gay, or bisexual. An estimated 0.3 percent of adults are transgender. This implies that there are approximately 9 million LGBT Americans.

Why are there such disparities in these numbers? A debate continues as to the true nature of sexual orientation and identity.[4] On one side of the debate are those essentialists who view sexual orientation and identity as "real," an essence that is universal that can be seen throughout history and across cultures. Such views often assume that sexual identity is both biologically based and static. In addition, most of the essentialist literature on sexual identity upholds a binary scheme of sexuality that suggests that individuals classify themselves as either heterosexual or homosexual. And homosexuals are "gay" if they are male, and "lesbian" if they are female. On the other side of the debate are social constructionists who hold that sexual orientation and identity are not fixed, but rather are historically contingent and culturally specific. Proponents of such views often suggest that sexual identities are shaped by social, political, economic, and cultural forces, and these identities can challenge or reinforce heterosexist notions of sexuality.[5]

Theorizing on this topic is varied and reflects the social location (e.g., race, class, and sexual orientation) of participants in the discourse. Although an increased awareness of LGBT sexual identities exists, contemporary analyses are often conducted by those who are located within several dominant societal groups (e.g., White, middle class, formally educated academics, etc.). As a consequence, there remains a shortage of systematic research focusing on the sexual identities of those who are not part of dominant social groups.[6] In order to promote a more complex understanding of those within subjugated groups, it is crucial to examine the experiences of those facing multiple oppressions.

Early scholarship and theorizing about sexual identity began with the juxtaposition of homosexuality and heterosexuality. In his article "The Invention of Heterosexuality," Jonathan Katz argues that contrary to what most believe or are taught, the idea of heterosexuality is a modern invention, dating to the late nineteenth century.[7] Katz supports his argument by tracing back the evolution of the acts and terms of heterosexuality and homosexuality. Heterosexuality and homosexuality should not be labeled as binary forms of sexual identity; rather, it is the act of sex that is hetero or homosexual, not the person. People were committing these acts of hetero and homosexuality before these terms were even invented. And back before medicine, psychology, and society wanted to label these acts, sex with people of different sex and the same sex was quite common. Dr. James G. Kiernan is known for first using the term heterosexuality in 1892. However, how he used the term in 1892 is different from today. Kiernan claimed heterosexuality to be "inclinations to both sexes." He did not have a name for those who demonstrated an inclination for only the opposite sex. However, Dr. Krafft-Ebing did not agree with Kiernan's ideas, and later that year he defined heterosexuality as it is currently understood: an erotic feeling toward the opposite sex. Krafft-Ebing defined homosexuality as an erotic feeling toward the same sex, and psychosexual hermaphroditism as an erotic impulse towards both sexes. Doctors normalized heterosexuality. However, Kinsey explains that there is no normal and abnormal in science. Kinsey claims that homosexuality and heterosexuality are nature's doing. He suggests that humans do not choose whether to be homosexual or heterosexual.

Along with the social construction of the categorization of these sexual identities came a hierarchal relationship between the two categories. Heterosexuality became the dominant, normal identity. Homosexuality came to be viewed as the abnormal, deviant identity. This could be due to the fact that intercourse with different sexes, between a man and a woman, produces procreation whereas sex between two men or two women does not. Early works viewed homosexuality as deviant and, at worst, pathological.[8] The essentialist perspective framed sexual identity within a binary system that is biologically based. It suggested that homosexuality is an abnormal condition which needs to be studied and cured. However, during the 1970s, research on sexual identity increased. This was due, in large part, to the gay and lesbian liberation movement, which focused on eradicating the stigma of homosexuality.[9]

Homophobia—negative feelings toward homosexuality and people who are identified or perceived as being homosexual—rather than the stigma of homosexuality *per se* is the true culprit that contributes to the silencing, abuse, and psychological and physical trauma faced by hundreds of thousands of members of the LGBT community.[10] The stigma of homosexuality is a reflection and product of homophobia rather than a separate social dynamic.

The symbolic interactionist framework provides some of the core concepts that inform contemporary social constructionists. For example, one might view LGBT status as a stigma—a "spoiled identity" in Erving Goffman's terms—that needs to be managed. Homophobia and the stigma of bisexuality may contribute to the "closet"-type behaviors exhibited among some LGBT people.[11] One way members of the LGBT community may manage their impressions is by controlling the naming process. In part, this is accomplished by choosing their own labels and encouraging others to make use of these names. "Bisexuals," for example, by identifying themselves as bisexuals rather than straight or gay, determine the degree to which their behaviors and ideas fit a heterosexual identity or a homosexual identity. They form the meanings that one attaches to one's self as an object, and they carry expectations for particular kinds of behaviors.[12]

As Paula Rust points out, however, scientists have attempted to elaborate developmental models of coming out that suggest that it is a linear process of self-discovery.[13] She argues that such depictions of a linear process are inaccurate. They usually replace a socially imposed notion of heterosexual identity with a lesbian or gay identity as the accurate reflection of the essence of the individual. But as Rust notes, these models rarely account for bisexual identity as an authentic identity. When they acknowledge bisexual identity at all, they usually cast it as a phase one might pass through on the way to adopting a lesbian or gay identity. Researchers operating within these linear developmental models of coming out usually ask people about the ages at which they experienced particular sexual milestones, and then, reporting the average ages, describe coming out as an ordered sequence of events. Such research suggests that lesbians first experience sexual attraction to other women at an average age of 12 or 13, but do not become aware of these sexual feelings until late adolescence. Rust argues that the portrait of sexual identity formation that is painted by these average ages is not only grossly simplified but factually inaccurate. Based on research with lesbian-identified and bisexual-identified women, she shows that average ages conceal a great deal of variation in the coming out process, both among and between lesbian and bisexual women. In contrast to the linear portrait painted by average ages, she suggests that lesbian and bisexual women experience each milestone event at a wide range of ages; many women do not experience all of the so-called milestone events; women who do experience these events experience them in various orders, and some women experience some events repeatedly.

Postmodern and queer theorists have problematized the notions of sexual identities as real categories. They argue that labeling one's self replicates the binary boundaries of sexuality and continues to establish hegemonic ideals of heterosexuality. Postmodern and queer theorists attempt to move beyond the labels and challenge the limits that sexual identities create.[14] They argue that people should abandon identities altogether and search to understand the social and political oppressions that labels recreate. Queer theory becomes a frontal assault on the notions of homosexuality as "deviant." Overall, these theorists analyze the underlying meanings of sex and sexual identity as socially constructed. A critique of queer theory is that postmodernists fail to "acknowledge the very real structures and physical bodies . . . in which individuals live."[15] This line of scholarship once again silences the voices of marginalized groups such as African American women who identify as gay, lesbian, and bisexual at a point in history when their voices have the greatest opportunity to be heard. It does so without creating space to acknowledge that these women continue to experience the world as if their identities are real and fixed within society. It is ironic that just as African-American women who sleep with women are gaining a toehold in the corridors of power, the authority of their voices as African-American gay, lesbian, or bisexual women is challenged through destabilizing these identities.

Revealing one's sexual identity places him or her in a position to be labeled as "lesbian," "gay," "bisexual," etc. These terms take on personal and political meanings that may or may not reflect the internalized views that individuals hold for themselves.[16] For example, Jeffery Weeks points out that homosexually inclined individuals may participate in the LGBT community and take on a homosexual identity while not engaging in homosexual behavior.[17] Others, however, may have sex with someone of the same gender and reject homosexual identity entirely. Weeks continues to remind us that homosexual identity depends on the meanings that the actors attribute to homosexuality, and that sexual identities are historically and culturally specific. Weeks also demonstrates that sexuality has become a potent political issue that creates the bases for political mobilizations among LGBT people. He asserts that lesbian identity, in particular, is constructed within Western society as a political choice that women make in order to demonstrate solidarity, sisterhood, and affection with other women and feminism, as well as an expression of sexual preference.

According to Shane Phelan, mainstream notions of lesbianism are often framed by essentialist ideals that construct lesbians as politically active, middle-class, anti-male feminists who have sex only with women.[18] Lesbianism, however, may not be simply a part of someone's essence. Nor does it necessarily exist outside of a specific historical period. Rather, it may be a critical space located within social structures that are more about challenging patriarchy and heteronormativity than sexual behavior.[19] Phelan asserts that identifying as lesbian involves a creation of the self in a community that guides the process of becoming lesbian.[20] Moreover, it involves enacting and inventing the meanings of lesbianism in a specific historical period which is both personal and political. Taking on a lesbian identity, then, reflects both individuals' internal beliefs about who they are as well as their politics.

Dwight McBride also discusses the role that politics play in the sexual identification of women who sleep with women, specifically when identifying as gay versus lesbian.[21] He reveals that even the mainstream media presents women such as Ellen DeGeneres as a non-threatening, all-American girl-next-door with whom Americans can be comfortable. In addition, referring to them as "gay" instead of "lesbian" creates the idea that homosexuals are just like heterosexuals. They want the same entrenched

American dream of the house with a picket fence and someone to love them (e.g., someone who shares similar values and politics).

Steve Valocchi claims that the construction of labels such as homosexual, gay, and lesbian is a class-inflected process that is the product of the class dynamics associated with the making of a capitalist state.[22] He states that the lesbian and gay movement of the 1970s worked from the premise of shattering the invisibility of gays and lesbians in order to support an essentialized identity through social institutions, practices, and cultural traditions. Advertisers within the consumer culture then monopolized these niche markets by constructing lesbian and gay identities around consumption. They conflated income with gay identity. The use of advertisement, then, enables individuals to claim their identities by the products they consume and the activities in which they partake. Individuals then associate gay/lesbian identity with middle-class status, ultimately moving these identities away from the political arena to a consumer category about style and fashion.

Revealing one's sexual identity is as much personal as it is political. Such identities are socially constructed. This ability to manage what some might view as a spoiled identity allows LGBT people to manage the impressions others have of them. But sexual identities are not binary or fixed; rather, they are historically contingent, culturally specific, and shaped by social, political, economic, and cultural forces.

SEXUAL ORIENTATION AND STRATIFICATION OUTCOMES

There are several theories that may help us to frame and understand the question of whether income and prestige are stratified according to sexual orientation. "Human capital" theory, for example, holds that education is a key to obtaining higher levels of income and occupational prestige. In this view, there is a direct relationship between educational attainment and increased income and status on the job. However, there is debate as to exactly how education matters for gains in income and status. Human capital theory argues that inequality occurs because some people make the choice to invest in themselves and their futures by gaining additional education and job-related skills while others do not. According to this theory, individuals invest in their stock of skills by paying or foregoing something in the present for the sake of some future gain. For example, people invest in education in order to increase their future wages. School involves the direct cost of tuition, and the opportunity-cost of foregone wages and foregone opportunities to use one's time for leisure. Human capital investments include such things as education, job training, seeking out information, willingness to relocate, making sure that one is healthy, etc. or any other factor that will make a person potentially more productive to his or her employer. Human capital theory suggests that some people earn more simply because they have invested more in themselves in terms of human capital. There is also the tendency for those who are "abler" to invest in themselves more than those who are not as capable. Talented people invest more in themselves than less talented people.

According to human capital theory, employers also act rationally. They seek to hire employees who will be the most productive so that their efforts will lead to greater profitability. If two workers show up for a job, the employer will select the worker who offers the greatest marginal productivity for a given wage. If the employer fails to do this, his competitor will do so and will be able to sell his widgets for less and ultimately drive the other employer out of business. Human capital theory, then, argues that higher education increases skills and makes people more productive on the job; thus, highly educated people will receive greater financial rewards and pay than those with less education and experience.[23]

But sometimes, even if groups are equally talented and have made equal investments in themselves, some employers still express tastes for discrimination. That is, they will prefer certain types of workers over others for non-rational reasons. While the employer may go out of business in the long run, in the short run, the discriminated-against worker will earn less. To the degree that this happens systematically against certain groups, there will be inequality (stratification).

In 2007, more than 12 percent of Americans were officially below the poverty line.[24] These statistics include people from every race, gender, age group, and region. As mentioned above, a popular stereotype suggests that lesbians and gay men are more affluent, more highly educated, and have higher incomes than do their heterosexual counterparts.

Research consistently shows, however, that LGBT people, especially lesbians and transgender people, endure vast income inequality compared to their heterosexual peers.[25] Lesbians, gays, and bisexuals are as likely to live in poverty as are heterosexual people and their families.[26] Lesbian couples, for example, tend to have much higher poverty rates than either heterosexual or male couples. They are twice as likely as straight married couples to live in poverty. Lesbian couples are especially hard-hit, as women continue to make 78 cents to every dollar that men make. Still, bisexual women are more than twice as likely as lesbians to live in poverty (17.7 versus 7.8 percent), and bisexual men are over 50 percent more likely to live in poverty than gay men (9.7 versus 6.2 percent). And nearly two in three (66 percent) transgender people make less than US$25,000 a year. The children of gay couples are twice as likely to be poor as are the offspring of straight, married couples. Randy Albelda and his colleagues suggest that "vulnerability to employment discrimination, lack of access to marriage, higher rates of being uninsured, less family support, or family conflict over coming out" all contribute to higher poverty rates among lesbians, gays, and bisexuals.

One of the solutions to such disparities is marriage equality and equalization of tax laws. Marriage equality is part of the solution, but there are other more basic measures, like passing the Employment Non-Discrimination Act (ENDA), eliminating LGBT discrimination in housing, making higher education and vocational training less expensive and more accessible, and improving education overall for everyone.

Albelda and his colleagues also suggest that "labor market reforms that help boost the wages of low-income workers will also benefit LGBT earners as well, such as higher minimum wages or larger earned income tax credits (EITC). Policies promoting equal pay for women would help raise the incomes of . . . lesbian couples, and might reduce the poverty gap for lesbian couples."[27]

LGBT INITIATIVES WITHIN CORPORATE AMERICA

Over the years, the federal government has enacted legislation to ensure that the rights of women, people of color, pregnant women, and employees with disabilities are protected in the workplace. Progressive companies then use these data to assess progress toward internal hiring and other diversity benchmarks. We believe that identifying work teams that need additional support, more education, and new policies and processes to improve employee engagement are important to organizations that are attempting to move from good to great in the diversity efforts. Unfortunately, many of these organizations lag behind when it comes to similar efforts with respect to sexuality. But the good news is that some best practices and factors have emerged as more companies implement LGBT Self-Identification programs. Many organizations have implemented nondiscrimination policies and provided benefits to LGBT employees. Frequently companies attend local LGBT Pride celebrations. Some sponsor programs that reach out to the emerging LGBT market. All of these programs are based on diversity, market share, and social responsibility goals.

How successful are companies in these efforts? How can you begin to evaluate LGBT initiatives within your company? It is important to have senior leaders within the organization acknowledge the significance of issues of equity and fairness, as well as the business case for inclusion as they relate to sexuality. A first step is the awareness that the data need to be collected. If an LGBT member or Employee Resource Group (ERG) exists within your organization, enlist their help to promote LGBT employees' willingness to self-identify. Be aware that many employees may not respond during the first year of a survey because they are unsure if their responses are anonymous or what the company will do with the information. Indeed, low return rates may occur in the first few years, but once a company shows a commitment to LGBT diversity, higher return rates will usually follow. A second step is for companies to realize what kind of data they need to collect and what they will do with the data in order to measure sexual orientation and gender so that they can take steps to make necessary improvements in the workplace. Allowing employees to opt in or opt out should be a goal of the program to develop a workplace where LGBT employees feel safe to "come out" and self-identify. A third step may include conducting an anonymous survey in order to assess the climate for LGBT employees. Anonymous climate surveys can include optional demographic questions on gender identity and sexual orientation that can then be reported through aggregated data broken down by business unit or function. Such surveys allow organizations to assess the climate of the workplace for LGBT employees. Results from such surveys can help guide changes that may lead to improved recruiting goals, higher promotion rates, and increased proportions of LGBT employees in management positions. As with any type of survey that involves demographic data (e.g., race, ethnicity, gender), organizational leaders should be prepared to take necessary corrective actions if and when the data reveal that discrimination is occurring.

The efforts of LGBT employee resource groups have been instrumental in initiating many of the changes that occur in organizations with respect to sexual orientation. We believe that developing leader-sanctioned resource groups is fundamental to building organizational culture-change processes. It is critically important to such resource groups to gain early support and endorsement of top organizational leaders. Often, a powerful strategy is for members of the LGBT resource groups to present the organizations' leaders with a clear "business case" for why sexual orientation matters in the workplace and in the larger community. It is also helpful for members of the LGBT resource group to meet with the organizations' leaders to discuss the impact of homophobia and heterosexism upon employees' lives. To gain the support of top leaders, some groups have collected and shared personal examples of how employees in their organization have been hurt by the current policies, business practices, or workplace dynamics. It is also instructive for LGBT members of the organization to explain how they and others have been passed over for promotions or how they have experienced harassing behaviors and homophobic comments so that they can help the organizations' leaders better understand and realize the depth and scope of the problems.

We believe there are several things organizations can do to improve the climate for LGBT members. In particular, as stated above, we believe that developing leader-sanctioned resource groups is important to generating organizational culture-change processes. We also believe that it is important that "leaders . . . use opportunities to re-emphasize their commitment to a policy of zero tolerance for homophobic harassment, discrimination and prejudice in the workplace, and state their expectation that all [members] strive to create a safe and productive . . . environment."[28]

We also believe that organizations can improve the climate for LGBT members by creating and then publicizing the existence of resource groups so that they can increase their membership. Usually, organizations can accomplish this by publishing articles in their newsletters or other outlets. They can also do so by advertising at Pride events or in the gay press. It is also possible to hold informal educational sessions for members. It may also be possible to conduct team-building sessions for group members. It is important to emphasize that such activities are open to all members.

Organizations should also offer awareness training programs to increase their members' knowledge about sexual orientation as an issue in the organization. Often, members of the LGBT resource group will take the lead in identifying potential speakers, educational topics, and group activities. These efforts should be partnered with the organization's diversity officers in order to include sexual orientation as a critical component of the organization's diversity training efforts. The goal of these efforts should be to help participants of various sexual orientations realize the similarities they share with each other. But consistent with the idea of critical diversity, such sessions should also shed light on the negative impact of prejudice and discrimination, especially on those who are LGBT. A challenge of such sessions is to show that the organization has no agenda in changing people's personal values or beliefs, but at the same time that it wants to create a safe and productive space for all organization members. Such sessions need to be geared toward providing members—especially senior leaders—with tools that will help them deepen their understanding and commitment to such issues.

Organizations should also consider developing LGBT Safe Zones. Such safe spaces are designed both to raise awareness about LGBT issues and to create space for people to voluntarily show their support for a LGBT-friendly environment. This should also be where members can openly hold conversations about issues related to sexual orientation. These LGBT Safe Zones may also be locations where rank-and-file members discuss LGBT issues of common concern.

Organizations also need to create policies that may help to manage homophobic behavior. Such policies need to include all relevant organizational policies that do not specifically include sexual orientation. Of course, these must include policies related to nondiscrimination and harassment. In keeping with critical diversity, they should also include policies related to fair business practices (recruiting, compensation, job assignments, promotions, and terminations), standards of conduct, and performance reviews. It is also important that organizations include benefit packages that ensure equitable benefits for LGBT members for themselves, their domestic partners, and their families. Such benefits may include things such as health, life, and disability insurance; family leave options; pensions, retirement plans, and stock options; emergency and bereavement options; flex time; and adoption assistance. Several organizations have come to realize that by offering equitable benefits they will increase their success at attracting and retaining talented members.

Finally, it is important that organizations communicate consistent messages. Leaders of LGBT resource groups often emphasize the need to communicate with managers and employees about the goals, activities, and purpose of their diversity efforts. It is important to raise issues about sexual orientation and to advertise educational events in newsletters, on webpages, on posters, and on list serves. As we mentioned previously, it is also important that members from the LGBT resource group meet personally with top leaders of the organization and diversity officers on a regular basis to keep the dialogue progressing on these issues. Even more, in order to sustain progress and organizational changes, it is critical that organizations create an infrastructure that ensures continued attention to and action on these issues.

NOTES

1. Badgett, 2001: 49
2. Day and Greene, 2006
3. Gates, 2011
4. Kohm and Yarhouse, 2002
5. Simon, 1996
6. Moore, 2008
7. Katz, 1990
8. Eliason, 2001; Esterberg, 1997; Lemelle and Battle, 2004; Newman, 2007; Bradford, 2004; and Collins, 2004
9. Stockdill, 2002
10. Battle and Bennett, 2000
11. Lemelle and Battle, 2004
12. Esterberg, 1997
13. Rust, 1996
14. Simon, 1996
15. Esterberg, 1997: 24
16. Lorde, 1982; and Takagi, 1996
17. Weeks, 1985
18. Phelan, 1993
19. Rich, 1980; and Phelan, 1993
20. Phelan, 1993
21. McBride, 2005
22. Valocchi, 1999
23. England, 1992
24. Albelda et al., 2009
25. Badgett, 2001; Badgett, Sears, and Ho, 2006; and Albelda et al., 2009
26. Albelda et al., 2009
27. Albelda et al., 2009: 15
28. Obear, 2000: 27

REFERENCES

Albelda, Randy, M. V. Lee Badgett, Alyssa Schneebaum, and Gary J. Gates, 2009. *Poverty in the Lesbian, Gay, and Bisexual Community.* Los Angeles, CA: The Williams Institute, UCLA School of Law.

Badgett, M. V. Lee. 2001. *Money, Myths, and Change: The Economic Lives of Lesbians and Gay Men.* Chicago, IL: University of Chicago Press.

Badgett, M. V. Lee, R. Bradley Sears, and Deborah Ho. 2006. "Supporting Families, Saving Funds: An Economic Analysis of Equality for Same-Sex Couples in Jersey." *Rutgers Journal of Law & Public Policy* 4 (1): 8–93.

Battle, Juan and Michael Bennett. 2000. "Research on Lesbian and Gay Populations within the African American Community: What Have We Learned?" *African American Research Perspectives* 6(2): 35–47.

Bradford, Mary. 2004. "The Bisexual Experience: Living in a Dichotomous Culture," in R. Fox (Ed.). *Current Research on Bisexuality: The Intersection of Race and Bisexuality: A Critical Overview of the Literature and Past, Present, and Future Directions of the "Borderlands".* Binghamton, NY: Harrington Park Press: 7–24.

Collins, Fuji. 2004. "The Intersection of Race and Bisexuality: A Critical Overview of the Literature and Past, Present, and Future Directions of the "Borderlands," in R. Fox (Ed.). *Current Research on Bisexuality: The Intersection of Race and Bisexuality: A Critical Overview of the Literature and Past, Present, and Future Directions of the "Borderlands".* Binghamton, NY: Harrington Park Press: 101.

Day, Nancy E. and Patricia G. Greene. 2006. "A Case for Sexual Orientation Diversity Management in Small and Large Organizations." *Human Resource Management* 47(3): 637–654.

Eliason, Michele. 2001. "Bi-Negativity: The Stigma Facing Bisexual Men." *Journal of Bisexuality* 1(2/3): 137–154.

England, Paula. 1992. *Comparable Worth: Theories and Evidence.* New York, NY: Aldine de Gruyter.

Esterberg, Kristin G. 1997. *Lesbian and Bisexual Identities: Constructing Communities, Constructing Selves.* Philadelphia, PA: Temple University Press.

Gates, Gary J. 2011. *How Many People Are Lesbian, Gay, Bisexual, and Transgender?* Los Angeles, CA: The Williams Institute, UCLA School of Law.

Katz, Jonathan Ned. 1990. "The Invention of Heterosexuality." *Socialist Review* 20(1): 7–34.

Kohm, Lynne Marie and Mark A. Yarhouse. 2002. "Fairness, Accuracy and Honesty in Discussing Homosexuality and Marriage." *Regent University Law Review* 14: 249–266.

Laumann, Edward, John Gagnon, Robert T. Michael, and Stuart Michaels. 2000. *The Social Organization of Sexuality: Sexual Practices in the United States.* Chicago, IL: University of Chicago Press.

Lemelle, Anthony and Juan Battle. 2004. "Black Masculinity Matters in Attitudes toward Gay Males." *Journal of Homosexuality* 47: 39–51.

Lorde, Audre. 1982. *Zami: A New Spelling of My Name.* Berkeley, CA: The Crossing Press.

McBride, Dwight. A. 2005. *Why I Hate Abercrombie & Fitch: Essays on Race and Sexuality.* New York, NY: New York University.

Moore, Mignon R. 2008. "Gendered Power Relations among Women: A Study of Household Decision Making in Black, Lesbian Stepfamilies." *American Sociological Review* 73 (April): 335–356.

Newman, David. 2007. *Identities and Inequalities: Exploring the Intersections of Race, Class, Gender and Sexuality.* New York, NY: McGraw-Hill.

Obear, Kathy. 2000. "Best Practices that Address Homophobia and Heterosexism in Corporations." *Diversity Factor:* 27.

Phelan, Shane. 1993. "(Be) Coming Out: Lesbian Identity and Politics." *Signs* 18(4):765–790.

Rich, Adrienne. 1980. "Compulsory Heterosexuality and Lesbian Experience." *Signs* 5: 631–660.

Rust, Paula C. 1996. "Sexual Identity and Bisexual Identities: The Struggle for Self-Description in a Changing Sexual Landscape," in B. Beeyman and M. Eliason (Eds). *Queer Studies: A Lesbian, Gay, Bisexual, and Transgender Anthology.* New York, NY: New York University Press: 64–86.

Simon, William. 1996. *Postmodern Sexualities.* London and New York: Routledge.

Stockdill, Brett. 2002. *Activism against AIDS: At the Intersection of Sexuality, Race, Gender, and Class.* Boulder, CO: Lynne Rienner.

Takagi, Dana Y. 1996. "Maiden Voyage: Excursion into Sexuality and Identity Politics in Asian America," in R. Leong (Ed.). *Asian American Sexualities.* New York and London: Routledge: 21–35.

Valocchi, Steve. 1999. "The Class-Inflected Nature of Gay Identity." *Social Problems* 46: 207–224.

Weeks, Jeffery. 1985. *Sexuality and Its Discontents: Meanings, Myths, and Modern Sexualities.* New York and London: Routledge.

——————————— ○ ———————————

END OF CHAPTER QUESTIONS

1. What is homophobia? What is heterosexism?
2. Who is Dr. James G. Kiernan? What is he known for?
3. Who is Dr. Krafft-Ebing? What is he known for?
4. What are three initiatives corporate America has implemented to protect the LGBT+ community in the workplace? In your opinion, what other initiatives could corporate America implement to protect the LGBT+ community in the workplace?

PART II

Secondary Marginalization

CHAPTER 5

How Gay Stays White and What Kind of White It Stays

Allan Bérubé; Birgit Brander Rasmussen, Eric Klinenberg,

Irene J. Nexica, and Matt Wray, eds.

MY WHITE DESIRES

Since the day I came out to my best friend in 1968, I have inhabited the social category "gay white man." As a historian, writer, and activist, I've examined the gay and the male parts of that identity, and more recently I've explored my working-class background and the Franco-American ethnicity that is so intertwined with it. But only recently have I identified with or seriously examined my gay male whiteness.[1]

Several years ago I made the decision to put race and class at the center of my gay writing and activism. I was frustrated at how my own gay social and activist circles reproduced larger patterns of racial separation by remaining almost entirely white. And I felt abandoned as the vision of the national gay movement and media narrowed from fighting for liberation, freedom, and social justice to expressing personal pride, achieving visibility, and lobbying for individual equality within existing institutions. What emerged was too often an exclusively gay rights agenda isolated from supposedly nongay issues, such as homelessness, unemployment, welfare, universal health care, union organizing, affirmative action, and abortion rights. To gain recognition and credibility, some gay organizations and media began to aggressively promote the so-called positive image of a generic gay community that is an upscale, mostly male, and mostly white consumer market with mainstream, even traditional, values. Such a strategy derives its power from an unexamined investment in whiteness and middle-class identification. As a result, its practitioners seemed not to take seriously or even notice how their gay visibility successes at times exploited and reinforced a racialized class divide that continues to tear our nation apart, including our lesbian and gay communities.

My decision to put race and class at the center of my gay work led me as a historian to pursue the history of a multiracial maritime union that in the 1930s and 1940s fought for racial equality and the dignity of openly gay workers.[2] And my decision opened doors that enabled me as an activist to join multiracial lesbian, gay, bisexual, and transgender groups whose members have been doing antiracist work for a long time and in which gay white men are not the majority—groups that included the Lesbian, Gay, Bisexual, and Transgender Advisory Committee to the San Francisco Human Rights Commission and the editorial board of the now-defunct national lesbian and gay quarterly journal *Out/Look*.

But doing this work also created new and ongoing conflicts in my relationships with other white men. I want to figure out how to handle these conflicts as I extend my antiracist work into those areas of my life where I still find myself among gay white men—especially when we form new activist and intellectual groups that once again turn out to be white. To do this I need "to clarify something for myself," as James Baldwin put it, when he gave his reason for writing his homosexual novel *Giovanni's Room* in the 1950s.[3]

I wanted to know how gay gets white, how it stays that way, and how whiteness is used both to win and attack gay rights campaigns.

I want to learn how to see my own whiteness when I am with gay white men and to understand what happens among us when one of us calls attention to our whiteness.

I want to know why I and other gay white men would want to challenge the racist structures of whiteness, what happens to us when we try, what makes me keep running away from the task, sometimes in silent despair, and what makes me want to go back to take up the task again.

I want to pursue these questions by drawing on a gay ability, developed over decades of figuring out how to "come out of the closet," to bring our hidden lives out into the open. But I want to do this without encouraging anyone to assign a greater degree of racism to gay white men, thus exposed, than to other white men more protected from exposure, and without inviting white men who are not gay to more safely see gay men's white racism rather than their own.

I want to know these things because gay white men have been among the men I have loved and will continue to love. I need them in my life and at my side as I try to make fighting racism a more central part of my work. And when students call out "white" to describe the typical gay man, and they see me standing right there in front of them, I want to figure out how, from where I am standing, I can intelligently fight the racist hierarchies that I and my students differently inhabit.

GAY WHITENING PRACTICES

Despite the stereotype, the gay male population is not as white as it appears to be in the images of gay men projected by the mainstream and gay media, or among the "out" men (including myself) who move into the public spotlight as representative gay activists, writers, commentators, and spokesmen. Gay men of color, working against the stereotype, have engaged in long, difficult struggles to gain some public recognition of their cultural heritages, political activism, and everyday existence. To educate gay white men, they've had to get our attention by interrupting our business as usual, then convince us that we don't speak for them or represent them or know enough about either their realities or our own racial assumptions and privileges. And when I and other gay white men don't educate ourselves, gay men of color have done the face-to-face work of educating us about their cultures, histories, oppression, and particular needs—the kind of personal work that tires us out when heterosexuals ask us to explain to them what it's like to be gay. Also working against their ability to put "gay" and "men of color" together in the broader white imagination are a great many other powerful *whitening practices* that daily construct, maintain, and fortify the idea that gay male means white.

How does the category "gay man" become white? What are the whitening practices that perpetuate this stereotype, often without awareness or comment by gay white men? How do these practices operate, and what racial work do they perform?

I begin by mining my own experience for clues.[4] I know that if I go where I'm surrounded by other gay white men, or if I'm having sex with a white man, it's unlikely that our race will come up in conversation. Such racially comfortable, racially familiar situations can make us mistakenly believe that there are such things as gay issues, spaces, culture, and relationships that are not "lived through" race, and that white gay life, so long as it is not named as such, is not about race.[5] These lived assumptions, and the privileges on which they are based, form a powerful camouflage woven from a web of unquestioned beliefs—that gay whiteness is unmarked and unremarkable, universal and representative, powerful and protective, a cohesive bond. The markings of this camouflage are pale—a characteristic that the wearer sees neither as entirely invisible nor as a racial "color," a shade that allows the wearer to blend into the seemingly neutral background of white worlds. When we wear this everyday camouflage into a gay political arena that white men already dominate, our activism comes wrapped in a *pale protective coloring* that we may not notice but which is clearly visible to those who don't enjoy its protection.

I start to remember specific situations in which I caught glimpses of how other gay whitening practices work.

One night, arriving at my favorite gay disco bar in San Francisco, I discovered outside a picket line of people protesting the triple-carding (requiring three photo ID's) of gay men of color at the door. This practice was a form of racial *exclusion*—policing the borders of white gay institutions to prevent people of color from entering. The management was using this discriminatory practice to keep the bar from "turning," as it's called—a process by which a "generically gay" bar (meaning a predominantly white bar) changes into a bar that loses status and income (meaning gay white men with money won't go there) because it has been "taken over" by black, Latino, or Asian gay men. For many white owners, managers, and patrons of gay bars, only a white gay bar can be *just* gay; a bar where men of color go is seen as racialized. As I joined the picket line, I felt the fears of a white man who has the privilege to choose on which side of a color line he will stand. I wanted to support my gay brothers of color who were being harassed at the door, yet I was afraid that the doorman might recognize me as a regular and refuse to let me back in. That night, I saw a gay bar's doorway become a racialized border, where a battle to preserve or challenge the whiteness of the clientele inside was fought among dozens of gay men who were either standing guard at the door, allowed to walk through it, or shouting and marching outside. (The protests eventually made the bar stop the triple-carding.)

I remember seeing how another gay whitening practice works when I watched, with other members of a sexual politics study group, an antigay video, "Gay Rights, Special Rights," produced in 1993 by The Report, a religious right organization. This practice was the *selling* of gay whiteness—the marketing of gays as white and wealthy to make money and increase political capital, either to raise funds for campaigns (in both progay and antigay benefits, advertising, and direct-mail appeals) or to gain economic power (by promoting or appealing to a gay consumer market). The antigay video we watched used racialized class to undermine alliances between a gay rights movement portrayed as white and movements of people of color portrayed as heterosexual. It showed charts comparing mutually exclusive categories of "homosexuals" and "African Americans," telling us that homosexuals are wealthy, college-educated white men who vacation more than anyone else and who demand even more "special rights and privileges" by taking civil rights away from low-income African Americans.[6] In this zero-sum, racialized world of the religious right, gay men are white; gay, lesbian, and bisexual people of color, along with poor or working-class white gay men, bisexuals, and lesbians, simply do not exist. The recently vigorous gay media promotion of the high income, brand-loyal gay consumer market—which is typically portrayed as a population of white, well-to-do, college-educated young men—only widens the racialized class divisions that the religious right so eagerly exploits.

During the 1993 Senate hearings on gays in the military, I saw how these and other whitening practices were used in concentrated form by another gay institution, the Campaign for Military Service (CMS).

The Campaign for Military Service was an ad hoc organization formed in Washington, D.C., by a group composed primarily of well-to-do, well-connected, professional men, including billionaires David Geffen and Barry Diller, corporate consultant and former antiwar activist David Mixner (a personal friend of Bill Clinton), and several gay and lesbian civil rights attorneys. Their mission was to work with the Clinton White House and sympathetic senators by coordinating the gay response to hearings held by the Senate Armed Services Committee, chaired by Sam Nunn. Their power was derived from their legal expertise, their access to wealthy donors, and their contacts with high-level personnel inside the White House, Senate, and Pentagon. The challenge they faced was to make strategic, pragmatic decisions in the heat of a rapidly changing national battle over what President Clinton called "our nation's policy toward homosexuals in the military."[7]

The world in and around the CMS that David Mixner describes in his memoir, *Stranger among Friends,* is a network of professionals passionately dedicated to gay rights who communicated with Washington insiders via telephone calls, memos, and meetings in the White House, the Pentagon, and private homes. Wearing the protective coloring of this predominantly white gay world, these professionals entered the similarly white and male but heterosexual world of the U.S. Senate, where their shared whiteness became a common ground on which the battle to lift the military's ban on homosexuals was fought—and lost.

The CMS used a set of arguments they called the *race analogy* to persuade senators and military officials to lift the military's antigay ban. The strategy was to get these powerful men to take antigay discrimination as seriously as they supposedly took racial discrimination, so they would lift the military ban on homosexuals as they had eliminated official policies requiring racial segregation. During the Senate hearings, the race analogy projected a set of comparisons that led to heated disputes over whether sexual orientation was analogous to race, whether sexual desire and conduct were like "skin color," or, most specifically, whether being homosexual was like being African American. (Rarely was "race" explicitly discussed as anything other than African American.) On their side, the CMS argued for a qualified analogy—what they called "haunting parallels" between "the words, rationale and rhetoric invoked in favor of racial discrimination in the past" and those used to "exclude gays in the military now." "The parallel is inexact," they cautioned, because "a person's skin color is not the same as a person's sexual identity; race is self-evident to many whereas sexual orientation is not. Moreover, the history of African Americans is not equivalent to the history of lesbian, gay and bisexual people in this country." Yet, despite these qualifications, the CMS held firm to the analogy. "The bigotry expressed is the same; the discrimination is the same."[8]

The military responded with an attack on the race analogy as self-serving, racist, and offensive. They were aided by Senator Nunn, who skillfully managed the hearings in ways that exploited the whiteness of the CMS and their witnesses to advance the military's antigay agenda. Working in their favor was the fact that, unlike the CMS, the military had high-ranking officials who were African American. The chairman of the Joint Chiefs of Staff, Gen. Colin L. Powell, who opposed lifting the ban, responded to the CMS with the argument that the antigay policy was not analogous to racial segregation because "skin color" was a "benign characteristic" while homosexuality constituted conduct that was neither benign nor condoned by most Americans.[9] Another African American Army officer, Lt. Gen. Calvin Waller, Gen. Norman Schwarzkopf's deputy commander and the highest-ranking African American officer in

Operation Desert Storm, attacked the race analogy with these words: "I had no choice regarding my race when I was delivered from my mother's womb. To compare my service in America's armed forces with the integration of avowed homosexuals is personally offensive to me."[10] Antigay white senators mimicked his outrage.

During the race analogy debates, the fact that only white witnesses made the analogy, drawing connections between antigay and racial discrimination without including people of color, reduced the power of their argument and the credibility it might have gained had it been made by advocates who had experienced the racial discrimination side of the analogy.[11] But without hearing these voices, everyone in the debate could imagine homosexuals as either people who do not experience racism (the military assumption) or as people who experience discrimination only as homosexuals (the progay assumption)—two different routes that ultimately led to the same destination: the place where gay stays white, the place where the CMS chose to make its stand.

According to Mixner's memoir, the Senate Armed Services Committee "had asked CMS to suggest witnesses."[12] As gay gatekeepers to the hearings, the CMS utilized another whitening practice—*mirroring.* This is a political strategy that reflects back the whiteness of the men who run powerful institutions to persuade them to take "us" seriously, accept "us," and let "us" in because "we are just like you." From the witnesses they selected, it appears that the CMS tried to project an idealized image of the openly gay service member that mirrored the senators' racial makeup and their publicly espoused social values and sexual mores—the image of the highly competent, patriotic, sexually abstinent, young, male officer who had earned the right to serve with a proud record and therefore deserved equality. The CMS selected for the gay panel a group of articulate and courageous veterans—all white men, except for one white woman.[13] Cleverly, Senator Nunn's staff selected a panel of African American ministers opposed to lifting the ban to precede the gay white panel, so that both sides constructed and participated in a racialized dramatic conflict that reinforced the twin myths that gay is white and African Americans are antigay.

Missing was the testimony of service members whose lives bridged the hearings' false divide between black and gay—veterans who were both African American and lesbian, gay, or bisexual. In this context, a significant whitening practice at the hearings was the exclusion of Sgt. Perry Watkins as a witness. Watkins was an openly gay, African American veteran considered by many to be a military hero. Kicked out of the army as a homosexual shortly before his retirement, he successfully appealed his discharge to the Supreme Court, becoming what one attorney called "the first out gay soldier to retire from the Army with full honors."[14]

To my knowledge, there is no public record of how or why the CMS did not invite Watkins to testify.[15] (This is another privilege that comes with whiteness—the ability to make decisions that seriously affect people of color and then protect that decision-making process from public scrutiny or accountability.) Sabrina Sojourner, who recalls that she was the only African American at the CMS among the nonsupport staff, told me that she "got moved further and further from the decision-making process" because she "brought up race," including the problem of the racial dynamic set up by presenting only white witnesses to testify.[16]

There was a moment when I was personally involved with this process. As the author of *Coming Out under Fire: The History of Gay Men and Women in World War Two,* I was asked by the CMS to prepare to fly from California to Washington to testify, but my appearance was not approved by the Senate staff, who allowed no open homosexuals to testify as expert witnesses.[17] During a phone conversation with a white CMS staff member, I remember getting up the courage to ask him why Watkins wasn't a witness and was told that "Perry is a difficult personality." I didn't push my question any further, getting the message that I shouldn't ask for complicated explanations during the heat of battle and deferring to their inside-the-beltway tactical decisions, thus forfeiting an important opportunity to seriously challenge Watkins's exclusion. More instances of this painful struggle over Watkins's participation in and around the hearings must have been going on behind the scenes.[18] Watkins believed he was shut out because he was a "queeny" African American.[19]

It seems that the CMS considered Watkins to be the opposite of their ideal witness. His military story was indeed more complicated than the generic coming-out story. During his 1968 induction physical exam in Tacoma, Washington, he had openly declared his homosexuality, checking "Yes" to the written question "Do you have homosexual tendencies?" and freely describing his sexual experiences to the induction psychiatrist. But the army drafted him nevertheless because it needed him to fight in Vietnam, along with other mostly working-class African American men, who, by 1966, accounted for 20 percent of U.S. combat deaths in that war, when African Americans made up 11 percent of the U.S. population and 12.6 percent of U.S. troops in Vietnam. Journalist Randy Shilts, who later interviewed Watkins, reported that Watkins believed "the doctor probably figured Watkins would . . . go to Vietnam, get killed, and nobody would ever hear about it again."[20] So Watkins's story was not a white narrative. "If I had not been black," he told Mary Ann Humphrey in an oral history interview, "my situation would not have happened as it did. . . . Every *white* person I knew from Tacoma who was gay and had checked that box 'Yes' did not have to go into the service."[21] Watkins's story resonated more with how men of color experience antigay racism in the military than with the story so many white servicemen tell. That white narrative begins with how a gay serviceman never experienced discrimination until he discovered his homosexuality in the service and ends with his fighting an antigay discharge, without referring to how he lived this experience through his whiteness. But Watkins explicitly talked about how he lived his gay military experience through race. "People ask me," he explained, " 'How have you managed to tolerate all that discrimination you have had to deal with in the military?' My immediate answer to them was, 'Hell, I grew up black. Give me a break.'"[22] Watkins had also, while in the military, danced and sang on U.S. Army bases as the flamboyant "Simone," his drag persona; as a veteran he was HIV-positive; and in some gay venues he wore body-piercings in public.[23]

Nevertheless, Watkins's testimony at the hearings could have struck familiar chords among many Americans, including working-class and African American communities, as the experience of someone who was *real* rather than an *ideal*. His story was so compelling, in fact, that after the hearings he was the subject of two films and a segment of the television news magazine "20/20."[24] But the story of his military career—which he so openly lived through race (as an African American), sexuality (had a sex life), and gender (performed in drag)—seems to have been considered by the CMS as too contaminated for congressional testimony and too distracting for the personal media stories that were supposed to focus only on the gay right to serve.

Watkins's absence was a lost opportunity to see and hear in nationally televised Senate hearings a gay African American legal hero talk about his victory over antigay discrimination in the military and expose the racist hypocrisy of how the antigay ban was in practice suspended for African Americans during wartime. The lack of testimony from any other lesbian, gay, or bisexual veteran of color was a lost opportunity to build alliances with communities of color and to do something about the "(largely accurate) perception of the gay activist leadership in Washington as overwhelmingly white."[25] Their collective absence reinforced another powerful myth that, even in a military population that is disproportionately African American and Latino, the representative gay soldier is a white officer, and the most presentable gay face of military competence is a white face.

As the hearings progressed, some CMS activists, speaking in public forums outside the hearings, took the race analogy a step further by promoting the idea that the gay rights movement was *like* the civil rights movement. During the hearings, those who argued the race analogy had drawn parallels between racist and antigay bigotry and discrimination. But those who extended the race analogy to the civil rights movement analogy had to take several more steps. First, they had to reconceptualize the civil rights movement. They took a multiracial movement for human equality and human rights, which included many lesbian, gay, and bisexual activists, and changed it into a nongay, black movement for African American racial equality. Next, they had to imagine the gay movement as a white movement for homosexual rights rather than as a multiracial movement that grew out of and continued the work of the civil rights movement. Then they could make the analogy between these two now-separated movements—one just about race, the other just about homosexuality. The last step was to symbolically recast gay white men in the roles of African American civil rights leaders. These moves tried to correct a problem inherent in such whitening practices as excluding people of color and the wearing, mirroring, and selling of gay whiteness. Because such practices draw directly on the privileges of whiteness, they do not on their own carry much moral weight. The extended race analogy compensates for this weightlessness by first invoking the moral authority of the civil rights movement (while erasing its actual history), and then transferring that unearned moral authority to a white gay movement, without giving anything back. At its worst, the race analogy can become a form of historical erasure, political cheating, and, ultimately, a theft of cultural capital and symbolic value.

David Mixner's memoir reveals how the extended race analogy was used in and around the Campaign for Military Service. When President Clinton, at a press conference, revealed that he wouldn't rule out separating homosexuals from heterosexuals within the military, Mixner first interpreted Clinton's comments as condoning gay segregation, then began equating it with racial segregation. Mixner's account of what happened next does not include attempts to seek advice from or build alliances with people whose histories include long struggles against legal segregation. This despite solid support for lifting the ban from civil rights veterans including Coretta Scott King and Roger Wilkins, the Black Lesbian and Gay Leadership Forum, the Congressional Black Caucus (including Ron Dellums, chairman of the House Armed Services Committee and a former marine who eventually held House hearings to counter Nunn's Senate hearings), and, in public opinion polls, a majority of African Americans (in contrast to a minority of white Americans).[26] Mixner instead describes a series of decisions and actions in which he invokes scenes from the history of racial segregation and the civil rights movement and appears to be reenacting those scenes as if he were a gay (white) version of a black civil rights leader.

A telling moment was when Mixner asked his friend Troy Perry, a gay white minister who founded and heads the gay Metropolitan Community Church, to let him use the Sunday pulpit at the MCC Cathedral in Dallas as a "platform from which to speak." Covered by network television, Mixner delivered a sermon to the nation about the gay "road to freedom." In his sermon he referred to the military's antigay policy as "ancient apartheid laws" and charged that "Sam Nunn is our George Wallace" and that "[b]igotry that wears a uniform is nothing more than a uniform with a hood." He angrily warned President Clinton, cast as antigay segregationist, that "with or without you we will be free . . . we will prevail!"[27] Shortly after the sermon, Tracy Thorne, a gay white navy veteran who had courageously faced verbal abuse at the Senate hearings and who flew to Dallas to support Mixner, said out loud what had been implied by Mixner's words and actions. David Mixner "could be our Martin Luther King, no questions asked," Thorne told a reporter from a gay newspaper.[28]

Such dramatic race-analogy scenarios performed by white activists beg some serious questions. Are actual, rather than "virtual," people of color present as major actors in these scenarios, and if not, why not? What are they saying or how are they being silenced? How is their actual leadership being supported or not supported by the white people who are reenacting this racialized history? And who is the "we" in this rhetoric? Mixner's "we," for example, did not account for those Americans—including lesbian, gay, bisexual, or transgender activists from many racial backgrounds—who did not finally have or indeed need "our own George Wallace" or "our own Martin Luther King." "Martin Luther King is the Martin Luther King of the gay community," Dr. Marjorie Hill, board president of Unity Fellowship Church and former director of the New York City Mayor's Office for Lesbian and Gay Issues, has pointedly replied in response to those who were looking for King's gay equivalent. "His lesson of equality and truth and non-violence was for everyone."[29] If the gay rights movement is already part of the ongoing struggle for the dignity of all people exemplified in the activism of Dr. Martin Luther King Jr., then there is no need for gay equivalents of Dr. King, racial segregation, or the civil rights movement. If the gay rights movement is not already part of the civil rights movement, then what is it? Answering this question from a white position with the race analogy—saying that white gay leaders and martyrs are "our" versions of African American civil rights leaders and martyrs—can't fix the problem and ultimately undermines the moral authority that is its aim. This use of the race analogy ends up reinforcing the whiteness of gay political campaigns rather than doing the work and holding onto the dream that would continue the legacy of Dr. King's leadership and activism.[30]

What would the gay movement look like if gay white men who use the race analogy took it more seriously? What work would we have to do to close the perceived moral authority gap between our gay activism and the race analogy, to directly establish the kind of moral authority we seek by analogy? What if we aspired to achieve the great vision, leadership qualities, grass-roots organizing skills, and union-solidarity of Dr. Martin Luther King Jr., together with his opposition to war and his dedication to fighting with the poor and disenfranchised against the deepening race and class divisions in America and the world? How could we fight, in the words of U.S. Supreme Court Justice Harry A. Blackmun, for the "fundamental interest all individuals have in controlling the nature of their intimate associations with others," in ways that build a broad civil rights movement rather than being "like" it, in ways that enable the gay movement to grow into one of many powerful and direct ways to achieve race, gender, and class justice?[31]

These, then, are only some of the many whitening practices that structure everyday life and politics in what is often called the "gay community" and the "gay movement"—making *race analogies; mirroring* the whiteness of men who run powerful institutions as a strategy for winning credibility, acceptance, and integration; *excluding* people of color from gay institutions; *selling* gay as white to raise money, make a profit, and gain economic power; and daily wearing the *pale protective coloring* that camouflages the unquestioned assumptions and unearned privileges of gay whiteness. These practices do serious damage to real people whenever they mobilize the power and privileges of whiteness to protect and strengthen gayness—including the privileges of gay whiteness—without using that power to fight racism—including gay white racism.

Most of the time, the hard work of identifying such practices, fighting racial discrimination and exclusion, critiquing the assumptions of whiteness, and racially integrating white gay worlds has been taken up by lesbian, gay, bisexual, and transgender people of color. Freed from this enforced daily recognition of race and confrontation with racism, some prominent white men in the gay movement have been able to advance a gay rights politics that, like the right to serve in the military, they imagine to be just gay, not about race. The gay rights movement can't afford to "dissipate our energies," Andrew Sullivan, former editor of the *New Republic,* warned on the Charlie Rose television program, by getting involved in disagreements over nongay issues such as "how one deals with race . . . how we might help the underclass . . . how we might deal with sexism."[32]

But a gay rights politics that is supposedly color-blind (and sex-neutral and classless) is in fact a politics of race (and gender and class). It assumes, without ever having to say it, that gay must equal white (and male and economically secure); that is, it assumes white (and male and middle-class) as the default categories that remain once one discounts those who as gay people must continually and primarily deal with racism (and sexism and class oppression), especially within gay communities. It is the politics that remains once one makes the strategic decision, as a gay activist, to stand outside the social justice movements for race, gender, or class equality, or to not stand with disenfranchised communities, among whom are lesbian, bisexual, gay, or transgender people who depend on these movements for dignity and survival.

For those few who act like, look like, and identify with the white men who still run our nation's major institutions, for those few who can meet with them, talk to them, and be heard by them as peers, the ability to draw on the enormous power of a shared but unacknowledged whiteness, the ability never to have to bring up race, must feel like a potentially sturdy shield against antigay discrimination. I can see how bringing up explicit critiques of white privilege during high-level gay rights conversations (such as the Senate debates over gays in the military), or making it possible for people of color to set the agenda of the gay rights movement, might weaken that white shield (which relies on racial division to protect)—might even, for some white activists, threaten to "turn" the gay movement into something less gay, as gay bars "turn" when they're no longer predominantly white.

The threat of losing the white shield that protects my own gay rights raises even more difficult questions that I need to "clarify . . . for myself": What would *I* say and do about racism if someday my own whiteness helped me gain such direct access to men in the centers of power, as it almost did during the Senate hearings, when all I did was ask why Perry Watkins wasn't testifying and accept the answer I was given? What privileges would I risk losing if I persistently tried to take activists of color with me into that high-level conversation? How, and with whom, could I begin planning for that day?

Gay white men who are committed to doing antiracist activism *as* gay men have to work within and against these and other powerful whitening practices. What can we do, and how can we support each other, when we once again find ourselves involved in gay social and political worlds that are white and male?

NOTES

1. "Caught in the Storm: AIDS and the Meaning of Natural Disaster," *Out/ Look: National Lesbian and Gay Quarterly* 1 (fall 1988), 8–19; "'Fitting In': Expanding Queer Studies beyond the *Closet* and *Coming Out*," paper presented at Contested Zone: Limitations and Possibilities of a Discourse on Lesbian and Gay Studies, Pitzer College, 6–7 April 1990, and at the Fourth Annual Lesbian, Bisexual, and Gay Studies Conference, Harvard University, 26–28 October 1990; "Intellectual Desire," paper presented at La Ville en rose: Le premier colloque Québécois d'études lesbienne et gaies (First Quebec Lesbian and Gay Studies Conference), Concordia University and the University of Quebec at Montreal, 12 November 1992, published in *GLQ: A Journal of Lesbian and Gay Studies* 3, no. 1 (February 1996): 139–57, reprinted in *Queerly Classed: Gay Men and Lesbians Write about Class,* ed. Susan Raffo (Boston: South End Press, 1997), 43–66; "Class Dismissed: Queer Storytelling Across the Economic Divide," keynote address at the Constructing Queer Cultures: Lesbian, Bisexual, Gay Studies Graduate Student Conference, Cornell University, 9 February 1995, and at the Seventeenth Gender Studies Symposium, Lewis and Clark College, 12 March 1998; "I Coulda Been a Whiny White Guy," *Gay Community News* 20 (spring 1995): 6–7, 28–30; and "Sunset Trailer Park," in *White Trash: Race and Class in America,* ed. Matt Wray and Annalee Newitz (New York: Routledge, 1997), 15–39.

2. *Dream Ships Sail Away* (forthcoming, Houghton Mifflin).

3. "'Go the Way Your Blood Beats': An Interview with James Baldwin (1984)," Richard Goldstein, in *James Baldwin: The Legacy,* ed. Quincy Troupe (New York: Simon and Schuster/Touchstone, 1989), 176.

4. Personal essays, often assembled in published collections, have become an important written form for investigating how whiteness works, especially in individual lives. Personal essays by lesbian, gay, and bisexual authors that have influenced my own thinking and writing about whiteness have been collected in James Baldwin, *The Price of the Ticket: Collected Nonfiction, 1948–1985* (New York: St. Martin's, 1985); Cherríe Moraga and Gloria Anzaldúa, eds., *This Bridge Called My Back: Writings by Radical Women of Color* (Watertown, Mass.: Persephone Press, 1981); Cherríe Moraga, *Loving in the War Years* (Boston: South End Press, 1983); Audre Lorde, *Sister Outsider* (Freedom, Calif.: Crossing Press, 1984); Elly Bulkin, Minnie Bruce Pratt, and Barbara Smith, *Yours in Struggle: Three Feminist Perspectives on Anti-Semitism and Racism* (Brooklyn: Long Haul Press, 1984); Essex Hemphill, ed., *Brother to Brother: New Writings by Black Gay Men* (Boston: Alyson, 1991); Mab Segrest, *Memoir of a Race Traitor* (Boston: South End Press, 1994); Dorothy Allison, *Skin: Talking about Sex, Class and Literature* (Ithaca, N.Y.: Firebrand, 1994); and Becky Thompson and Sangeeta Tyagi, eds., *Names We Call Home: Autobiography on Racial Identity* (New York: Routledge, 1996).

5. For discussion of how sexual identities are "lived through race and class," see Robin D. G. Kelley, *Yo' Mama's Dysfunktional!* (Boston: Beacon, 1997), 114.

6. Whiteness can grant economic advantages to gay as well as straight men, and gay male couples can sometimes earn more on two men's incomes than can straight couples or lesbian couples. But being gay can restrict a man to lower-paying jobs, and most gay white men are not wealthy; like the larger male population, they are lower-middle-class, working-class, or poor. For discussions of the difficulties of developing an accurate economic profile of the "gay community," and of how both the religious right and gay marketers promote the idea that gay men are wealthy, see Amy Gluckman and Betsy Reed, eds., *Homo Economics: Capitalism, Community, and Lesbian and Gay Life* (New York: Routledge, 1997).

7. David Mixner, *Stranger among Friends* (New York: Bantam, 1996), 291. For accounts of how the Campaign for Military Service was formed, see Mixner's memoir and Urvashi Vaid, *Virtual Equality: The Mainstreaming of Lesbian and Gay Equality* (New York: Anchor, 1995). Preceding the ad hoc formation of the Campaign for Military Service in January 1993 was the Military Freedom Project, formed in early 1989 by a group composed primarily of white feminist lesbians. Overshadowed during the Senate hearings by the predominantly male Campaign for Military Service, these activists had raised issues relating the military's antigay policy to gender, race, and class; specifically, that lesbians are discharged at a higher rate than are gay men; that lesbian-baiting is a form of sexual harassment against women; and that African American and Latino citizens, including those who are gay, bisexual, or lesbian, are disproportionately represented in the military, which offers poor and working-class youth access to a job, education, and health care that are often unavailable to them elsewhere. Vaid, *Virtual Equality*, 153–59.

8. "The Race Analogy: Fact Sheet comparing the Military's Policy of Racial Segregation in the 1940s to the Current Ban on Lesbians, Gay Men and Bisexuals," in *Briefing Book*, prepared by the Legal/Policy Department of the Campaign for Military Service, Washington, D.C. (1993).

9. Quoted from the *Legal Times*, 8 February 1993, in Mixner, *Stranger among Friends*, 286. Professor of history and civil rights veteran Roger Wilkins, responding to Powell's statement, argued that "Lots of white people don't think that being black is benign even in 1993." Mixner, *Stranger among Friends*, 286.

10. Henry Louis Gates Jr., "Blacklash?" *New Yorker*, 17 May 1993.

11. For brief discussions of how the whiteness of those making the race analogy reduced the power of their arguments, see Gates, "Blacklash?" and David Rayside, *On the Fringe: Gays and Lesbians in Politics* (Ithaca, N.Y.: Cornell University Press, 1998), 243.

12. Mixner, *Stranger among Friends*, 319.

13. The gay service members on this panel were former Staff Sgt. Thomas Pannicia, Sgt. Justin Elzie, and Col. Margarethe Cammermeyer. Margarethe Cammermeyer, with Chris Fisher, *Serving in Silence* (New York: Penguin, 1994), 299. Other former gay service members who testified at the hearings were Sgt. Tracy Thorne and PO Keith Meinhold. Active-duty lesbian, gay, or bisexual service members could not testify without being discharged from the military as homosexuals, a situation that still exists under the current "don't ask, don't tell" military policy.

14. Mary Dunlap, "Reminiscences: Honoring Our Legal Hero, Gay Sgt. Perry Watkins 1949–1996," *Gay Community News* (winter 1996): 21.

15. In his memoir, *Stranger among Friends*, Mixner makes no mention of Watkins.

16. Author's personal conversation with Sabrina Sojourner, 19 October 1998.

17. An expert witness who was white, male, and not a gay historian was allowed to introduce a brief written synopsis of historical evidence from my book.

    I was one of the white men working with the CMS behind the scenes and from afar. Early in the hearings, Senator Edward Kennedy's staff asked me to compile a list of questions for him to ask during the hearings. In July, after the hearings were over and the "don't ask, don't tell" policy had been adopted, I submitted to the House Armed Services Committee written testimony, titled "Historical Overview of the Origins of the Military's Ban on Homosexuals," that critiqued the new policy and identified heterosexual masculinity, rather than the competence or behavior of homosexual service members, as the military problem requiring investigation. And I sent the CMS a copy of a paper I had given in April, "Stripping Down: Undressing the Military's Anti-Gay Policy," that used historical documents and feminist analysis to argue for investigating the military's crisis in heterosexual masculinity. In all these writings, I was trying, unsuccessfully, to get the CMS and the Senate to adopt a gender and sexuality analysis of the military policy; I used race and class analysis only to argue that the antigay policies disproportionately affected service members who were people of color and/or working-class.

18. After Watkins's death in 1996 from complications due to HIV, Mary Dunlap, a white civil rights attorney who for years had followed his appeal case, in a tribute addressed to him, called him a "generous, tireless leader" who expressed "open and emphatic criticism and unabashed indictment of the racism of those among us who so blatantly and hurtfully excluded your voice and face and words from the publicity surrounding the gaylesbitrans community's challenge to 'Don't Ask, Don't Tell' in the early 90s." Dunlap, "Reminiscences," 21.

19. Shamara Riley, "Perry Watkins, 1948-1996: A Military Trailblazer," *Outlines*, 8 May 1996.

20. Randy Shilts, *Conduct Unbecoming: Gays and Lesbians in the U.S. Military* (New York: St. Martin's, 1993), 60, 65; Mary Ann Humphrey, *My Country, My Right to Serve* (New York: HarperCollins, 1990), 248-57. Statistics are from D. Michael Shafer, "The Vietnam-Era Draft: Who Went, Who Didn't, and Why It Matters," in *The Legacy: The Vietnam War in the American Imagination*, ed. D. Michael Shafer (Boston: Beacon Press, 1990), 69.

21. Humphrey, *My Country*, 255-56.

22. Ibid.

23. Dunlap, "Reminiscences"; Shilts, *Conduct Unbecoming*, 155-56; Humphrey, *My Country*, 253-54.

24. A 1996 documentary film, "Sis: The Perry Watkins Story," was coproduced by Chiqui Cartagena and Suzanne Newman. On the "20/20" segment and a feature film on Watkins that was in preproduction, see Jim Knippenberg, "Gay Soldier Story to Be Filmed," *Cincinnati Enquirer*, 23 December 1997.

25. Rayside, *On the Fringe*, 243.

26. Keith Boykin, *One More River to Cross: Black and Gay In America* (New York: Anchor, 1996), 186-92.

27. Mixner, *Stranger among Friends*, 301-2, 308-10.

28. Garland Tillery, "Interview with Top Gun Pilot Tracy Thorne," *Our Own*, 18 May 1993.

29. Quoted from the documentary film "All God's Children," produced by Dee Mosbacher, Frances Reid, and Sylvia Rhue (Women Vision, 1996). I wish to thank Lisa Kahaleole Hall, Stephanie Smith, and Linda Alban for directing me to this quotation.

30. One way to measure how much moral authority the race analogy tries to take from the civil rights movement and transfuse it into a predominantly white gay movement is to see what moral authority remains when the race analogy is removed. David Mixner would be the David Mixner of the gay movement, the military's antigay policy would be a form of antigay bigotry, and Sam Nunn would be "our" Sam Nunn. Or, to reverse the terms, other movements for social change would try to gain moral authority by using a "gay analogy," declaring that their movement was "like" the gay movement. These moves do not seem to carry the moral weight of the race analogy.

31. Quoted from Justice Blackmun's dissenting opinion in the U.S. Supreme Court's 1986 *Bowers v. Hardwick* decision. "Blackmun's Opinions Reflect His Evolution over the 24 Court Years," *New York Times*, 5 March 1999. I wish to thank Lisa Kahaleole Hall for the conversation we had on 24 October 1998,

out of which emerged the ideas in this essay about how the civil rights movement analogy works and is used as a strategy for gaining unearned moral authority, although I am responsible for how they are presented here.

32. "Stonewall 25," *The Charlie Rose Show*, Public Broadcasting System, 24 June 1994. I wish to thank Barbara Smith for lending me her videotape copy of this program.

———————————— ○ ————————————

END OF CHAPTER QUESTIONS

1. What is white privilege?
2. How can the author use his white privilege to empower and give voice to people of color in the LGBT+ community?
3. What does the author mean by "whitening practices"?

CHAPTER 6

Homophobia in Black Communities

bell hooks

Recently I was at my parents' home and heard teenage nieces and nephews expressing their hatred for homosexuals, saying that they could never like anybody who was homosexual. In response I told them, "There are already people who you love and care about who are gay, so just come off it!" They wanted to know who. I said, "The who is not important. If they wanted you to know, they would tell you. But you need to think about the shit you've been saying and ask yourself where it's coming from."

Their vehement expression of hatred startled and frightened me, even more so when I contemplated the hurt that would have been experienced had our loved ones who are gay heard their words. When we were growing up, we would not have had the nerve to make such comments. We were not allowed to say negative, hateful comments about the people we knew who were gay. We knew their names, their sexual preference. They were our neighbors, our friends, our family. They were us—a part of our black community.

The gay people we knew then did not live in separate subcultures, not in the small, segregated black community where work was difficult to find, where many of us were poor. Poverty was important; it created a social context in which structures of dependence were important for everyday survival. Sheer economic necessity and fierce white racism, as well as the joy of being there with the black folks known and loved, compelled many gay blacks to live close to home and family. That meant however that gay people created a way to live out sexual preferences within the boundaries of circumstances that were rarely ideal no matter how affirming. In some cases, this meant a closeted sexual life. In other families, an individual could be openly expressive, quite out.

The homophobia expressed by my nieces and nephews coupled with the assumption in many feminist circles that black communities are somehow more homophobic than other communities in the United States, more opposed to gay rights, provided the stimulus for me to write this piece. Initially, I considered calling it "homophobia in the black community." Yet it is precisely the notion that there is a monolithic black community that must be challenged. Black communities vary—urban and rural experiences create diversity of culture and lifestyle.

I have talked with black folks who were raised in southern communities where gay people were openly expressive of their sexual preference and participated fully in the life of the community. I have also spoken with folks who say just the opposite.

In the particular black community where I was raised there was a real double standard. Black male homosexuals were often known, were talked about, were seen positively, and played important roles in community life, whereas lesbians were talked about solely in negative terms, and the women identified as lesbians were usually married. Often, acceptance of male homosexuality was mediated by material privilege—that is to say that homosexual men with money were part of the materially privileged ruling black group and were accorded the regard and respect given that group. They were influential people in the community. This was not the case with any women.

In those days homophobia directed at lesbians was rooted in deep religious and moral belief that women defined their womanness through bearing children. The prevailing assumption was that to be a lesbian was "unnatural" because one would not be participating in child-bearing. There were no identified lesbian "parents" even though there were gay men known to be caretakers of other folks' children. I have talked with black folks who recall similar circumstances in their communities. Overall, a majority of older black people I spoke with, raised in small, tightly knit southern black communities, suggested there was tolerance and acceptance of different sexual practices and preferences. One black gay male I spoke with felt that it was more important for him to live within a supportive black community, where his sexual preferences were known but not acted out in an overt, public way, than to live away from a community in a gay subculture where this aspect of his identity could be openly expressed.

Recently, I talked with a black lesbian from New Orleans who boasted that the black community has never had any "orange person like Anita Bryant running around trying to attack gay people." Her experience coming out to a black male roommate was positive and caring. But for every positive story one might hear about gay life in black communities, there are also negative ones. Yet these positive accounts call into question the assumption that black people and black communities are necessarily more homophobic than other groups of people in this society. They also compel us to recognize that there are diversities of black experience. Unfortunately, there are very few oral histories and autobiographies which explore the lives of black gay people in diverse black communities. This is a research project that must be carried out if we are to fully understand the complex experience of being black and gay in this white-supremacist, patriarchal, capitalist society. Often we hear more from black gay people who have chosen to live in predominantly white communities, whose choices may have been affected by undue harassment in black communities. We hear hardly anything from black gay people who live contentedly in black communities.

Black communities may be perceived as more homophobic than other communities because there is a tendency for individuals in black communities to verbally express in an outspoken way anti-gay sentiments. I talked with a straight black male in a California community who acknowledged that though he has often made jokes poking fun at gays or expressing contempt, as a means of bonding in group settings, in his private life he was a central support person for a gay sister. Such contradictory behavior seems pervasive in black communities. It speaks to ambivalence about sexuality in general, about sex as a subject of conversation, and to ambivalent feelings and attitudes toward homosexuality. Various structures of emotional and economic dependence create gaps between attitudes and actions. Yet a distinction must be made between black people overtly expressing prejudice toward homosexuals and homophobic white people who never make homophobic comments but who have the power to actively exploit and oppress gay people in areas of housing, employment, etc. While both groups perpetuate and reinforce each other and this cannot be denied or downplayed, the truth is that the greatest threat to gay rights does not reside in black communities.

It is far more likely that homophobic attitudes can be altered or changed in environments where they have not become rigidly institutionalized. Rather than suggesting that black communities are more homophobic than other communities, and dismissing them, it is important for feminist activists (especially black folks) to examine the nature of that homophobia, to challenge it in constructive ways that lead to change. Clearly religious beliefs and practices in many black communities promote and encourage homophobia. Many Christian black folks (like other Christians in this society) are taught in churches that it is a sin to be gay, ironically sometimes by ministers who are themselves gay or bisexual.

In the past year I talked with a black woman Baptist minister, who, although concerned about feminist issues, expressed very negative attitudes about homosexuality, because, she explained, the Bible teaches that it is wrong. Yet in her daily life she is tremendously supportive and caring of gay friends. When I asked her to explain this contradiction, she argued that it was not a contradiction, that the Bible also teaches her to identify with those who are exploited and oppressed, and to demand that they be treated justly. To her way of thinking, committing a sin did not mean that one should be exploited or oppressed.

The contradictions, the homophobic attitudes that underlie her attitudes, indicate that there is a great need for progressive black theologians to examine the role black churches play in encouraging persecution of gay people. Individual members of certain churches in black communities should protest when worship services become a platform for teaching antigay sentiments. Often individuals sit and listen to preachers raging against gay people and think the views expressed are amusing and outmoded, and dismiss them without challenge. But if homophobia is to be eradicated in black communities, such attitudes must be challenged.

Recently, especially as black people all over the United States discussed the film version of Alice Walker's novel *The Color Purple,* as well as the book itself (which includes a positive portrayal of two black women being sexual with each other), the notion that homosexuality threatens the continuation of black families seems to have gained new momentum. In some cases, black males in prominent positions, especially those in media, have helped to perpetuate this notion. Tony Brown stated in one editorial, "No lesbian relationship can take the place of a positive love relationship between black women and black men." It is both a misreading of Walker's novel and an expression of homophobia for any reader to project into this work the idea that lesbian relationships exist as a competitive response to heterosexual encounters. Walker suggests quite the contrary.

Just a few weeks ago I sat with two black women friends eating bagels as one of us expressed her intense belief that white people were encouraging black people to be homosexuals so as to further divide black folks. She was attributing the difficulties many professional heterosexual black women have finding lovers, companions, husbands, to homosexuality. We listened to her and then the other woman said, "Now you know we are not going to sit here and listen to this homophobic bull without challenging it."

We pointed to the reality that many black gay people are parents, hence their sexual preference does not threaten the continuation of black families. We stressed that many black gay people have white lovers and that there is no guarantee that were they heterosexual they would be partnered with other black people. We argued that people should be able to choose and claim the sexual preference that best expresses their being, suggesting that while it is probably true that positive portrayals of gay people encourage people to see this as a viable sexual preference or lifestyle, it is equally true that compulsory heterosexuality is promoted to a far greater extent. We suggested that we should all be struggling to create a climate where there is freedom of sexual expression.

She was not immediately persuaded by our arguments, but at least she had different perspectives to consider. Supporters of gay rights in black communities must recognize that education for critical consciousness that explains and critiques prevailing stereotypes is necessary for us to eradicate homophobia. A central myth that must be explored and addressed is the notion that homosexuality means genocide for black families. And in conjunction with discussions of this issue, black people must confront the reality of bisexuality and the extent to which the spread of AIDS in black communities is connected to bisexual transmission of the HIV virus.

To strengthen solidarity between black folks irrespective of our sexual preferences, allegiance must be discussed. This is especially critical as more and more black gay people live outside black communities. Just as black women are often compelled to answer the question—which is more important: feminist movement or black liberation struggle?—women's rights or civil rights?—which are you first: black or female?—gay people face similar questions. Are you more identified with the political struggle of your race and ethnic group or gay rights struggle? This question is not a simple one. For some people it is raised in such a way that they are compelled to choose one identity over another.

In one case, when a black family learned of their daughter's lesbianism, they did not question her sexual preference (saying they weren't stupid, they had known she was gay), but the racial identity of her lovers. Why white women and not black women? Her gayness, expressed exclusively in relationships with white women, was deemed threatening because it was perceived as estranging her from blackness.

Little is written about this struggle. Often black families who can acknowledge and accept gayness find inter-racial coupling harder to accept. Certainly among black lesbians, the issue of black women preferring solely white lovers is discussed but usually in private conversation. These relationships, like all cross-racial intimate relationships are informed by the dynamics of racism and white supremacy. Black lesbians have spoken about absence of acknowledgement of one another at social gatherings where the majority of black women present are with white women lovers. Unfortunately, such incidents reinforce the notion that one must choose between solidarity with one's ethnic group and solidarity with those with whom one shares sexual preference, irrespective of class and ethnic difference or differences in political perspective.

Black liberation struggle and gay liberation struggle are both undermined when these divisions are promoted and encouraged. Both gay and straight black people must work to resist the politics of domination as expressed in sexism and racism that lead people to think that supporting one liberation struggle diminishes one's support for another or stands one in opposition to another. As part of education for critical consciousness in black communities, it must be continually stressed that our struggle against racism, our struggle to recover from oppression and exploitation are inextricably linked to all struggles to resist domination—including gay liberation struggle.

Often black people, especially non-gay folks, become enraged when they hear a white person who is gay suggest that homosexuality is synonymous with the suffering people experience as a consequence of racial exploitation and oppression. The need to make gay experience and black experience of oppression synonymous seems to be one that surfaces much more in the minds of white people. Too often, it is seen as a way of minimizing or diminishing the particular problems people of color face in a white-supremacist society, especially the problems encountered because one does not have white skin. Many of us have been in discussions where a non-white person—a black person—struggles to explain to white folks that while we can acknowledge that gay people of all colors are harassed and suffer exploitation and domination, we also recognize that there is a significant difference that arises because of the visibility of dark skin. Often homophobic attacks on gay people occur in situations where knowledge of sexual preference is indicated or established—outside of gay bars, for example. While it in no way lessens the severity of such suffering for gay people, or the fear that it causes, it does mean that in a given situation the apparatus of protection and survival may be simply not identifying as gay.

In contrast, most people of color have no choice. No one can hide, change, or mask dark skin color. White people, gay and straight, could show greater understanding of the impact of racial oppression on people of color by not attempting to make these oppressions synonymous, but rather by showing the ways they are linked and yet differ. Concurrently, the attempt by white people to make synonymous experience of homophobic aggression with racial oppression deflects attention away from the particular dual dilemma that non-white gay people face, as individuals who confront both racism and homophobia.

Often black gay folk feel extremely isolated because there are tensions in their relationships with the larger, predominately white gay community created by racism, and tensions within black communities around issues of homophobia. Sometimes, it is easier to respond to such tensions by simply withdrawing from both groups, by refusing to participate or identify oneself politically with any struggle to end domination. By affirming and supporting black people who are gay within our communities, as well as outside our communities, we can help reduce and change the pain of such isolation.

Significantly, attitudes toward sexuality and sexual preference are changing. There is greater acknowledgement that people have different sexual preferences and diverse sexual practices. Given this reality, it is a waste of energy for anyone to assume that their condemnation will ensure that people do not express varied sexual preferences. Many gay people of all races, raised within this homophobic society, struggle to confront and accept themselves, to recover or gain the core of self-love and well-being that is constantly threatened and attacked both from within and without. This is particularly true for people of color who are gay. It is essential that non-gay black people recognize and respect the hardships, the difficulties gay black people experience, extending the love and understanding that is essential for the making of authentic black community. One way we show our care is by vigilant protest of homophobia. By acknowledging the union between black liberation struggle and gay liberation struggle, we strengthen our solidarity, enhance the scope and power of our allegiances, and further our resistance.

—————————— o ——————————

END OF CHAPTER QUESTIONS

1. In your own words, define "black liberation struggle."
2. In your own words, define "gay liberation struggle."
3. In your opinion, should the black liberation struggle and the gay liberation struggle be linked?
4. Is the suffering that comes from homosexuality synonymous with the suffering that comes with being a person of color?

Strangers Among "Us"

Secondary Marginalization and "LGBT" Politics

Shane Phelan

The questions of assimilation and of group presentation bear not only on lesbians and gays, but on all those marked as sexual strangers. Claiming respectability for one group of strangers often proceeds by implicitly or explicitly contrasting that group to others, constructing relations of similarity between those seeking entry and their gatekeepers while simultaneously articulating that group as "normal" compared to other groups. This happens both within groups, as when "good homosexuals" make their bid for entry by condemning "bad queers," and among groups that many see as closely allied. Indeed, whether a collection of people is seen as a group or as several groups depends largely on the process of articulation of group identity and politics (Laclau and Mouffe 1985). Such articulation is an ongoing, dynamic part of the politics of sexual strangers.

In recent years, gay and lesbian activists have received pressure for greater recognition from bisexuals and transgendered people. Decrying their quite different modes and bases for exclusion, these groups have challenged lesbians and gays to broaden their understandings of their communities and their politics. In response, many groups and individuals now regularly refer to "LGBT" communities and politics. Partisans of "queer," on the other hand, often claim that queer offers greater inclusiveness to all these groups by calling into question the very identities initialed in LGBT. Whether queer or LGBT, the casual observer might well conclude that the project of inclusion is well under way. This conclusion, however, would be mistaken.

In communities subject to advanced marginalization, the access and privilege of some is conditional on the secondary marginalization of "the most vulnerable and stigmatized in their communities" (Cohen 1999, 27). Although bisexuals and transgendered people are not the only stigmatized groups within lesbian and gay communities, I focus here on these groups as larger signs of what is lost in the process of sexual marginalization. I will argue that although real inclusion seems politically risky, the risk is worth taking. Such inclusion requires some fundamental changes in existing lesbian and gay communities. These changes amount to a queering of communities that have been in retreat from their own queerness.

The history of relations among the four groups initialed in LGBT is hardly that of a community, unless we use that term in the vaguest manner. Lesbians and gays have often come together for a variety of reasons, but they have just as often separated from one another. How and why they come together is a result of conceptions of identity and social standing within communities. These conceptions in turn have structured the reception of bisexuals and transgendered people. I will argue here that, rather than extending existing understandings of sexual orientation and gender to "include" bisexuals and transgendered people, lesbians and gays should use the understandings of bi and trans people to reexamine their assumptions about what it means to be lesbian or gay. They should do this not in order to elim-inate meaningful differences among the groups, but in order to envision an ontology and a politics that actively confront the position of strangeness in modernity rather than running from it or reacting to it.

REJECTION AND APPROPRIATION

Bisexuals and transgendered people appear as strangers within lesbian and gay communities in ways star-tlingly similar to how lesbians and gays appear in heteronormative society. Strangers threaten because of their ambiguity rather than simply their difference. They look like "us," but they aren't; or, they might be, but for this one (or more) difference(s), the importance of which is continually under negotiation. Unlike the strangeness of queers in general in mainstream societies, though, the position of these two groups is characterized by an ambivalent dynamic of rejection and appropriation. Most strangers are simply overlooked in or rejected from community or polity imaginaries. Because the current construc-tion of lesbian and gay identities and histories has been so bound to these two groups, however, they cannot be rejected in any simple sense. Rather, the dual processes of rejection and appropriation signal the importance of these groups to the construction of lesbian and gay identities as well as continuing ambiguity about the relations between sex, gender, and sexuality.

Bisexuals are strangers in lesbian and gay communities because they sometimes seem to fit in, then at other times don't; or, perhaps more threatening, they embody the possibility of simultaneously fitting and not fitting. In communities defined by object choice, a desire that fluctuates must necessarily be problematic. Nonetheless, many bisexuals are appropriated for lesbian and gay history, rewritten as gay or lesbian, when it serves the purpose of proving that "we are everywhere." This historical appropria-tion is in sharp contrast with the invisibility of contemporary bisexuals in lesbian and gay scholarship and activism (or the invisibility of their bisexuality). This dual reception is not surprising. Ancestors have spoken, and can no longer speak back; contemporaries continually present their strangeness and its challenges.

Perhaps not surprisingly, transgendered people suffer a similar stigma. Like bisexuals, they are alternately disavowed and appropriated by lesbians and gays: if dead, they are hailed as ancestors or martyrs; if alive, they are vilified as embarrassments to the "normal" homosexuals. Contemporary homosexual politics has worked to separate gender from sexuality so as to enable homosexuals to claim normal manhood or womanhood. Transgendered people do not belong in this normal community. Gay bars that welcome transgendered embodiments continue to be those at the bottom of the homosexual social scale, in the worst neighborhoods, facing the greatest violence. For many normal homos, the presence of transgendered embodiment is the key element marking off certain bars as "low class" or pride parades as "over the top." Ki Namaste (1997, 185–89) has noted how drag queens and transsexuals are relegated to the status of "entertainment" in gay communities, not speakers on a podium or equal political participants but performers. In many communities, these "low-class" trans/drag bars have the strongest politics, best participation, and highest fundraising in the community—and in return they are ignored and hidden away.

This marginalization has recently shown signs of giving way to a broader politics. Since 1995, the Human Rights Campaign has increasingly reached out to transgendered people and has pledged to support an amendment to the proposed Employment Non-Discrimination Act (ENDA) that would add transgendered status as a protected category. In May 1999 the National Gay and Lesbian Task Force adopted the stronger position of pledging not to support ENDA unless "sexual expression" as well as "sexual orientation" is included. This comes partly in response to a survey that found that over a quarter of those lesbians, gays, and bisexuals who experienced job discrimination reported that the discrimination was due in part to their gender expression. The survey makes clear that the strangeness of sexual minorities is deeply bound to their perceived deviance from gender norms.

Nonetheless, neither the large organizations nor most of the new gay discourse questions the reification of "sexual orientation" as an issue distinct from that of transgender. The drive to assert the distinction between gender and sexual orientation is part of a larger campaign to establish the normality of lesbians and gays, a normality in which transgendered people do not share. Nor, for that matter, do bisexuals; because bisexuals challenge the idea of a fixed sexual orientation, the cultural metaphors of instability surrounding bisexuality make them less than desirable allies.

The exclusion of bisexuals and transgendered people from lesbian or gay communities and politics is thus a product of two forces. First, the push to assimilate into existing cultural and legal categories is facilitated by notions of sexual orientation as fixed and binary. If homosexuals are "born that way," their presence does not pose a challenge to the heterosexual identities and futures of others. This point has been prominent in legal arguments for equality as well as in media presentations (Currah 1996; Herman 1997). As Paisley Currah (1996, 58) has argued, "immutability arguments" "correspond not only to popular fictions about rights and immutability but also to the prevailing legal standards in US constitutional law." Legal standards for protection from discrimination, largely derived from the model of racial oppression, require that the group in question manifest "immutable characteristics" that make it a "discrete and insular minority." Thus, opponents of equality claim that homosexuality is chosen (although, as Herman notes, the argument over immutability is gradually receding within Christian Right discourse) (Herman 1997, 69–75, 120–25). Among the public, there is a correlation between acceptance of immutability and sympathy for equality (*New York Times* 5 March 1993, cited in Currah 1996, 82 n. 20).

The law, however, is not the only reason that gay and lesbian advocates have insisted on immutability. Although other minorities such as religious minorities are not required to show that they are immutable, life-long members of their sects, lesbian and gay activists have been reluctant to make the analogy between religion and sexuality. Because majorities of Americans continue to find homosexuality immoral, even as they endorse equal political and economic rights, activists have been reluctant to make arguments that might offend judges and the heterosexual majority. Further, many if not most American gays and lesbians now believe that sexual orientation is immutable, so they might be reluctant to adopt arguments that neglect what they see as a central element of their identity and their oppression.

The second element in the crafting of mainstream arguments is the assertion that gays and lesbians do not challenge prevailing gender structures. If they are, as many insist, just like heterosexuals in their gender conformity, then they are not a threat to existing conceptions of masculinity, femininity, or sexual difference. Andrew Sullivan's narrative of masculinity lost and found (1995), in which gender deviance is a product of the closet that is naturally left behind upon finding acceptance from heterosexuals, explicitly aligns him with "normal" men and against transgendered people. The Human Rights Campaign's closeting of butch lesbians and drag queens similarly reassures its constituencies that inclusion will require no reconsideration of gender.

As Joshua Gamson (1998) has shown, the stigmatization of bisexuals and transgendered people on talk shows, stigmatization in which lesbians and gay men participate, has been essential to the construction of homosexuality as normal. Gamson argues that "the moral defense of homosexuality, in fact, is shaped by the frequent dismissal of transgendered and bisexual people on TV talk. When same-sex desire is linked to nonmonogamy (as it so often is on programs dealing with bisexuality), or when it is closely associated with gender-crossing . . . we hit a brick wall in the drive toward a morality of love, freedom, and acceptance" (135). Nor, he notes, was this limit reached only by heterosexual viewers, audiences, or producers: gay and lesbian participants, whether "experts" or everyday people, solidify their normality on these shows by contrasting their stable, gender-conforming lives to these "others."

It is no coincidence, therefore, that the mainstream strategies of some gay and lesbian activists elide the existence of bisexuals and transgendered people. The absence of these groups is essential to the success of the two arguments upon which these activists base their claims for normality. The challenges that bisexuals and transgendered people bring to gay and lesbian politics are distinct, but they converge on the inability of gay and lesbian activists to come to grips with the position of strangers in heteronormative society. The exclusion of bisexual and transgendered people is not solely a result of political strategizing based on ideas about what heterosexuals will tolerate, but this factor is not absent: as Gamson notes, many argue that legal changes such as the Employment Non-Discrimination Act will not be achieved unless bisexuals and transgendered people are left out. But the major national organizations have largely changed their tune over the last five years. Rather than being a product of political calculation, the marginalization of these groups is intimately related to the quest for an identity on the part of lesbians and gays. The modern intolerance of ambivalence, what Zygmunt Bauman (1991) calls the "legislative" attitude of modernity in which apparent chaos is ordered through successive inside/outside distinctions, is not absent from gay and lesbian communities and individuals. Nor is it present only in those who might be called assimilationist; although organizations such as the Human Rights Campaign and writers such as Sullivan provide highly visible examples of such intolerance, it manifests in a wide range of abjections, abhorrences, and fears. Although they are not more biphobic or transphobic than heterosexuals, and many are less so, lesbian and gay communities participate in larger modern fears about ambivalence and boundary crossing. As participants in the modern "legislation" of and discourse about homosexuality, they have both challenged and accepted hegemonic ideas about gender, sexuality, race, and class. Ending the exclusion of bisexuals and transgendered people requires moving from liberal notions of tolerance to an understanding of and challenge to popular models of homosexuality as well as race, class, and gender. A short history is in order.

PARADIGMS AND/OF EXCLUSION

Modern treatments of homosexuality have operated through two main models. The first model considers homosexuality as sexual inversion. In this model, lesbians desire women because they are "really" men, or at least are more like men than are heterosexual women. Sexologists such as Richard von Krafft-Ebing and Havelock Ellis presented perhaps the clearest treatments of this model. Even Freud, who strenuously argued against conflating sexual object choice and physical or psychic gender in men, agreed that "real" lesbians are inevitably more masculine than non-lesbians. This heterosexualized model, for all its logical inconsistencies, remains the dominant understanding among heterosexuals, and among many gays and lesbians.

The second model focuses on the "homo" in homosexuality, the quest for the same, to suggest that lesbians are more womanly than heterosexuals, and gay men more manly than straight men, because they form bonds unadulterated by the other. This model is evident in early twentieth-century gay organizations such as the Committee of the Special in Germany and the Paris lesbian circle of Natalie Barney, and in contemporary lesbian-feminism. This homoerotic model essentializes masculinity and femininity while rejecting the ideology of complementarity that lies at the heart of modern heteronormativity.

The political consequences of these two models are quite different. The first model suggests that gays and lesbians are more alike than not, sharing a middle space on a gender continuum. Karl Ulrichs's nineteenth-century conception of a continuum from "real (heterosexual, masculine) men" to masculine gays to feminine gays to masculine lesbians and finally to "real women" exemplifies this thinking. Edward Carpenter's conception of homosexuals as a "third sex" popularized this understanding among gays and lesbians. Claiming Native American *berdaches* and Indian *hjiras* as ancestors, adherents to this conception claim commonality for gays and lesbians on the basis of their presumed gender inversion.

This idea of a common ground is easily reinforced by laws and other hegemonic practices that stigmatize homosexuality in both men and women. Thus "homosexuality" becomes the name for an axis of sociopolitical identification and action. That identification has been least problematic for gay white men, who have seen homosexuality as their distinguishing characteristic. For this group, all homosexuals have a common oppression and a common goal. Issues of gender, racial, or class inequality take a back seat to this presumed common interest.

The politics of the second model is perhaps the opposite of this. For the homoerotic man, homosexuality provides a shared masculine bond and way of life. Drawing on ancient Greece as a model, writers in this vein have celebrated the manliness of men together (Blasius and Phelan 1997, 152–69). Lesbian-feminists likewise have argued that they have little in common with gay men, as gay men's sexual practices and culture are quite different from lesbian mores and often involve dismissal and exclusion of women (Blasius and Phelan 1997, 498–521).

We thus have two models of what homosexual desire involves and implies. Neither has been at all satisfactory. As totalities, they have largely colluded in dominant ideas about gender. The idea that loving women is evidence of masculinity is not only heterosexist, it is contradicted by daily evidence. However, loving women is also not evidence of one's greater womanliness. If lesbian desire is not necessarily masculine desire, neither is it clearly feminine or feminist. As the writing and activism of bi and trans people makes clear, and as I will explain more later, we are not just one sex or one gender, nor are those we desire.

Both of these models fail insofar as they fail to problematize the categories of woman and man. By assuming that all "women" are the same in some key way, a way that is usually left undefined, they occlude the variety of ways of being a woman, as well as the myriad identifications and gaps of identification that are experienced by those who claim or are assigned the status of woman. These assumptions are illuminated at certain moments, most conspicuously when transgendered people's inclusion is at stake. The exclusion of male-to-female (MTF) trans people from "women's" events has initiated important discussions about the status of woman as a category. More recent controversy over female-to-male (FTM) trans people incites different, though related, problems with our categories of gender.

Exclusion is not simply a matter of residual marginalization, however. As Kathleen Chapman and Michael du Plessis (1997) have recently argued, attacks on and exclusion of transgendered people have played an integral role in securing a binary sex/gender system within feminism: "the use of transgender issues, concerns, subjectivities, and representations as markers of the limits against which feminist and lesbian selves and communities are defined" is part of a larger project to secure the identity of "woman" in a potentially chaotic environment (170). Rather than following from a prior construction of woman, transgendered people are crucial others for the construction of women in such lesbian-feminist discourse. That this is the case is demonstrated perhaps most clearly by the reception of Janice Raymond's anti-trans *The Transsexual Empire*. This book, published in 1979 and reissued in 1994, became a central text in lesbian-feminist theorizing about "woman" long before a visible and effective trans community developed. Sheila Jeffreys's *The Lesbian Heresy* (1993) and her more recent work have continued this theme, arguing that transsexuality and transgender are antifeminist—for MTF transsexuals because they appropriate women's space and "pretend" to be women, for FTM transsexuals because they abandon women for manhood. For both Jeffreys and Raymond, the social construction of gender and sexuality reaches its limits at the body.

Lesbian-feminists are not, of course, alone in this use of transgender to consolidate their identities. Modern gay politics since Freud has insisted on the distinction between sexual object choice and gender identity, and gay politics has implicitly contrasted the otherwise "normal" homosexual to the "gender dysphoric" transsexual. The diagnosis of gender dysphoria in the Diagnostic and Statistical Manual followed the removal of homosexuality as a pathology, and its continued pathologization has not been an object of discussion in gay or lesbian communities except insofar as gender dysphoria has been coded as gay (Sedgwick 1993, 154–64). Most public gay discourse continues to treat gender nonconformity as a lie spread by anti-gay forces, a slur on respectable men and women. The healthy homo has been constructed throughout the twentieth century, whether in Freud, homophile discourse, gay liberation (with some significant exceptions), or current public discourse, by explicit contrast with and renunciation of the sick gender nonconformist.

If the treatment of transgendered people illuminates the extent to which lesbians and gays remain attached to traditional gender categories, the reception of bisexuals offers insight into the continued commitment to ideas of a fixed sexual orientation. Bisexuals continue to be presented in public under the sign of promiscuity and all the evils believed to follow from it, most notably sexually transmitted diseases, especially AIDS. More fundamentally threatening, however, is the way that bisexuals disrupt the dichotomy between immutability and choice, not because all bisexuals deny that they were "born bisexual" (many insist that they were, and some argue that all humans are innately bisexual), but because their "orientation" crosses the lines of gender that immutability holds inviolate. If one can be attracted to either men or women, the lines that separate or link gender and desire cannot be stabilized. This becomes a direct sexual threat to heterosexuals: having been promised that lesbians are born, not made, seems to promise safety for heterosexual women. Even if a lesbian is attracted to a heterosexual woman, that woman may rest comfortably with the defense that she can't change any more than the lesbian can. But if bisexuality is a possibility, current heterosexuals might have to consider whether a flirtation might not change them in ways that they find distressing.

Bisexuality also confounds the model of homosexuality as gender inversion: If gay men are "like women," are bi men between hetero and gay men? The recent study that found that lesbians' inner ears are more like men's than the ears of heterosexual women left open the question of bisexuals. They were said to be "in between"—but in between what? Lesbians and straight women, or dykes and men? How neat the world would be if we could mark off territories in this way, as scientists hope to do. In fact, the dominant gendered discourse about homosexuality largely leaves bisexuality invisible, as it assumes that we all "are" one way or another.

In contrast to mainstream ideas of "in-betweenness," the position of bisexuals in lesbian communities has been developed through the homoerotic model of sexual orientation, extended to a homosolidaristic political community. If lesbians are most womanly, and most feminist, then bisexuals are less womanly and less feminist than lesbians (Rust 1995). Tainted by their association with men, bisexual women endanger the otherwise pure community. Insufficiently "inverted," bisexuals are also seen as politically unreliable. Both the inversion model and the theory of homoeroticism thus place bisexuality in a troubled and troubling position. If the homoerotic model presents bisexuals as unreliable allies, the inversion model participates in the assumption that everyone is either straight or gay. Thus, bisexuals are either gays who won't or can't admit that fact, or they are sexual tourists. Stereotyped as immature, unstable, unwilling to commit, untrustworthy, bisexual people are demonized in both dominant and lesbian and gay discourses.

TOO QUEER? QUEER ENOUGH?

Both trans and bi people have fought these exclusions. Their fights are not identical by any means. Bisexuals debate between the need to form their own communities and the desire to be included in lesbian and gay ones. Trans discussions are more ambivalent about inclusion, focusing more on constructing gender communities that cross lines of sexuality. Both groups have, however, an important political and conceptual relation to lesbian and gay communities. In response, many locations and communities have witnessed a sea change in the 1990s. Following the loss of hegemony of lesbian-feminism and the ascendancy of "queer," many lesbians and gays have tried to be inclusive. The label LGBT is an example of this new inclusiveness. A coalitional label, LGBT asserts a common goal. In conjunction with the term "community," LGBT suggests spaces where these four groups live and work together and create new meanings. This is an important shift from previous regimes of principled, explicit rejection and exclusion.

So far, however, I am not convinced by LGBT. As an inclusive label, LGBT enables lesbians and gays to deny charges of exclusion without actually changing their understandings or their lives. B and T are not only at the end of the line of initials; they remain the conceptual and political periphery of L and G communities.

This marginalization is present in queer theory as well as in political practice. Jay Prosser (1998, 14) has recently noted the ways in which transsexuals have been treated both as "literalizing the body" and therefore supporting gender systems, and as "deliteralizing" and subverting the assumed link between sex and gender. Transsexuals therefore become both not queer enough and the prototype of queer. The collapse of trans into queer, Prosser argues, serves queer more than it does trans subjects: inclusion becomes "the mechanism by which queer can sustain its very queerness—prolong the queerness of the moment—by periodically adding subjects who appear ever queerer precisely by virtue of their marginality in relation to queer" (58). With a theoretical investment that is perhaps the opposite of political efforts at normalization and inclusion, queer theory nonetheless appropriates trans subjects without acknowledging their perspectives.

The treatment of bisexuality in queer theory is equally fraught with difficulty, though of a different kind. Bisexuality, it seems, is not quite queer enough for queer theory. Judith Butler's entire treatment of bisexuality in *Gender Trouble* (1990) consists of a repudiation of the idea of an original, prediscursive bisexual disposition. Butler's description of heterosexual melancholia and her failure (refusal?) to account for homosexuality in psychoanalytic terms leave readers with a binary between heterosexual and queer (for which homosexuality is the privileged term) that once again leaves us to wonder whether bisexuality as an adult subject position can be anything other than "in between" or "some of each." Are bisexuals sort of melancholic? What is the dynamic of loss and introjection for bisexuals? Butler does not elaborate. Nor, for that matter, does Eve Sedgwick (indeed, bisexuality does not appear in the indexes to *Epistemology of the Closet* [1990] or *Tendencies* [1993], two volumes extensively concerned with binaries).

The difficulty with bisexuality in these texts is not due to any limitations on the part of their authors. Bisexuality consistently falls outside of both the medical model and the homoerotic one, thus confounding analyses that implicitly rely on either. Behind most recent queer theorizing, for all its valorization of agency, lies the continued belief that homosexuals just are that way, that to question how they appeared is to participate in homophobia. Likewise, bisexuality appears to be of interest only as an anomalous failure to "be all you can be." The homoerotic model, on the other hand, treats heterosexuality as interesting only to the extent that it is a cover for homoerotic bonding or an engagement of convenience (as Shakespeare would have it, the earth must be peopled). Thus, while transgender may be both not queer enough and too queer, within either prevailing model bisexuality is just not queer enough.

OSCILLATING AGENCY

The marginalization of bisexuality and transgender produces a loss not only for those "in" those categories, but for everyone. Bisexuality and transgender are the phenomena operating most strongly today to challenge and transform ideas about gender and sexuality. The promise of bisexuality and transgender lies precisely in the string of words used as epithets—unstable, uncommitted, fence-sitters—as well as in the inescapability of agency they both entail. These are insults to those who remain convinced that salvation and inclusion must come from establishing a clear identity and fighting for its inclusion. To these people instability is an insult and a threat. If our sexuality defines a line of battle, then being uncommitted becomes proof of unreliability. If, however, we understand the stakes of sexual politics in more universal terms, we see that the questions of mobility and choice are exactly the ones we must focus on.

Elizabeth Daumer (1992, 98) has argued that the perspective of bisexuality offers the chance to illuminate "the gaps and contradictions of all identity" and "the at times radical discontinuities between an individual's sexual acts and affectional choices, on the one hand, and her or his affirmed political identity, on the other." Daumer argues that destabilizing identity moves us toward a more progressive politics for several reasons. First, awareness of identity's incompleteness fosters appreciation for diversity both within and between individuals. Second, disarticulating identity, sexual act, and desire forces us to find a political ground for alliances, a vision for the future rather than a simple claim of identity. Without disavowing identity politics, we are led to incorporate our identities into a politics of ideas (Highleyman 1995). Our political dreams cannot rest with our own affirmation and comfort, because we might change our identities and desires. We need to build a politics that allows for shifts even as we affirm present identities.

What are the vision and the center of this politics? Most fundamentally, they are choice and agency. The threat of bisexuality has always been choice. Bisexuality seems to call inescapably for choices about whom and how to love. For lesbian-feminists, the threat is that bisexuals will choose a man. For heterosexuals, the threat is that bisexuals will choose a same-sex lover. For lesbians and gays, the threat is that bisexuals belie the claim that we can't help our desire. While the current rallying cry for gay rights is that of the 1950s and 1960s—namely that we have no choice, we're born this way, we can't help it—bisexuals imply that desire does not negate agency.

This does not mean that bisexuals experience desire and commitment less fully than others. Desire, affection, and other attractions do not appear for the bisexual as less intense or less commanding than they do for others—indeed, part of the pain attested to by bi writers is the product of being told to choose the appropriate partner when their desire is not so easily commanded. Nonetheless, bi people are forced into positions of choice and agency by the mutual exclusions they face. What do I do when those I live with and find community with reject my love?

Of course, some might say that we all face choices such as this. When our friends don't like our lovers we hope we won't have to choose between them, but we sometimes do. However, only rarely do such choices force a fundamental shift in one's identity. Those who find their desire and their identity firmly within lesbian parameters rarely have to change their whole identity because of their lover. Nonetheless, there are cases analogous to this one. Communities are not homogeneous wholes, but clusters of overlapping networks conveniently reified by key names. A lesbian who stops drinking may find that her identity and her friendships change quite dramatically, or a career change may move her from one network to another. These are major shifts with important implications for personal identity. They are not, however, burdened by the significance we place on sexuality. In our culture, where sexuality supposedly tells us crucial information about individuals, and where lines between sexualities and sexual communities are still strongly policed, the gender of our lover(s) defines us in spite of our personal construction of the meaning of that gender.

One response to this, of course, is to say "I am bisexual" in order to invoke a new identity and found a new community. This has been an important and often successful strategy in the 1990s, as bisexuals have fought for inclusion in lesbian and gay organizations and communities. However, instituting bisexuality as a third (or fourth) sexual identity simply expands the list of identities without building common ground or new visions for the future. It leads to the formation of LGB communities, but it does not call into question the identities contained in those initials.

Others find a more transgressive potential in bisexuality. Figured not as another sexual identity but as the negation of sexual identity, bisexuality manifests its full threat, not to lesbian or gay communities, politics, or sex, but to identity itself. As Jo Eadie says, "to say 'I am bisexual' is to say 'I am not I'" (1993, 129). If identity is secured by sexual object choice, and if bisexuality embodies a choice that is shifting and never-completed, then the position of bisexuality is indeed a position of an I that is never fully I. Bisexuals appear as "double agents" (130). We should note here not only the image of the double agent as a figure in war and politics, but the doubled agent, the agent of choice who is never self-identical. To say "I am not I" is not to say that I don't exist, or that I am not an agent, but that I am never only one, self-contained and neatly bounded. I choose, I exercise agency, but I do so not as the Enlightenment subject who knows her desires and motivations, but rather as an incomplete being in a sea of possibility.

Bisexuals appear, then, as coyote figures roaming the sexual frontier (Phelan 1996). Bisexuality, however, does not have a monopoly on this coyote identity. Transgendered people manifest double agency as well. As border figures, faithful neither to femaleness nor to maleness, trans people unmoor the "I" that is secured by gender. Faced with regimes of binary gender, trans people cross the boundary and confound life narratives. As Jacob Hale (1998) notes, this is not a matter of "high-spirited celebration or revelry," not a position of exuberance, but is a result of the fact that trans "embodiments and our subjectivities are abjected from social ontology: we cannot fit ourselves into extant categories without denying, eliding, erasing, or otherwise abjecting personally significant aspects of ourselves. ... When we choose to live with and in our dislocatedness, fractured from social ontology, we choose to forgo intelligibility: lost in language and in social life, we become virtually unintelligible, even to ourselves" (336).

Double agents, we remember, are often disavowed by both sides and killed upon discovery. Before capture, they might well find themselves unclear at times where their loyalties lie or about how to proceed in a bipolar world. Doubled sexual agents are continually threatened by the demand to show one's papers, to declare one's allegiance, and to be recognizable to the authorities. Perhaps, however, double agents might coalesce to form non-aligned territories. How, and whether, to do that is the subject to which I now turn.

CONFRONTING THE STRANGER WITHIN

When a border zone denizen's corpse is claimed by those with firmer categorical location, border zones become less habitable for those who are trying to live in the nearly unspeakable spaces created by the overlapping margins of distinct categories. Border zone inhabitants infer reasonably that their lack of fixed location within categories is prohibited by the more firmly located, that such absence will be used as grounds for subjecting them to multiple indiscriminate erasures, and that their sullen resistant silence and their dissenting cries alike will be folded into the discourses of those with more solid categorical and thus social locations. (Hale 1998, 319)

The seriousness of the position of the double agent is often disavowed in queer theory. Despite the prominence of transgender in recent queer theory, as Prosser notes, the physical danger and emotional and ontological anguish of dislocation are often glossed over in favor of either celebrations of the frisson of dissonance or claims for the political productivity of gender trouble. If lesbians and gays are to actively attend to the situations of bi and trans people and to develop a new politics from that attention, they must include a willingness to bear that danger and that anguish.

The process of forming alliances, of acknowledging kinship with double agents or the doubling in every agent, is fraught with danger. The quest to be allies can be subverted rather than strengthened by gestures of incorporation. The inversion model assimilates sexuality into gender, making all lesbians transgendered. The assumption of fixed, exclusive sexual orientations makes bisexuals "really" lesbians or gays who won't admit it or, if in the past, didn't have the permission or privilege that would have enabled them to live as lesbian or gay. When lesbians and gays claim bisexual or transgendered people as ancestors and current members of a community against their self-understandings they do not make themselves better allies, but cannibals, as Hale describes. Claimed as lesbians or gays when that serves the purposes of those groups, disavowed when they become a source of uneasiness, bi and trans people find themselves within "LGBT communities," forced either to assimilate or to stake out more distinct territory.

Rather than consuming and subsuming bi and trans people into models of homosexuality, I suggest that we begin from the perspective of bi and trans in order to challenge traditional ideas about sexuality and gender. Bi and trans are not the same perspective by any means, but they present some similar lessons about the limitations of current lesbian and gay politics.

The first lesson of bi and trans is that sexuality is imbricated with gender, but not in any simple way. This works against both lesbian-feminist understandings, in which sexuality is about gender, and against opponents such as Gayle Rubin (1984) who argue that sexuality and gender are entirely separable (see also Rich 1980). Too much queer theory has analyzed sexuality in isolation from gender, returning us to a sort of prefeminist homosexuality (Martin 1994). Our sexuality is always partly about gender, though not in any simple sense. Gender, conversely, is partly about sexuality. Whatever our bodily equipment, our configurations as masculine or feminine carry with them expectations about who does what, with what, with whom. We need not, however, reduce these cultural entwinements to heterosexist images of masculine beings seeking out feminine ones or homoerotic images of similar beings finding reflection and validation together. Neither should we assume that important pleasures are not derived from confounding those expectations about gender and sexuality. Recognizing that sex and gender are not isomorphic, and that neither sex nor gender is itself self-identical and clearly bounded, affords the possibility of creating new identities that are valorized, not by their "naturalness," but by their expression of agency and creativity.

The second lesson we see more clearly from the viewpoint of bi or trans thinkers is that the demand for clear boundaries and borders hurts rather than strengthens us. Boundaries appeal to our need for order, and this is a necessary part of human functioning. When we make it our life's work to defend the boundaries rather than shift them to accommodate the continually evolving excess of human life, however, we sacrifice too much to order. Boundary policing in sex and gender communities is not only authoritarian, it leads us into conceptual lacunae that are better used as inspiration. When lesbians sleep with men, sometimes the men they sleep with turn out to be FTM. Or perhaps the man is a woman (or vice versa). And maybe the lesbian is MTF, or is another kind of man. It is certainly not the job of feminists to defend boundaries and borders, to reify order; there are others who are better trained and equipped, and we will not win at that game. Our job is to continue to question boundaries, to open ourselves to the change we say we seek. Making our communities into armed camps is not good politics; rather than shoring our borders to prevent infection, we must work on infecting the body politic with the dangerous virus of irreverent democracy.

It is important to note how these "lessons" differ from forms of appropriation that cannibalize bisexuals or transgendered people. Learning lessons is an important part of democratic politics. Those who come to politics only as pre-formed subjects ready to articulate their own (preformed and clearly bounded) interests will never be able to explain why others should support them in their cause. The democratic articulation of interests is that process wherein people's description of their situation and their needs becomes a public matter, of concern not only to those in that situation and holding those interests but also to those with whom their fate is linked. The two lessons listed above may indeed be learned at a number of sites, but mainstream lesbian and gay politics has failed to learn or has forgotten them. Those engaged in such politics establish their commonality with the heterosexual majority by denying both the complicated relations between gender and sexuality and the ways in which the borders of lesbian and gay communities contain and bleed with many others.

The essence of appropriation is non-reciprocity. Failing to listen to and fight for others, while claiming their achievements and their pain as one's own, is not inclusion but appropriation. It is thus crucial that learning from bisexuals and transgendered people does not become a matter of claiming "we are all transsexuals" or that bisexuals are "of course" part of lesbian and gay communities while failing to attend to the specificities of different experiences. I do not offer these two lessons in order to say that we are all the same, all united in opposition to heteronormativity, but rather to suggest that we need to note the particular ways in which these general principles play out in different locations and experiences.

The first lesson suggests that the separation of sexual object choice from gender identity, the core of the construction of the modern homosexual, is both false and pernicious. Both the internal transcripts of gay and lesbian communities and the dominant heteronormative transcript have always recognized this and allowed for a multitude of links and gaps between gender and sexuality. The gay and lesbian communities' public transcript has denied it in a bid for respectability, but this denial has served only a very small group. Learning the principle of imbrication would enable the multiple groups that interpellate themselves as part of a potential community to begin to build a politics on the recognition of these imbrications as illuminating and fruitful rather than shameful.

In building such a politics, the second lesson points to a crucial element for organization and maintenance. Rather than trying to identify an agenda and a constituency a priori and then fighting to maintain the integrity of that agenda and constituency, radical sexual politics should operate through continued public discussion and negotiation about which agendas might catalyze and mobilize the broadest possible constituency. This does not mean that all groups have to affiliate with all other groups, that they must accept as allies everyone who expresses a desire to ally or makes a claim to a common agenda. The principle of porous borders should not translate into a simple command that judgments or separations are regressive. It does imply that decisions to separate or disavow others should not be based on simple identity categories, which probably fail to capture the reality of all members (and likely violate the principle established by the first lesson), but rather on statements of principle and policy about particular issues.

As a particularly thorny example, I'd like to turn to the ILGA/NAMBLA controversy of 1994. In the face of stereotypes that all gay men are pedophiles, most lesbian and gay organizations have not only disavowed groups such as the North American Man-Boy Love Association (NAMBLA) but have argued for distinguishing pedophilia from homosexuality on the grounds that heterosexuality and homosexuality designate adult orientations while pedophilia is neither heterosexual nor homosexual. This position actively resists NAMBLA's assertions of community membership and the objections of many activists to their exclusion from groups such as the International Lesbian and Gay Organization (ILGA). NAMBLA was barred from ILGA after the U.S. government made NAMBLA's membership a basis for denying non-governmental organization (NGO) status to ILGA at the United Nations. Whether such exclusion is a matter of secondary marginalization within a marginalized community or a "legitimate" distinction will not be decided by a priori definitions of community boundaries and membership but by discussions about principles and goals. If the dominant principle becomes articulated as the rights of consenting adults to love one another without discrimination, then NAMBLA will find itself out of that community. If, on the other hand, the organizing principle of a coalition or alliance is framed as the universal right to sexual freedom, then it will be much harder to justify exclusion on the grounds of age or "inappropriate object." Currently, although ILGA and its affiliated groups implicitly appeal to the principle of rights, the groups' explicit frame of identity ("lesbians and gays") leaves them continually subject to the charge that they have "turned on their own" to gain legitimacy.

The ILGA/NAMBLA case is instructive for another reason. Not only is it a case of contentious exclusion in order to buy legitimacy, it is also an example of the failure to acquire legitimacy through exclusion. After the NAMBLA expulsion, which was justified entirely by the importance of acquiring NGO status, the United States still barred ILGA. The Clinton Administration was clearly not convinced that the remaining member groups around the world were not in fact havens for perverts. Without articulated principles, ILGA was left simply with sharper, narrower boundaries. ILGA did not gain allies from the exclusion—those who opposed ILGA before continued to do so—but lost some of those who understand themselves to be part of the identity named in the organization's title and stated mission. Both those who were excluded and those who remained were disciplined just a little more, as those who remained were reminded of the boundaries of "normal" homosexuality.

When the Right comes after lesbians and gays, we who identify with or are targeted by those labels understandably fight for our right to equality. We fight for "lesbian and gay rights." We thus consolidate identities formed under duress, identities that are nonetheless rich in meaning. Yet many, if not most, lesbians and gays do not find themselves living within LGBT communities, or even in lesbian and gay communities, and they do not derive deep meaning from their sexuality except as stigma. These folks go to work, come home, engage in friendships and civic groups, and hope to be part of their home communities. For them, the point of equality is not to find validation for a particular identity, but to be what they are, to have their sexuality mean as much or as little as they choose. Making this possible involves more than demonstrating that they are as normal as their neighbors; it also requires something other than consolidating identities and adding them to a list of boundaried units deserving of rights. It requires wholesale resistance to heteronormativity and to gender tyranny, both outside and inside our communities.

QUEER COMMUNITIES, QUEER UTOPIAS

Susan Stryker, a transgender activist and scholar, has noted that what she finds most compelling about the idea of "queer" is "the sense of a utopian, all-encompassing point of resistance to heteronormativity and . . . a 'posthomosexual' refiguration of communities of people marginalized by sexuality, embodiment, and gender" (1998, 151). In such a refiguration, queer communities would not be bounded by initials, but would become spaces for experimentation and visioning of new possibilities for self-creation. In order for this to become possible either conceptually or in practice, however, "queer" needs to mean more than "lesbian or gay," more even than resistance and marginality. Such a starting point continues to define queer in terms of what it is not rather than in terms of its (our) own possibilities. Perhaps inevitably, queer communities will form first among those marginalized by hegemonic cultural formations; but becoming queer must involve a remapping of the social world so that marginalization, assimilation, and resistance (each of which is defined by a posited center) are all transformed into new cultural locations and forms.

This project, of course, is not new. Throughout the nineteenth and twentieth centuries, groups of gender-variant or sexually variant people worked to create new cultures and counterpublics. The vision of queerness articulated by Stryker is a vision shared in various ways by gay liberation, lesbian-feminism, and early homosexual theorists and organizers such as Harry Hay and Edward Carpenter, as well as utopian thinkers such as Herbert Marcuse. The history of these movements and ideas illuminates the difficulties faced by such visions, as the quest for cultural autonomy is (perhaps inevitably) bound and re-bound to the hegemonic. Lesbian-feminism's attempt to produce gynocentric cultures relied, implicitly and often explicitly, on a demonization of men and masculinity (Phelan 1989; Shugar 1995). Gay liberation opened with volleys against "straight society" as well as the call to create new gay cultures. Such reaction is neither regrettable nor avoidable; the utopian drive is inescapably bound to protest against existing arrangements. Nonetheless, there are dangers in reaction. Not only is one bound emotionally, looking over one's shoulder in anger, but one is also bound conceptually. Those engaged in assimilationist projects are not the only ones who measure themselves against the dominant standard. Those engaged in countercultural programs may and do equally concern themselves with whether they "look like straights." The rejection of both bisexuals and transgendered/transsexual people has followed this pattern, as lesbians view bisexuals in terms of men rather than as creators of new possibilities, and see in trans people only the reflection of heterosexual femininity and masculinity (Raymond 1979; Rust 1995). Again, this is unavoidable to an extent: we read the new through eyes accustomed to the old, and we never see without organizing vision into patterns based on already-existing elements. Nonetheless, there are moments when, like new languages, common roots shift into new patterns and variations.

Queer should be not the banner of evasion, of some caricatured postmodern irresponsibility, but the sign of a non-identitarian utopian universalism. It is non-identitarian not in rejecting all identities, but in recognizing that no identity is self-sufficient and adequate to the job that language forces upon it. No hyphenation, no string of modifiers or extensions of identities will overcome that fundamental constitutive inadequacy. Queer communities would be those in which this inadequacy is honored and given central place rather than covered up or tolerated in the margins. Queer communities should be utopian, both in the drive for a better world and in the knowledge that the dream will never fully take shape, the day of reconciliation will never arrive. Utopianism requires a good deal of humility and patience to avoid becoming dogmatic and impractical. Finally, queer communities should be universalist, open for all, seeking to produce the values upon which everyone could find recognition and inclusion. These values cannot reduce themselves to identities, both because of the incompleteness of identity and because identity does not guarantee shared values. Much of the confusion and sense of betrayal in our communities is the result of the assumption that those with shared identities will share a sense of what those identities entail. Shared identities, however, are no substitute for shared politics. The reification of community hides this from us, but queered communities would enable us to recognize and address it. Community is not a thing or a place in which we find ourselves by birth or ascriptive attributes, but is a process by which we build commonality and difference (Phelan 1994, ch. 5). Queer community is a process of democratic values, in which lesbians and gays and trans people and bisexuals and, yes, heterosexuals participate to loosen the bonds of gender.

Would such communities be "home" to anyone? By this I mean to ask, not whether anyone would be eligible for membership, but rather whether such communities would provide the stability and belonging that humans (even postmodern ones) need. Prosser's insistence that sexual difference is a persistent and basic feature of human societies, and that crossings as well as fixity sustain this difference, is well taken. The bonds of gender are experienced very differently for different sorts of people: for some they are a burden and a constriction, for others (very often trans people) they are a crucial support for personal identity and self-esteem. Loosening the bonds of gender cannot mean, then, a forced regime of resistance to assignment, as lesbian-feminists such as Jeffreys (1997) seem to advocate, but loosening the demand to be recognizable *or not,* as well as prior understandings of what one's partner(s) reveals about one's gender identity or political or cultural commitments. Such a community, I believe, could indeed be a home: not a hall of mirrors, reflecting oneself back consistently, but a place where one could be recognized as a person with both a history and a future that has not yet been written.

Attempts to valorize our sexual identities, to give ourselves legitimacy through constructing histories or making claims to our superior nature or culture, always work by excluding important people and questions. Mainstream lesbians and gays have hidden bisexuals because they seem to present the possibility that we could be straight if we wanted. But there is no pleasure in a movement based on the claim that we can't help it. Imagine, instead, a movement to foster agency and variety in sexuality. Feminists have spearheaded such movements, but these movements have too often been contained at points where we are forced to confront our own fears and abjections. But forming real BTLG communities would mean pushing past the discomfort to the place of creativity. In this place we could ask one another, Who lives inside of you? What do those selves dream of and desire? How can we do justice to all of them? Silencing bi and trans people is part of the silencing of all of us—the butches who can't admit to the boys and men (and little girls and hot babes) in them, the femmes who fear for their feminist credentials, the androgynes who long for other androgynes, the lesbian-feminists who get hot talking politics, and all the others inside and around us.

Beliefs that bisexuals are unreliable or that MTF or FTM lesbians are agents of patriarchy rest on an ideology born of fear and despair. It is time to abandon those parents and move with the knowledge that citizenship will not be bought by drawing new boundaries. We also have to challenge our fears, to consider seriously that the certainty about our identities that citizenship seems to offer comes at the cost of falsifying and denying the strangeness within each of us, of every sexuality. This is not a step into equality, but a renunciation for which we will all pay dearly.

BIBLIOGRAPHY

Bauman, Zygmunt. 1991. *Modernity and Ambivalence.* Ithaca, NY: Cornell University Press.

Blasius, Mark, and Shane Phelan, eds. 1997. *We Are Everywhere: A Historical Sourcebook of Gay and Lesbian Politics.* New York: Routledge.

Butler, Judith. 1990. *Gender Trouble: Feminism and the Subversion of Identity.* New York: Routledge.

Chapman, Kathleen, and Michael Du Plessis. 1997. "'Don't Call Me *Girl*': Lesbian Theory, Feminist Theory, and Transsexual Identities." In *Cross Purposes: Lesbians, Feminists, and the Limits of Alliance,* ed. Dana Heller, 169–85. Bloomington: Indiana University Press.

Cohen, Cathy. 1999. *The Boundaries of Blackness.* Chicago: University of Chicago Press.

Currah, Paisley. 1996. "Searching for Immutability: Homosexuality, Race and Rights Discourse." In *A Simple Matter of Justice?* ed. Angelia R. Wilson. London: Cassell.

Daumer, Elizabeth. 1992. "Queer Ethics, or The Challenge of Bisexuality to Lesbian Ethics." *Hypatia: A Journal of Feminist Philosophy* 7/4:91–105.

Eadie, Jo. 1993. "Activating Bisexuality: Towards a Bi/Sexual Politics." In *Activating Theory: Lesbian, Gay, Bisexual Politics*, ed. Joseph Bristow and Angelia Wilson. London: Lawrence and Wishart.

Gamson, Joshua. 1998. *Freaks Talk Back: Tabloid Talk Shows and Sexual Nonconformity*. Chicago: University of Chicago Press.

Hale, C. Jacob. 1998. "Consuming the Living, Dis(re)membering the Dead in the Butch/Ftm Borderlands." *GLQ: A Journal of Lesbian and Gay Studies* 4/2:311–48.

Herman, Didi. 1997. *The Anti-Gay Agenda: Orthodox Vision and the Christian Right*. Chicago: University of Chicago Press.

Highleyman, Liz A. 1995. "Identity and Ideas: Strategies for Bisexuals." In *Bisexual Politics: Theories, Queries, and Visions*, ed. Naomi Tucker with Liz Highleyman and Rebecca Kaplan, 73–92. New York: Harrington Park Press.

Jeffreys, Sheila. 1993. *The Lesbian Heresy.* North Melbourne: Spinifex.

_____. 1997. "Transgender Activism: A Lesbian Feminist Perspective." *Journal of Lesbian Studies* 1/3–4:55–74.

Laclau, Ernesto, and Chantal Mouffe. 1985. *Hegemony and Socialist Strategy*. London: Verso.

Martin, Biddy. 1994. "Sexualities without Genders and Other Queer Utopias." *diacritics* 24/2–3:104–21.

Namaste, Ki. 1997. "'Tragic Misreadings': Queer Theory's Erasure of Transgender Subjectivity." In *Queer Studies: A Lesbian, Gay, Bisexual, and Transgender Anthology*, ed. Brett Beemyn and Mickey Eliason. New York: New York University Press.

Phelan, Shane. 1989. *Identity Politics: Lesbian Feminism and the Limits of Community*. Philadelphia: Temple University Press.

_____. 1994. *Getting Specific: Postmodern Lesbian Politics*. Minneapolis: University of Minnesota Press.

_____. 1996. "Coyote Politics: Trickster Tales and Feminist Futures." *Hypatia: A Journal of Feminist Philosophy* 11/3:130–149.

Prosser, Jay. 1998. *Second Skins: The Body Narratives of Transsexuality*. New York: Columbia University Press.

Raymond, Janice. 1979. *The Transsexual Empire: The Making of the She-Male*. Boston: Beacon.

Rich, Adrienne. 1980. "Compulsory Heterosexuality and Lesbian Existence. *Signs: Journal of Women in Culture and Society* 5/1:631–660.

Rubin, Gayle. 1984. "Thinking Sex: Notes for a Radical Theory of the Politics of Sexuality." In *Pleasure and Danger: Exploring Female Sexuality*, ed. Carole Vance. Boston: Routledge and Kegan Paul.

Rust, Paula. 1995. *Bisexuality and the Challenge to Lesbian Politics: Sex, Loyalty, and Revolution*. New York: New York University Press.

Sedgwick, Eve. 1990. *Epistemology of the Closet*. Berkeley: University of California Press.

_____. 1993. *Tendencies*. Durham, NC: Duke University Press.

Shugar, Dana. 1995. *Separatism and Women's Community*. Lincoln: University of Nebraska Press.

Stryker, Susan. 1998. "The Transgender Issue: An Introduction." *GLQ: A Journal of Lesbian and Gay Studies* 4/2:145–58.

Sullivan, Andrew. 1995. *Virtually Normal: An Argument about Homosexuality*. New York: Knopf.

———————————— ○ ————————————

END OF CHAPTER QUESTIONS

1. How have bisexual and transgender people pressured gay and lesbian activists for greater recognition?
2. How are bisexual and transgender people stigmatized by gay and lesbian people?
3. Who is Judith Butler? What did she say about bisexuality?
4. What is meant by bisexuality as a "double agent"? In what ways does "double agent" further stigmatize bisexuality?

Gay American Indian Men's Mobility and Sexual Sedentarism in the United States Census Rules of Residence

Brian Joseph Gilley

INTRODUCTION

The intense debate about recognizing same-sex marriage on the 2010 United States Census reaffirms skeptics' views of counting the nation's citizens (and non-citizens) as a political device. The debate was centered around counting same-sex marriages, particularly those who are legally recognized by states, on the 2010 Census. In the past—including the data presented here—individuals who were in domestic partnerships were merely counted as coresidents. For example, the 2000 United States Census forms required a "primary resident" be named in situations where more than one unmarried person lived in the same domicile. For same-sex couples living in domestic partnerships, this meant that one or the other had to be recorded as the primary owner of the home and the primary resident of the domicile, which generally did not reflect the actual living arrangements of the couple. In the summer of 2009, under pressure from activists, the Obama administration decided that same-sex marriages in states where unions are recognized would be counted on the 2010 United States Census. In *The New York Times*, a spokesman for the Census Bureau, said ". . . [T]hey ought to report the way they see themselves" (The Associated Press 2009).

Clearly, having the United States census "recognize" same-sex marriage is a political victory for advocates. Yet, a policy relying on White upper middle-class coupling and legalistic discourses further exacerbates the depoliticization of social inequality among United States minorities pushing gay, lesbian, bisexual, transgender, and queer (GLBTQ) people of color further to the margins. United States census rules of residence do exclude individuals who do not view their relationships as "partnerships" but instead emphasize sex as motivating their co-habitation. Prioritizing marriage, or committed coupling, potentially disrupts the ability for sexuality—as a set of practices—to reveal the ways in which culture and routines of the body affect GLBTQ demography. Using politicized forms of dominant constructions of sexuality and space may not produce the "quality of life" and lifestyle indicators required to obtain a portrait of the nation's GLBTQ population much less the ways sexuality circulates through residence patterns (Purdam et al. 2008). The category of "same-sex marriage" as a legal consciousness discourse produces an asexual understanding of "residence." Same-sex marriage avoids the aspects of gay men's social-sexual practices, which are no doubt less palatable to society at large and may be more significant in determining mobility (Nicol and Smith 2008). When other class, race, ethnicity, and geographic factors are taken into account, the compounding effects of normalized categories of knowledge production, such as "rules of residence," exacerbate the marginalization of non-normative social-sexual practices. The confluence of historic cultural practices, male mobility, and contemporary sexuality generates a situational reality placing American Indian men's sexuality at the margins of gay social agendas and debates. With the 10-year prohibition ending on publishing ethnographic data I collected under the Statistical Research Division's "Highly Mobile Peoples" project during the 2000 Census, I finally hope to be able to add to our understanding of the ways sexual circulation, HIV/AIDS, and residency overlap for American Indian men.

A GAY AMERICAN INDIAN MEN'S INTERACTIVE SOCIAL NETWORK

In 2000, I conducted research under the United States Census Bureau Statistical Research Division's (SRD) Ethnographic Social Network Tracing Project (ESNTP). The group I worked with was known as the Highly Mobile Peoples Project and included studies on multiple United States populations who were historically underenumerated on the annual United States census. The interest in highly mobile peoples was built on a growing concern about the intersection of social disenfranchisement, cultural factors, and bias in United States census information gathering. The SRD funded ethnographers to trace the residence patterns of multiple populations in order to understand the ways in which individuals' life circumstances, such as class, race, and culture, might affect their being missed by United States census enumerators. Research was conducted with populations such as migrant field hands, fishermen, and homeless American Indians. The connection between life circumstances and residential mobility was supported anecdotally, but the ESNTP sought to apply social network data directly to the 2010 United States Census (Brownrigg 2003). Ethnographers were asked to provide as much data on research subjects' memories of where they were on Census Day, April 1, every year for the previous five years. They also traced the movements of the members of the particular social network under study for nine months, which included overnight stays, changes in primary domicile, transitions in housing, and causes for transition in housing.

The field site for the census data presented here was a Native American men's group in Oklahoma sponsored by a non-profit clinic in an urban center. Twenty men from the group were tracked, interviewed, and observed. Bi-monthly men's group meetings acted as the hub of social life from which spokes of social activities radiated, such as powwows and campouts/retreats, gay bar outings, and bath house or sexual cruising excursions. These meetings, which continue to be held 10 years later, are designed to bring together gay, bi-sexual, transgender, queer, and Two-Spirit (GBTQ2) Native men who are experiencing personal issues and allow them to deal with their concerns in a specifically Indian way. Two-Spirit, for readers unfamiliar with the term, is a relatively new American Indian activist oriented moniker designating oneself as gay and indigenous. GBTQ2 men's meetings at the clinic usually focus on activities to provide a constructive and low pressure environment. Participants will make beadwork, finger weave, or sew while the leaders of the group engage participants in talk about their current situation. It is the incidental conversations during group meetings where many individuals discuss informally their money, housing, relationship, and work problems. However, members of the group interact outside of the formal group meeting context as well, which includes retreats sponsored by the formal group, group and individual trips to powwows and ceremonies, and ad hoc gatherings at individuals' homes to make crafts or sing. Ad hoc gatherings are less formal and the leaders of the formal group meetings are no longer in the forefront of the activities. The change in context from the formal group setting to more public events such as powwows and ceremonies alters the way individuals interact with one another. In the more public context, individuals tend to reveal much less about their personal lives and focus more on the social event they are attending. Therefore, the combined activities of the support group with the additional gatherings create a distinctive sense of social cohesiveness. The social cohesiveness is further supported by the fact that many of the members of the group have been attending the bi-monthly meetings and interacting socially for in excess of 10 years.

As Lobo observed for the Bay Area Indian community, such support groups form a "community" based on self-identification. The community is not constituted by neighborhood residency, but rather "it is a widely scattered and frequently shifting network of relationships with location nodes found in organizations and activity sites" (Lobo 1990:2). Men join the group because they self-identify as gay and Native American and secondarily because they seek the support of individuals who share their particular situation. Tribal identities are not primary in the creation and maintenance of the support group, but rather a shared identity of Indian and gay is the basic organizing factor. The United States government's relocation program in the 1950s was a major factor in the urbanization of Native peoples, and to a large extent non-tribally oriented organizations and communities were a result of the out migration from rural and reservation communities (Burt 1986; Jobe 2003; Lobo 1990, 2001). However, government coerced relocation was not a major factor in urban relocation for Oklahoma Natives, but rather was a result of economic conditions in rural communities. In the beginning of the 20th century, many of the Native communities were isolated and economically depressed. Also, many Natives made their living participating in rural-based economic activities like farming, while others barely scraped by. Younger members of the community began to seek employment closer to urban and industrial areas. Our assumptions about the mobility of Native American populations tend to favor a portrait of economic forced rural to urban mobility. Rather, the data found in this study show that the mobility of Native Americans has its own set of spatial orientations and movements along a rural-urban continuum often determined by social, cultural, and personal involvements. The sexual wants and practices of the study group further complicates understanding the continuum at the same time it illuminates particular aspects of its patterns. This continuum is thought of by many Natives as "Indian Country" which is about geographic space as much as it is about a conceptual and social landscape.

GLBTQ2 Natives often relocate seeking more freedom from community surveillance of gender and sexuality, while many of their heterosexual peers moved away from rural community centers for economic reasons. Despite geographic displacement, both groups maintain social and familial relationships within their communities (Gilley 2006). For much of the 20th century, Indian Country was the rural space occupied by allotment and reservation Indian communities, often associated with poverty. However, within the last 50 years, Native geographic and conceptual space has become associated with urban communities as well as geographic areas that are seen as "home" on reservation and in rural communities (Lobo 2001). However, the present situation of Native communities calls for recognition of Native geography as a space, not specifically urban or rural, but a space of social and political interaction. Whether it is a gymnasium at a local high school, a lodge in someone's backyard, or a carload of people on a highway, that space becomes what Appadurai (1990) would call an "ethnoscape" and an "ideoscape." Ethnoscapes and ideoscapes represent "imagined worlds ... the multiple worlds which are constituted by the historically situated imaginations of persons and groups spread around the globe"

(Appadurai 1990:7). The imagined worlds of the ethnoscape and ideoscape that is Indian Country are the landscapes formed by people who conduct their lives among the seemingly stable communities of identity. However, as such communities appear stable, disjunctures within them emphasize the deterritorialization of nationalist (tribal) identities where "heritage politics" are often perceived as uniformly constituted among and between individuals. It is in the space called Indian Country where group hegemony over difference is regulated as well as resisted (Appadurai 1990). Furthermore, Indian Country as an ethno-ideological space is a product of the disjuncture between what is seen as Indian society and that of White society, where sameness and difference are performed and reified in everyday activity. The ways in which Natives construct and move through geographic space have implications for how residence is determined. Residence in Native concepts is a much more fluid idea where kinship, community, and, as illustrated here, sexual practices are at work.

Besides their community "residences," many of the men in the group have or share residences in urban areas or in outlying suburbs. Some group members live in rural areas and come into the urban center for group meetings and activities. A few of the men continue to be "homeless" in that they have a history of migration between friends' or family members' houses as well as taking up residence in the urban YMCA. The highest time of mobility is during the summer months when social, ceremonial, and tribal obligations increase. Throughout the summer and early fall, many community members reside part-time, for a few days or up to three months, at a relative or friend's house in a rural area adjacent to their tribal homelands or at very remote ceremonial spaces, often referred to as "ceremonial grounds" by Oklahoma Natives. Demographically, the age range of the group begins in the early 20s and extends to men in their mid-50s, with individuals in their 40s and 50s predominating. Based on field data, it appears that the concentration of ages in the 40s and 50s is the result of men with more experience in the gay community and more comfort with their identity, desiring to shift their social associations away from the gay bar scene and toward their cultural identity. Men in their 40s and 50s in 2000 were also the population of GBTQ2 men who had sustained the initial devastation of the AIDS epidemic and, thus, were the most prevalent population living with AIDS at the time. The 20 members who were tracked and interviewed during my fieldwork represent American Indians from mostly Southeastern peoples including Cherokee, Creek, Seminole, Lumbee, and Chickasaw, with a certain number of individuals representing western and plains groups such as the Lakota and Apache. The tribal makeup of members is reflective of the East Oklahoma geographic concentration of the study group. The education, occupation, and income level of participants varies widely as well. About 50 percent of the group members are college educated, with most having incomes less than $30,000 a year. The high number of post-secondary education among the group is high as compared to the Native American male population in general and was even relatively high for White gay-identified men in 2000 (Black et al. 2000). Income levels are slightly higher than average American Indian men, but lower as compared with non-Natives who possess post-secondary education (Gregory, Abello, and Johnson 1997). Most individuals in the group hold full-time jobs in various industries, while some individuals are receiving Social Security disability or are employed sporadically. Because the group was based in a clinic formed by HIV/AIDS educators, the number of American Indian men living with HIV or AIDS consistently hovered around 60 percent. Individual circumstances informed the talk at bi-monthly meetings, which generally centered on current issues in members' lives. Information about mobility came from discussions about current problems or changes in members' life situations and activities required by an individual's tribal community participation. Trips to ceremonial grounds or powwows, as well as changing from one particular living situation to another because of domestic issues, loss of employment, and illness were all factors in mobility. Participant observation of mobility was expanded to attendance of men's group sponsored events, such as ceremonies and retreats. Through participant observation, I traced the episodes of contact between interaction network members, as well as correlated episodes of contact with domicile change. Participant observation also allowed me to document potential reasons that certain individuals were "highly mobile" while others' mobility was fairly "stable."

Interviews of interaction network members were primarily based on recording the characteristics from the 2000 Census Short Form with additional questions about employment and personal characteristics from the 2000 Census Long Form. The United States Census Short Form collects the most basic demographic data, such as age, race, ethnicity, sex/gender, marital status, and basic employment. The Short Form also collects data on where an individual was living five years before to generate generalizable data about mobility. The United States Census Long Form gathers more detailed information with twice as many questions collecting information on individuals such as property ownership, income, previous employment, previous incomes, and as many past addresses as individuals can remember. The Long Form also collects data on specific domiciles, such as when a home was built and the estimated value of the property. Any characteristics gathered by Long and Short Forms relating to mobility were used to gather information from the GBTQ2 network along with characteristics I anticipated would be important to individuals within the community, such as sexuality, relationship status, and access to housing. The Long and Short Form information did not provide enough data to produce statistical generalizations about mobility patterns. However, interviews and participant observation provided invaluable narratives about instances of mobility as well as reasons for domicile change not covered by the United States census forms or the data mandated by the SRD for study. Informants were asked questions concerning: how they viewed temporary and permanent residents, activities that took them away from their primary domiciles, and times of the year when they traveled the most. The SRD of the Census Bureau provided Decennial Census 2000 outcomes and computational social network analyses to analyze the relationship between the enumeration of individuals at domiciles and mobility from the Short and Long Form data. The data and analysis provided by the SRD attempted to match records of individuals and domiciles based on census form information that I gathered with information gathered from the Decennial Census outcomes. Emerging from the SRD's data capture were several of what are considered "misfits" between the reporting of residents and co-residents for particular domiciles and the ethnographic data collected from the social interaction network.

In the data capture conducted by the SRD, the domiciles and personal records I reported from the social interaction network were compared with Decennial Census outcomes from Census 2000 forms returned to the Census Bureau and from field enumerators. From the comparison, the SRD produced matched and unmatched records for domiciles and persons. Of the 22 individuals for whom I submitted Short and Long Form data, 13 individuals and their domiciles came up as matched records with the Decennial Census outcomes. The unmatched persons and domiciles posed a few interesting questions that could only be answered through the ethnographic data. At least three individuals who were living with domestic partners, parents, and friends on Census Day 2000 were omitted from domiciles in information gathered by returned forms or enumerators. According to the data capture generated by the SRD, three individuals who had reported living at particular domiciles during the ethnographic interview on Census Day 2000 were not counted at that domicile on the Decennial Census outcomes. However, their residence at the domicile was confirmed by my field visit as well as by the individual with whom they lived. It appears that these social network members staying in another individual's domicile on Census Day were not counted because they were not perceived of as permanent residents by the owner of the home. All three of the individuals not counted were co-residents of the home owner/renter and were either paying rent or "helping out" with the utility and rent payments in exchange for living in the home. In all three cases, the primary home owner/renter excluded any co-residents in the 2000 Census enumeration. At the time the original analysis was conducted, I was not able to include other information collected during ethnographic interviews, home visits, and participant observation. Two themes in particular emerged from the un-included data. First, many co-residents were thought of as temporary residents because they were either temporary lovers or were men trading sex for overnight stays or short-term housing. Second, I observed many HIV positive men, particularly the newly diagnosed seropositives, having difficulty in obtaining housing. Some of the men who were too sick to work, but had not yet received Social Security disability, were staying with lovers or friends. Most of these individuals could not rely on family after their diagnosis and chose to move from one friend's house to another's or to trade sex for temporary housing.

Difficulties surrounding sexuality and HIV/AIDS were further compounded by the unique residential patterns of the Native American population that had been documented by previous census underenumeration studies (Bonvillain 1989; de la Puente n.d.; Lobo 1990; Lujan 1990; Moore 1992). Most have concluded that the residential habits and mobility of American Indians makes them likely to be undercounted for economic reasons, resistance to the government, and extended family living situations. All of these reasons emerged as potential mitigating factors in mobility and undercount in this study. However, sexuality and sexual circulation impacted the ways in which domicile owners viewed their co-resident's stay (in this instance the interaction network member's stay) in their home. The parameters of census rules of residence played a major role in whether or not individuals were counted in the 2000 Census enumeration and in this study's case, limited the data collection on men's mobility.

UNMATCHED MEN

"Usual residence" has been defined by the United States Census Bureau as the place where the person lives and sleeps most of the time. Rules of residence for a person without housing of their own state that they are to be counted where they were staying on Census Day 2000. As Lobo (1990:23) points out for the Native community in Oakland: "Men, particularly single men, may move between households, particularly among a series of female headed households." With this observation in mind, the data I collected also showed a high residential mobility among single American Indian men. To a large extent, a sociohistorical tendency of single Indian men to move frequently and take up residence with another person or family informed the ways in which heads of households viewed network member's stays. That is, the concept of usual residence was not culturally applicable to these particular living situations because the person holding tenure of the domicile interpreted a co-resident's stay as temporary: be that seasonal, overnight, or an emergency extended stay. Further complicating an already culturally specific pattern of mobility is the intersection of sexuality and American Indian residential patterns.

In the research on highly mobile populations, "unmatched" persons represent a significant concern. Unmatched individuals are those who did not return census forms or did not appear on the returned form of their primary residence. In some cases, people are living in places not recognized as "residences." Within the confines of census categories, a person is "unmatched" because they were not counted, and highly mobile people are the most difficult to match with domiciles. Looking at matching from a more dynamic perspective, we recognize that for many of the men represented in this study, being "unmatched" is an intentional state. Being considered matched or unmatched as a census category articulates with non-committed domestic relationships, transience, illegal employment such as sex work, or the desire to avoid being located. The demographic data found that many of the non-matched places that network members are reported to be staying are in rural parts of Oklahoma and are difficult to find. The unmatched locations of stays are oriented to ceremonial grounds and opportunities that the rural outdoors can only provide such as open pit fires and streams. In one example, the SRD could not produce a match for ceremonial grounds in Northern Oklahoma that was at one time on the Osage reservation. The ceremonial grounds include homes, a graveyard, and a ceremonial arbor. Around the ceremonial arbor, there are at least six or seven homes that have residents living there year-round. The residents of these homes are usually elderly people who have owned the homes since they were built. I was told that originally there were many more homes built in this area, and at one time certain tribal officials lived at this location. However, during the 1930s, many of the homes were abandoned as many Osages moved to California. Alternative to having a home at the ceremonial site, many families opted for arbors that surround the ceremonial grounds. Many families take up residence at the ceremonial site for as long as a month and seldom less than one week every year for ceremonial dances in early June. Individuals whose family owns a home on the ceremonial grounds may move in with their relatives for the months of June and July during the ceremonial season. These domiciles and camp areas may not have been previously counted because there are no signs showing where the ceremonial grounds are located from the highway and are mostly kept secret except by word of mouth. In another instance of this during the month of May, 35 members of the social interaction network attended a ceremony at a state and federally run park in Oklahoma for one week. The park itself did not come up on the SRD data capture as possessing domiciles. However, the park contains at least 30 cabins as well as government housing for Park Service employees. The interaction network chose this park to have their ceremonial meeting because of the remote location, the ability to build large ceremonial fires, the sacred aspect that the outdoors adds to ceremonies, and the ability to house and feed a large number of persons. At this particular ceremonial gathering, individuals from the social network stayed three to a cabin, ate in the mess hall, and spent most of the week preparing for ceremony, socializing, or participating in ceremonies.

The social relationships required for maintaining one's identity as Native American plays a major role in movements of individuals. The largest factor in seasonal adjustments is participation in family-oriented ceremonial obligations, tribal social/ceremonial obligations, powwows, and men's group activities. As Lobo (1990:23) observed for American Indians in the Bay Area, ". . . [M]obility is frequently viewed as an advantage in capturing resources, and in maintaining and cultivating an active and extensive network of relations." These seasonal adjustments are the result of the maintenance of one's identity as Native American through the fulfillment of social obligations. Therefore, episodes and instances of domicile change and mobility were directly correlated with the various ways in which individuals sought to fulfill social obligations as they intersected with individual needs at that time. There are two major factors that connect increased community participation with undercount: a high rate of seasonal mobility and access to multiple places to stay while traveling. Characteristically, many of the non-matched persons are some of the most active in the social and ceremonial aspects of the Native American community. Although the availability of monetary resources played into one's ability to attend events, most of the socially involved highly mobile people obtained their livelihood from services provided to the community, or supplemented government assistance, such as Social Security disability, with resources from the social interaction network, relatives, and community members. For the population discussed here, census rules of residence reveal the intersections of mobility or residence and the dilemmas of sexuality and HIV/AIDS infection for American Indian men who already move about the landscape in culturally determined ways. Sexuality and HIV/AIDS are an additional causal factor producing particular effects which produce unique forms of mobility.

NATIVE SEASONAL MOBILITY INTERSECTS AIDS AND SEXUALITY

One network member and unmatched person, 33-year-old Will, was well known among the Indian community to the extent that he was able to move to multiple states and seldom be concerned with having a place to stay. While tracking Will, I recorded three moves for him, each time living with another group of people sharing similar social participations. In one such move, Will was participating in a weeklong ceremonial event in the Rocky Mountains in early August. While at this ceremony, Will arranged to move in with James and Matt with the promise of helping Matt assemble his regalia for powwow dancing. He was also in an "open relationship" with both men. In his characterization of the "relationship," he preferred James over Matt, but Matt owned the house and "wore the pants," thus he felt obligated to have intercourse with Matt as well as James. The timing of this move was important in that Will had spent from the early Spring until late summer traveling to powwows and various ceremonial events. Will's travels directly correlated with the powwow and ceremonial season but also tracked with a "seasonal sexual circulation." That is, his sexual circulation followed an explicitly Native pattern of seasonal mobility determined by cultural participations. Will was mostly closeted while living close to his family and community; however, during the summer months, he traveled throughout the West and Southwest attending powwows, staying with established friends and sexual partners, as well as making new sexual-based acquaintances. Traditionally, the first major powwow in the West and Central West begins in mid-March, with powwow activity hitting its peak in mid-July and leveling off the first of August. When I asked Will about his last move, he stated that his sister was temporarily moving back to the reservation and would be renting out her apartment where he stayed in the fall and winter. The powwow season was nearly over and Will needed a place to "regroup" for the off-season in fall and winter. Will stayed with James and Matt until early May 2000, but was not counted as living there on Census Day. To no one's surprise, Will's temporary sexual-based residency with James and Matt did not fit census rules of residence. At the same time, Will's culturally motivated mobility did not fit census rules of residence. As such, sexuality as well as cultural identity converged to "unmatch" him and allow him to not be counted.

Another example of an unmatched person engaged in seasonal mobility is Chuck, a highly active traditional healer. Chuck maintained a home in the Southwest, but was seldom absent from any ceremonial event or powwow in which the men's group was participating. Chuck's services as a healer were sought by many people, and he traveled extensively throughout the Southwest, West, and Great Plains conducting ceremonies. He usually stayed for a couple days with the person who had required his services or with friends in the area before moving to the next location. The financial support Chuck received for the treatments—cash, food, clothing, and items he could sell or pawn—supplemented his Social Security disability for being HIV positive and in the early stages of AIDS. Chuck would combine several healing-service trips into longer trips that would inevitably include powwows, GLBTQ2 events, and community ceremonies. As with many of the other interaction network members, Chuck's mobility was largely during the Spring and Summer ceremonial and powwow season. Chuck attempted to make ceremonial trips coincide with social events, again mostly occurring during the summer months. In one example from July 2000, Chuck spent two weeks working his way through the Southwest conducting ceremonies and staying with different families. The families would provide him with food, basic supplies, gas money, and a place to stay in exchange for his ceremonial services. Chuck's commitment as a healer and highly active participant in the social interaction network precipitated only part of his seasonal movements. Chuck reported living in his rented home on Census Day 2000, but later after observing his extensive mobility, I asked him where he remembers sleeping on April 1, 2000. In the data Chuck gave for himself, he reported staying at an individual's house for which he was conducting a healing ceremony in New Mexico. In reality, Chuck had become severely ill while "on the road" and took up residence with a longtime acquaintance. He had stopped taking his medication because he had not been able to work in a trip back to his home city and, thus, to his doctor for refills of antiretroviral medication. Chuck further explained that he had "taken up" with his host as a way to insure "decent living conditions" until he was well enough to travel again. Chuck's personal survival was greatly dependent on his ability to be mobile, but also to circulate back through his home town every 30 days to refill his medications as he used tribal health care and had limited resources to secure a longer-term supply of drugs.

The SRD of the Census Bureau labeled Will and Chuck as "highly mobile peoples" due to their frequent changing of residences over the nine month study period and their self-reported residence patterns over the previous five years. The two men's sociocultural participations and racial identification as American Indian also informed the ways in which their "mobility" was analyzed and justified. Yet, because sexuality is not taken as an "official" indicator of residency, the stories told above were explicitly missing from the reported analysis. Sexuality, particularly non-heteronormative forms, when it intersects other social categories such as race complicates residential patterns for populations identifying as GLBTQ2 and may produce "enclaves" and necessitate more complex ways of self-identification (Baumle 2010). Same-sex marriage or other normalized categories of "partnering" would not have captured data on Chuck or Will simply because they did not conceive of themselves as engaged in a relationship defined in permanent ways. For the very same reasons, they were understood as "residents" by the primary resident of the domicile. Even though they occupied a space defined by sexual engagement, they were living in ways demographers would consider a kind of residency.

SEXUAL SEDENTARISM AND RESIDENCE

The intersection of sexuality, mobility, and "residence" in the two ethnographic examples of Will and Chuck give insight to the ways the marriage category, or any "partnership" category, would not engage a critical motivator for residence: sexuality. The spatiality of gay American Indians in general and especially those who identify in contrast to the "homonationalist" tendencies of the same-sex marriage movement are incompatible with the "immobility" of a racially and sexually normalized category. Nationstate censuses already view aboriginal spatial patterns as complicating citizenship given the immobility required of visible national subjects (Prout 2009). Indigenous citizens become invisible through "unquantifiable" forms of mobility challenging demographic categories and, thus, disrupting their "inclusion" in multicultural settler states (Norris and Clatworthy 2003; Povinelli 2002). According to Jasbir Puar (2007:2), this exclusion is "contingent upon the segregation and disqualification of racial and sexual others from the national imaginary." A "national homosexuality," through census(ed) same-sex rules of residence has the effect of reproducing an "official" sedentarism for GLBTQ peoples which requires a domesticated or "rooted" sexuality. Native sexualities, hetero and gay, in general are considered "unrooted" and transitory in practices of serial monogamy and resistance to state intervention in kinship and marital relations. The transitory sexuality of the average non-other gay man is also at odds with a dominant produced asexual domestic coupling. By bringing same-embodied persons into the national fold under the rubric of "same-sex marriage," the United States census again reproduces the ability of the White "homosettler" to abrogate sexuality from their national identity and reaffirm political viability. Yet for the already socioculturally mobile American Indian, sexual mobility is an extension of an existing set of values intersecting points of desire and practice.

The sexual "uprootedness" of Will and Chuck provide a pathologized form of residential behavior lying in contrast to the "national order of things." By refusing the sexual sedentarism of same-sex domesticity, the sexually mobile American Indian man may escape census "enumeration" of their lives and habits, refusing a "territorialization" of their sexuality (Malkki 1997). Yet, underenumeration is also a form of consent to invisibility, which functions agentively as well as an unintentional exclusion from "being counted." The "rules of residence" have the effect of exclusion through underenumerating particular categories of personhood, experience, and bodily acts, while actively enumerating sedentary sexualities transformed into dominant gay domesticated categories. As Valentine (2007:235) points out, "Over the course of the 20th century, certain social actors in the United States, with relatively more ability to challenge meanings and practices, have actively worked to produce innovative cultural models . . . conceptualizing gender variance and homosexual desire." The social actors in question have been able to effectively use census enumeration of same-sex coupling as either an additional shield to dominant societal moral intervention or another form of discipline for the gay male body.

REFERENCES

Appadurai, A. 1990. Disjunctive and difference in the global culture economy. *Theory, Culture, and Society*. 7: 295–310.

Associated Press, The 2009. Census to Recognize Same-Sex Marriages in '10 Count. *The New York Times* (New York, N.Y.), June 21 :A20.

Baumle, Amanda K. 2010. Border Identities: Intersections of Ethnicity and Sexual Orientation in the US-Mexico Borderland. *Social Science Research* 39(2):231–245 .

Black, Dan, Gary Gates, Seth Sanders, and Lowell Taylor 2000. Demographics of the Gay and Lesbian Population in the United States. *Demography* 37(2): 139–154.

Bonvillain, Nancy 1989. Residence Patterns at the St. Regis Reservation. Preliminary Report for Joint Statistical Agreement 89-15. Washington, D.C.: Center for Survey Methods Research, United States Bureau of the Census.

Brownrigg, Leslie A. 2003. Ethnographic Social Network Tracing of Highly Mobile People, Census 2000 Evaluation J.2, SRD. Washington, D.C.: United States Census Bureau.

Burt, Larry 1986. Roots of the Native American Urban Experience. *American Indian Quarterly* 10(2):85–99.

de la Puente, Manuel n.d. Using Ethnography to Explain Why People Are Missed or Erroneously Included By the Census: Evidence From Small Area Ethnographic Studies. Washington, D.C.: Center for Survey Methods Research, United States Bureau of the Census.

Gilley, Brian J. 2006. *Becoming Two-Spirit*. Lincoln: University of Nebraska Press.

Gregory, Robert G., Annie C. Abello. and Jamie Johnson 1997. The Individual Economic Well-Being of Native American Men and Women During the 1980s: A Decade of Moving Backwards. *Population Research and Policy Review* 16(1–2): 115–145.

Jobe, Margaret M. 2003. Native Americans and the US Census: A Brief Historical Survey. *Journal of Government Information* 30(1):66–80.

Lobo. Susan 2001. Introduction, In *American Indians and the Urban Experience*. S. Lobo and K. Peters, eds. Walnut Creek, CA: AltaMira Press 3–5.

____1990. Oakland's American Indian Community: History, Social Organization, and Factors that Contribute to Census Undercount. Ethnographic Exploratory Research Report #12. Washington, D.C.: United States Bureau of the Census.

Lujan, Carol 1990. As Simple as One, Two, Three: Census Underenumeration Among the American Indians and Alaska Natives. Undercount Behavioral Research Group Staff Working Paper #2. Washington, D.C.: United States Bureau of the Census.

Malkki. Lisa H. 1997. National Geographic: The Rooting of Peoples and the Territorialization of National Identity Among Scholars and Refugees. In *Culture, Power, Place: Explorations in Critical Anthropology*. Akhil Gupta and James Ferguson, eds. pp. 52–74. Durham, N.C.: Duke University Press.

Moore, John H. 1992. Determine Extent of Census Undercounting Among Certain Rural Creek Indians of Oklahoma. Coverage Evaluation Report for the US Census Bureau, EV 92-10. Washington, D.C.: United States Bureau of the Census.

Nicol, Nancy, and Miriam Smith 2008. Legal Struggles and Political Resistance: Same-Sex Marriage in Canada and the USA. *Sexualities* 11 (6):667–687.

Norris, Mary Jane, and Stewart Clatworthy 2003. Aboriginal Mobility and Migration Within Urban Canada: Outcomes, Factors, and Implications. *In* Not Strangers in These Parts: Urban Aboriginal Peoples. David Newhouse and Evelyn J. Peters, eds. pp. 51–78. Ottawa, Canada: Policy Research Initiative.

Povinelli, Elizabeth A. 2002. *The Cunning of Recognition*. Durham, N.C.: Duke University Press.

Prout, Sarah 2009. Vacuums and Veils: Engaging with Statistically "Invisible" Indigenous Population Dynamics in Yamatji Country, Western Australia. *Geographical Research* 47(4):408–42l.

Puar, Jasbir K. 2007. *Terrorist Assemblages*. Durham, N.C.: Duke University Press.

Purdam, Kingsley, Angelia R. Wilson, Reza Afkhami, and Wendy Olsen 2008. Surveying Sexual Orientation: Asking Difficult Questions and Providing Useful Answers. *Culture, Health, and Sexuality* 10(2): 127–141.

Templin, Jonathon., and Stanley. Wasserman 2001. Unpublished Manuscript. Washington, D.C.: Statistical Research Division, United States Bureau of the Census.

Valentine, David 2007. *Imaging Transgender*. Durham, N.C.: Duke University Press.

———————————— ○ ————————————

END OF CHAPTER QUESTIONS

1. What is "usual residence"?
2. How does mobility intersect with sexuality?
3. How have Will and Chuck dismantled the mainstream image of domestic coupling?

PART III
Finding Community

Out in the Mountains

Exploring Lesbian and Gay Lives

Kate Black and Marc A. Rhorer; Carlos Dews, ed.

T his essay focuses on the lives of gays and lesbians and their experiences growing up in the Appalachian mountains. The idea for this project began when I wanted to do a research paper on lesbians and gays in Appalachia and asked Kate, then curator of the University of Kentucky Appalachian Collection, about prior research on the subject. Kate said, "There isn't anything." A few months later, while returning from the 1993 Appalachian Studies conference, we decided to present something about lesbians and gays at the 1994 conference. We knew we could find people to ask about their experiences of growing up gay in Appalachia. We wanted to give a voice to that experience, while at the same time giving ourselves voices as a lesbian and gay man at the Appalachian Studies Conference.

Until this research, gays and lesbians did not exist in the context of Appalachian scholarship. Because of the ubiquitous "hillbilly" stereotype, issues of representation are frequently explored in Appalachian studies. Even though scholars worked diligently to establish the richness and diversity of Appalachian social life and history, lesbian and gay representation in Appalachian culture had been ignored. We hope that this exploratory work will stimulate other researchers to include gays and lesbians in the conversation of Appalachian Studies.

Though neither of us is from the mountains, we both grew up in the rural South. As longtime residents of Lexington, Kentucky, we both knew other lesbians and gays in Lexington who grew up in the mountains and migrated to Kentucky cities to study, work, and live. We talked with five lesbians and four gay men, all white, from Eastern Kentucky, West Virginia, East Tennessee, and Western North Carolina, ranging in age from twenty to forty-five. Only one of them continues to live in the mountains; the other eight live in Lexington and Louisville. Pseudonyms are used for all interviewees. These interviews are now part of the oral history collection at the University of Kentucky.

Before the interviews, we agreed on areas to explore: coming-out experiences, homophobia, AIDS-phobia, and community building. We felt that these were key issues based on our autobiographies and those of our friends who grew up in the rural South. It is the process of navigating these issues that, in part, forms our identities as lesbians and gay men. We found several common themes in the rich stories of the participants: feelings of isolation, the importance of community, fears from inside and outside the closet, various forms of oppression and discrimination, and multiple, fluid identities based on place and sexuality, in a dynamic relationship with one another.

FEELINGS OF ISOLATION

When we asked people to talk about the differences between being gay in the mountains and in urban areas, all expressed feelings of isolation in the mountains. While growing up, they had no one to turn to for guidance, support, and information when they began realizing they were homosexual. They felt there were no others with same-sex attractions, even to the extreme that some did not know gays or lesbians existed. When some interviewees mentioned the possibility of moving back to the mountains, they noted that the most difficult part would be coping with the isolation from other gays and lesbians. One person made contacts in Lexington before moving back home to insure some access to the gay community. A few participants had a sense that mass-communication technology (particularly cable and satellite television) has the potential to reduce feelings of isolation by providing young lesbians and gays in the mountains access to nonheterosexist images.

These feelings of isolation were expressed in a variety of ways. Karla, a lesbian put on academic probation her first year at Morehead State University in Morehead, Kentucky, said: "A lot of the problem was I discovered the gay community. I never knew one existed. It was unbelievable! Every other person was gay." As a young person in high school, Allan also thought he didn't know any gay people. Speaking of high school friends who he now knows are gay, Allan remembered: "At the time I thought they were people I got along well with, but I didn't realize why. ... I didn't know people who were gay."

A forty-five-year-old lesbian, Phyllis, who often gives talks on homophobia at Kentucky colleges, told us a story reiterating the sense of aloneness that young mountain people struggling to come out may experience. Once when Phyllis was speaking at Morehead State University, a young man came up to her afterward and asked, "How old did you say you were?" She answered, "Forty-two." Then he said: "You're the same age as my Mama. I didn't know there were any gay or lesbian people as old as my mama!"

But being isolated and silenced by heterosexual hegemony can have serious repercussions, as Ann described:. "The saddest part to me about growing up in the mountains as a gay person is that ... you end up feeling like an outsider; you've got no one to talk to about these strange feelings you have, and you have to end up like lots of young people growing up gay, being isolated, and you think about killing yourself cause you're so strange."

Some of the interviewees described resourceful ways in which they managed to give a name to the sexual feelings they embodied. For example, Karla came out to herself when she was thirteen. She found out the definition of "lesbian" when she "went to the public library and looked up 'homosexuality.'. . . There was absolutely no one to talk to."

Brent also elaborated on the characteristics of isolation, while considering the difference between his rural Powell County and its county seat: "To be gay in Clay City [Kentucky], it's hard," but it is harder out in the county where there isn't access to cable TV. "MTV is preaching 'Free Your Mind,' [but] your mind is not going to be free if you don't live inside the city limits."

FINDING A COMMUNITY

This sense of isolation diminished when people moved from the mountains to the city, because in the urban setting they could meet and be with other gays and lesbians. While finding a community of other gays and lesbians was crucial, paradoxically an increased feeling of anonymity in the city was equally important. Anonymity, which many could not obtain at home, allowed greater freedom from the scrutiny of those who might condemn them; most people expressed a much greater sense of comfort about being out in the city. In contrast, at home people felt as if they were under surveillance and subjects of the gossip networks, even after moving away to the city. However, several people mentioned a positive aspect of the tight-knit nature of rural community: if a person came from an established family lineage in the mountains, she or he was less likely to be harassed for being lesbian or gay.

While discussing the differences between being gay in the mountains and in Lexington, Donald mused about the nature of urban anonymity and rural visibility. "When you move to a bigger city, your reputation doesn't necessarily have that much weight," he said, implying that reputation has different definitions and meanings in these two worlds. What is a boon in one place may be a hindrance in another. But Karla saw the rural community with a more steely gaze: "Appalachian queers migrate out of there . . . the few that do live there are usually not totally rejected by the family but rejected by the community. They'll be real kind [to your face] but still say stuff behind your back." Thus you might be despised but not necessarily be treated as if you are.

Ann, a woman in her forties who came out in the late 1960s and often drove to the gay bar in Lexington from the mountain home where she still lives, described her forays as a familial quest: "You had community [at The Bar], which gave you family, family of choice." Two decades later, twenty-year-old Greg made a similar assessment about his life in Lexington; "Living here, there's a lot more opportunities to meet those of your kind—a lover, a boyfriend, a fuck buddy. To live in Clay City, I wouldn't want to do that . . . it's just not open enough."

One interviewee sees himself as both mountain insider and outsider, a perspective from which he can examine the tension between the two. When Donald was eight, he and his mother moved back to her family's Eastern Kentucky community after years of living in Ohio. He described both his parents as coming from old mountain families. Theorizing about the relationship between being gay or lesbian and what constitutes social status in the mountains, he said, "If someone conies in from the outside— straight or gay—it doesn't make any difference. They are going to have a very difficult time fitting into the community. If, however, they are from this long lineage, they will find it much easier to be who they are, regardless if they're gay or straight."

Because finding lesbian and gay community, especially as a newcomer, depends on identifying others who are lesbian and gay, we asked the interviewees to talk about how they found other lesbians and gays, either in the mountains or in their city homes. We heard a variety of creative responses. While several people mentioned being invited to lesbian and gay parties, especially in mountain college towns, others seemed to rely on their instincts and what might be dubbed a homosexual common sense: "You go to the gym, you find gym rats." "[I]t takes one to know one." "Gaydar." But Allan, a thoughtful, garrulous twenty-eight-year-old, came up with multiple, less instinctual, ways in which his generation of lesbians and gays found each other in Boone, North Carolina, home of Appalachian State University. "[T]here was a lesbian softball league It wasn't an official lesbian softball league, it just happened that most people on it were probably lesbian. There was a student group. A lot of people would go to a regional gay bar. Recently, I know of people in Boone who get on e-mail and try to meet people that way."

IDENTITY AND COMMUNITY

We believe that identity and community are intricately linked. In fact, identities are formed and informed by communities. Conversely, communities both affect and can be an effect of identities. Many people are members of more than one community simultaneously or through a life span, just as many of us consider ourselves to have multiple identities. In short, since community and identity are not necessarily tidy concepts—both in our everyday lives and in the abstract sense—the process of identity and community formation can often be a tense one. One identity can be at odds with another one. In the worlds we live in, for example, urban gays or lesbians may judge us to be too "country," too rural, or just outright hicks. At home, that is, the place where we grew up, we may still be considered persona non grata as a lesbian and gay man.

We were curious about how people reconciled these tensions. For example, we wondered if people identified themselves as both gay and Appalachian. While everyone readily identified themselves as gay or lesbian, we found that many of the interviewees seemed to avoid directly addressing their Appalachian identities. In addition, some had not resolved their sense of conflict over being from the mountains.

Brent was among those who remained conflicted about the place where he grew up. He referred to his "trapped" life in the mountains, equating living in the mountains with cultural isolation: "If I was trapped in Clay City, I would be myself, just like I was when I was trapped there. Information and exposure to different cultures and different people is what really changes minds. That's what causes accents, when people are trapped up in the mountains." Brent obviously saw being from the mountains as a kind of "mark of the beast" and something of which to feel ashamed. The youngest of the interviewees, twenty-year-old Greg, told us proudly, "People are surprised when they find out where I'm from. [My friends] say, 'I can't believe you turned out the way you did.'" In other words, Greg "passes" and feels pleased about his transformation.

Ann, the one interviewee who has continuously lived in Eastern Kentucky, readily identified herself as Appalachian. Without embarrassment or remorse she declared, "It's home, this is where the roots are." Another lesbian, Karla, described matter-of-factly what being Appalachian means to her: "It's the family, the heritage." One man who used to live in Boone, North Carolina, toyed with the idea of moving back there while questioning whether such a move was possible for him. In Lexington, Allan is part of a vibrant gay and lesbian community in which he has made a place for himself, most notably in gay politics. Yet in Boone, he feels a certain freedom not found in Lexington, which he expressed pensively: "I feel sometimes people [in Boone] know me more as a person than as a gay person."

FACING FEARS

Because all the people we talked to expressed an overwhelmingly greater sense of freedom and ability to be out in the city, we wanted to know how the dimensions of the closet change with a move to the city. People talked about what was scary or fearful about being out at home versus being out in the city. Though fear of being out was experienced in the city, everyone generally felt that the situation was more hostile in the mountains for gays and lesbians. Men experienced much more physical aggression at home and seemed to have a limited definition of the term "fear," equating it with the threat of physical violence. Males also endured much verbal taunting in junior high and high school. Both men and women told us stories of physical violence and verbal taunting directed toward gay males in the mountains.

Interestingly but not surprisingly, women tended to include psychological as well as physical violence in their descriptions of fearful situations. Women seemed to sustain more social ostracism (that is, from family, friends, and church), were forced into psychiatric care for a "cure," or both. None of the men reported being sent to a therapist. Men were tormented because those around them suspected they were gay, while women were more likely to face threatening conditions if they were caught actually being sexual with a woman. However, one woman contradicted this representation when she told us a story of her local police cruising places where teenagers parked. She said when she was caught making out with her girlfriend, the police would generally laugh and tell them to go home, but when her gay male friends were caught, they were likely to be brutalized.

When asked about what had produced fear when he lived in the mountains, Allan said: "I've been scared that people would find out. I've been scared that if people knew I was gay, I would lose my job, people would say something to me, that I wouldn't have any recourse, wouldn't have any place to go." He went on to say how he was scared to kiss his lover goodbye when he dropped him off for work. Also, Allan was afraid that "they'd hear my partner and I and they would come and bust down the doors and get us," a fear grounded in the North Carolina sodomy law.

Donald, who talked about physical violence in the mountains, told us that he'd "heard stories of incredible physical violence against [gay] people." One of the more horrific incidents Donald remembered took place in Breathitt County, Kentucky, where a man was dismembered and killed by local people because he was thought to be gay. Kelly, a young lesbian, said that one of her gay male friends was stabbed twenty-seven times while shopping in a country store in West Virginia, solely because he was homosexual. In another hostile incident, Kelly left her truck overnight at a body shop and "while it was there someone painted on the tailgate [near the pink triangle and rainbow decals] 'die fag' and slashed the two back tires." Because of the reference to "fag," she thought that the perpetrator probably assumed the truck was owned by a man. Several men noted they were persistently taunted with words like "fag" and "sissy" throughout their adolescent schooling.

Lesbians, in particular, said that the social ostracism they endured as young people was often orchestrated by adults. "When I was in the eighth grade," Kelly told us, "because I came out to a couple of my friends, that proceeded to get me ostracized from overnight parties and church." One of the women we talked with had a relationship during high school that was discovered by her girlfriend's parents. The parents, driving a long distance in the middle of the night, arrived at the motel room where the two young women were staying for a softball tournament and pulled their daughter out of the room at 4:00 A.M.

One of the interviewees, Ann, attended Berea College, located on the edge of the Kentucky mountains and known for its student industries of crafts production and hotel keeping. While a student there, Ann had a relationship with one of her teachers. After Berea College officials exposed her to her parents, Ann was caught by her mother at the lover's house at 1:00 AM "If turned out to be pretty devastating for both of us. She lost her job over it. I became this crisis point in my family. They decided I needed psychiatric help." With her typical wit and the advantage of age, Ann concluded, "Here was this woman corrupting some poor little Appalachian girl who obviously didn't know what she was doing." At this point Kate, the interviewer, and Ann began to giggle, and Kate said, "Yeah, you're supposed to be making brooms." Ann came back with, "Yeah, or spoon bread at the Tavern!"

LEVELS OF DISCRIMINATION

Gays and lesbians face discrimination both in the mountains and in the city. We defined "discrimination" as the public or civil face of homophobia because the people we talked with defined it that way. Not surprisingly, those who work with children or young adults appear very susceptible to discrimination. We heard the story of two teachers in the mountains who were fired because they were rumored to be homosexual. Karla, who is out in most parts of her life, says she would never come out at her job working with schoolchildren in Eastern Kentucky because she "would be fired in a heartbeat."

Many people expressed fear of being out at their jobs in the city, even when they did not work with children, because they were afraid of being fired or passed over for raises or promotions. Two people told stories about gay bars that involved discrimination or the threat of it. These incidents gain even more importance because bars as public meeting places are historically central to the gay and lesbian community. Ann remembered police surveillance behind The Bar, a gay nightclub in Lexington, Kentucky, to observe those who went in and out. One man spoke about a bar owner in Huntington, West Virginia, who was gay, who did not want to be associated with anything "political," in this case having an AIDS literature table in his bar. The interviewee explained that the bar owner felt too vulnerable to actions of the local authorities and, therefore, did not want to do anything to call attention to his bar or his clientele.

In most rural and small town communities, churches and public schools are often the most important and influential social institutions. A man told us of how a lesbian high school teacher in North Carolina lost her job just because one of her students perceived that she was a lesbian and proceeded to openly accuse her. Allan explained how people in the community "prayed for her" publicly at church. The teacher was fired "on the pretext that she cussed in class, but it was well known that it was because she was a lesbian," Allan concluded.

Kelly related how she experienced discrimination at her Lexington workplace. "I can't prove anything from this, but I would swear I'm being discriminated against at my job." Kelly elaborated: "After I'd been working there for three months, one of the people who was in middle management took me into his office and told me that I shouldn't be working there because of my sexual orientation and that there was no reason for me to come back. ... Apparently he forgot to tell anyone else this and the next time my shift rolled around I got a call asking me where I was. So I went in, didn't say anything about it, and I've been working there ever since."

Several of the people we talked with told stories of discrimination at public meeting places. In Boone, North Carolina, in the late 1980s, a group of gays who were not students wanted to start an off-campus gay organization and meeting place. Bomb and death threats were made. Allan, who lived in Boone at the time, said the police provided protection and "were pretty good about dealing with it [but that] people would have to come in around the police when these meetings first went on." Recalling earlier times, Ann described how she frequently went to the gay bar in Lexington, Kentucky, during the early 1970s: "It was frightening, going to The Bar. It was rough, tough. Police cars parked out back. People said, 'Don't drive your car, they're taking down license plate numbers,' so there was all that harassment. So coming to the bar was not only an act of celebration, but an act of defiance."

AIDS-PHOBIA

We also asked people to talk about AIDS. We included AIDS-phobia in the discussions about various forms of homophobia, since the two have been viciously linked ever since the early days of the epidemic when AIDS was called GRID-Gay-Related Immune Deficiency. Surprisingly, one of the gay men we interviewed did not know anyone who is HIV positive or has AIDS. Everyone acknowledged that AIDS-phobia exists, but they did not seem to think it was more rampant in one place or the other, except for one man who said he'd experienced more AIDS-phobia in Lexington—by both the straight and gay community—than in the mountains. He correlated AIDS-phobia with a higher HIV incidence in Lexington. Two people said that because they stick closely to the lesbian and gay community or are outspoken advocates for the lesbian/gay community and for people with AIDS, they are not as likely to hear AIDS-phobic remarks and discussions.

When we asked Karla if she heard AIDS-phobic statements at home, she said, "More than anything else. More than homophobia, more than racist things. ... It's not really [expressed] as trashing people with AIDS, it is just terror that they're gonna get it." A few people said they had experienced people correlating AIDS directly with homosexuality. Greg told us that when he came out to his grandmother, she responded irrationally by exclaiming, "You're gonna get AIDS!" He noted that she is an intelligent, politically aware woman, yet she immediately connected being gay with being HIV positive.

Kelly said that when she comes out to people, they often respond with "Aren't you afraid of AIDS?" She also told us a story of AIDS-phobia, not explicitly tied to homophobia. In her workplace, an urban YMCA, all employees are required to take an AIDS awareness class. This Y's policy is to notify the supervisor if an HIV-positive person is in a class or program. This information is then passed up the ladder to the executive director. Kelly pointed out to her co-workers at a postclass discussion that no one needed to know this information since one of the tenets of the AIDS awareness course was to treat anyone who is injured as infected to prevent infecting anyone else. In short, universal precautions should be universal. Kelly "was knocked down by everyone else in the room, saying that it didn't matter, they [YMCA employees] deserve to know because they work with these children and adults and if they were infected they [YMCA employees] were going to treat them differently."

INTERNALIZING HOMOPHOBIA

Like racism, homophobia not only is perpetrated by those who dominate but also can be internalized by those who are dominated. Because organized religion played an important part in most of the interviewees' lives—socially, morally, and spiritually—we found that many had deep inner struggles over their homosexuality rooted in religious notions of sin and guilt. This powerful underpinning of internalized homophobia was sometimes acted out in religious proselytizing. One of our interviewees told us that before she came out in high school, she used the Bible to try to convince a lesbian couple she knew that their sexuality was a sin.

Two of the lesbians we talked with, however, resisted the oppression and repression of the church by questioning and railing against it. Kelly described her church experience this way: "The church was the only social outlet in the town. So I wasn't going to church so much for religious/spiritual reasons as I was for social reasons. In fact, I learned quite early in keep my mouth shut when discussing the

Bible and other issues because I asked too many questions that the answer was always 'Pray about it, and you'll see the truth.'" For Karla, the conflict was not reconciled for many years. She told us that she "really struggled with religion and going to hell. I really did not want to be gay. I've had a hard time accepting it. Probably [over] the last five years, it has gotten easy." Finally, another woman, at a young age, was able to transform her questioning into a belief in social justice.

For most of the interviewees, the extreme isolation from other lesbians and gays contributed to their internalized homophobia. Many spoke movingly of the need to help lesbian and gay young people in the mountains know they are not abnormal or alone. Many suggested lesbian and gay visibility as a partial solution to this problem. One of the youngest interviewees, Brent, connected the isolation with organized religion, seeing it as a potent force for his own suffering and confusion. Brent, who went to mass every day when he was thirteen, prayed, "Why do I have to be different? Why can't I be like everyone else?" He poignantly concluded:

> I would hate for another generation of gay people to have to grow up and feel alienated, to feel like they are outcasts. I consider myself, in a way, one of the lucky people who have finally been able to draw themselves into another community and find other people like themselves, so that they don't end up being drug addicts or jumping off a bridge or hanging themselves, just because they have no role models, have no other friends that they can come out to. They need someone to show them that they're okay, that they're not bad, that they're not going to hell.

SOME LAST THOUGHTS

Over the course of these interviews, fresh questions for subsequent interviews and new conceptual categories began to emerge. For example, class differences and perspectives surfaced from the interviews even though we did not probe our interviewees with questions about class. One of the interviewees, Karla, for instance, conflated class and gender roles when she described her lesbian community at a state University as being divided into the A, B, and C crowds. The A crowd consisted of "the pretty ones who were well dressed and acted like they were better than other people. Then there was just the average people in the B. In the C, of course, was the real butch people."

While we neither explicitly nor implicitly asked people to talk about their whiteness or notions of race, a few interviewees freely offered the information that their families were more racist than homophobic.

Neither did we ask questions directly about gender identities, yet several people brought up the categories of "butch" and "fem" for lesbians and "butch" and "queen" for gay men. For example, Allan theorized: "People [he means gay men] in rural areas of Kentucky and North Carolina tend to be queenier. It is like they try to mesh with the stereotype of gay people more than people in larger cities, who feel free to emulate other things." This statement possibly provides a window into class and gender differences, roles—both chosen and prescribed—internalized homophobia (the interviewee's), varying notions about power and resistance, and, perhaps, rural and urban dissonance. In addition, several people talked about the contentious role religion played in their lives. In short, this exploratory project begs for more exploration.

Nine interviews hardly constitute a scientifically valid sampling. But they reveal much difference among these nine people who grew up lesbian and gay in the Appalachian mountains. Their identities are multiple, sometimes contradictory, and always complex. Rural and small town people—in Appalachia and in the South—are far more complicated than the media and, often, scholarship portray them. These nine people were, in fact, grappling with creating a synthesis of multiple identities—class, race, gender, place, religion, and, of course, sexuality. Even in this preliminary research, the evidence cautions all of us against categorizing lesbians and gays as a homogenous group, and for that matter, Appalachians, also.

The common threads among the interviewees were the pain that synthesizing can evoke (though the pain seemed to be experienced and coped with variously) and their desire—desire for same-sex relations, sex, love, community. Together, the pain and desire seemed to produce this incredible resistance—albeit manifested by varying strategies and tactics—to the ever lurking and ever pressing homophobia and heterosexism.

---○---

END OF CHAPTER QUESTIONS

1. What is internalized homophobia?
2. What were some challenges the authors faced as sexual minorities in Appalachia?
3. How are identity and community linked?
4. Why is community important to non-heterosexual people?

Gay Oklahoma Sooners Pole Vaulter Drives 553 Miles to Marry His Husband

Tanner Williams

Tanner Williams grew up a Southern Baptist and struggled
with his sexuality. He says pole vaulting and God saved
him. He celebrates his wedding anniversary in June.

On June 19, 2014, I got married. To a man. And both of us live in Oklahoma.

It was something I wouldn't have thought possible a couple of years ago. But on June 16, 2014, my future husband, Scott Williams, and I got up at 5 a.m. and drove my 2012 ruby red Yukon Denali 553 miles in 8 hours and 16 minutes to the Land of Enchantment. At that time, it was not legal to marry in the state of Oklahoma. We decided we were not going to wait on someone else's agenda and decided to get married legally in Santa Fe, New Mexico.

Our ceremony took all of 10 minutes in front of a judge and two witnesses who worked in the Santa Fe Municipal Court. We said our vows and told each other how much we were in love and how nothing, not even family, would come between us. Just like that we were legally married.

We were in Santa Fe for three days for our honeymoon. We went horseback riding in the mountains for hours and spent a lot of time by the pool drinking jalapeno margaritas. We became used to restaurants asking "red or green?," referring to the type of chilis we wanted. We shopped at Navajo art stores and watched Native American dances. We drove to the top of the Truchas Peak (13,102 feet), where it was the first time this Oklahoma boy had seen a true mountain. It was the trip of a lifetime and quite a journey for me in accepting my sexuality.

Scott and I met at an OU football game on Sept. 7, 2013, against West Virginia at Gaylord Family Memorial Stadium in Norman. We began dating the day after celebrating the win. It was not until I was 19 that I finally decided to be true to myself and love the way love was meant. I dated many girls in the past, but knew that it would never work out. It only encouraged me to want to open up and be who I believe God created me to be. At the game, I met Scott, an amazingly gorgeous and sweet man. He was my first real boyfriend. He treated me like a king and began to love me like anyone could ever want to be loved. Then and there I realized that I would spend the rest of my life with him.

On May 7, 2014, he asked me to marry him. I was so excited but also so scared. It wasn't even legal in Oklahoma for two men to marry yet. All these thoughts went through my head: What would my family think of this? Even more so, what would my teammates and coaching staff on the University of Oklahoma track and field team—where I am a pole vaulter—think of me? I hadn't told any of them other than my three best friends at the time—one whom was very unaccepting and said he was only trying to "protect me."

Tanner Williams, right, and Scott Williams with their marriage license in Santa Fe

I THINK THAT BEING GAY DOESN'T MAKE YOU ANY LESS OF MAN. IF ANYTHING, IT MAKES YOU A BETTER MAN.

With a tap on the screen of my iPhone, I posted the engagement news on Facebook and my secret was out to the entire world. Within five minutes, I had 10 people calling, even more texting me asking if it was real or if it was a joke. I had never even seen myself coming out to anyone. Now I was known as gay to everyone.

That same day at practice I was nervous. Nervous to walk through the doors, nervous to walk into the locker room, and even more nervous to make eye contact with anyone on the team. I felt that I would be judged and ridiculed. But the opposite happened. Congratulations came to me from almost every person that I saw. I even received hugs from some of the guys on my team, including from one who I thought might bully me. All of my coaches were incredibly happy for me and so were all of my teammates.

The relief that overwhelmed me was incredible. I was a little nervous when competition came around because I knew how quickly that the news of the engagement spread. But I went on to score fifth at the 2014 outdoor Big 12 track and field competition, jumping a personal record height of 17 feet, 1 inch. What a difference from earlier in the season when I did not clear the bar five times out of six track meets. After coming out, I was a completely new man. I think that being gay doesn't make you any less of man. If anything, it makes you a better man.

Within the months to follow, the University of Oklahoma's Athletic Department set up training for LGBTQ allies, known to us as "Sooner Ally." Athletes and faculty were given the opportunity to train themselves on how to stop discrimination and hate and create a culture of inclusion. Stickers for the Human Rights Campaign began to appear, and they even created stickers for the Sooner Ally. I got to step up and be heard with other Sooner student-athletes from other minorities in a group called Bridge Builders—becoming friends with football player and rights activist Eric Striker, women's basketball player Kaylon Williams and others who stand together "OUnited."

My coaches see me as brave and as a leader to our team. They treat me with more respect now than they did when I was in the closet. Sometimes I feel like they do not take my marriage seriously, but after a few talks I made it quite clear that my marriage is just as real and just as legal as any of theirs.

Almost a year into my marriage I can report that it is very challenging, but also very fun. Because I did marry early, I get to grow up with my husband. I get to learn from him, and he gets to learn from me. We are at different places in our lives (he's 30), but that just makes the marriage even more exciting. My teammates trust me and, even more, they love my husband.

I have never felt more comfortable in my skin. I would not be where I am today without the help of my best friend and teammate Alex Morgan, who is a beauti-

Tanner Williams set his personal best vault after coming out to his team.

ful woman from California and who has been there through every step of my coming out and marriage. If it were not for being an athlete for the University of Oklahoma, I would not have had the courage or the ability to come out and be true to myself and to everyone around me. Coming out was the greatest thing to ever happen to me, and I wouldn't trade a single second for anything in the world.

I was also blessed to have Chloe Thompson—whom I consider to be my sister from Ardmore, Oklahoma (where I was born and raised)—and her family throw us a belated wedding shower. Some of our

closest friends made the trip to celebrate our marriage, where we shared laughs, memories, wine and cake. Before this celebration, we were planning to have an actual wedding ceremony, but thought better of the idea, since some in our families disapproved (one called the idea of a reception "silly for two men"). We told everyone at that shower that they were also celebrating our reception as well. It was crushing to find the lack of family support, but it only made us a stronger couple. If we could handle the negativity, we could handle anything.

Growing up in Southern Oklahoma was a challenge. I was raised in a Southern Baptist family and always had to hide my feelings while putting a fake smile on my face. I was bullied as a child because I was quiet. Others teased me, calling me "gay" or a "fag." The impact on me was almost beyond repair.

I was depressed beyond belief, and even considered suicide at times. These times led me to find a savior of any kind. I found God and pole vaulting, and to this day I still say they both saved my life. I found peace with who I was in pole vaulting, and also leaned on God's shoulder during some of the darkest times in my life.

It wasn't always easy attending church. The pastor and congregation would lecture us on things such as: "Homosexuality is not funny, it is not a joke. Why would we find 'Will & Grace' funny? We need to save them from hell." I would beat myself up trying to hide those feelings. I dated any girl that would have me. I tried to build up a relationship with God so strong that I would just simply eliminate the gay feelings inside. But I learned you cannot pray away the gay. You cannot convert a gay child to be straight.

I was never true to myself or to any of my friends and family. I grew up in a household where family members wouldn't even watch Ellen DeGeneres because she was a lesbian and it "disgusted" them.

Other family members would call each other "fags" and throw the word around like it was going out of style.

Most of my family was very homophobic. It even seemed as if every one of my friends in my school (class size of 83) were homophobic as well. You are not born hateful, racist, or against any person or race in this world. We were simply taught that it is "wrong to be gay" or that "black people deserve police brutality" and even telling women that they belong in the kitchen.

Everyone deserves to be treated equally, and to use the Bible against us is hypocritical to what a Christian should do. Love is the answer; love is what God wants us to share together as brothers and sisters in Christ. As is says in Romans 13:10: "Love does no harm to its neighbor. Therefore, love is the fulfillment of the law."

It's basically impossible when people get treated the way they do just by the color of their skin, or who they want to spend the rest of their lives with. In southern Oklahoma, it is seen as right to hate because others don't conform to the same religious beliefs. But this kind of discrimination and hate does not live only in Oklahoma; it is in every other state, country, continent in this world.

It was not until I was 19 that I finally decided to be true to myself and love the way love was meant. I dated many girls in the past, but knew that it would never work out. It only encouraged me to want to open up and be who I believe God created me to be.

I look forward to this June 19, when Scott and I get to mark our first anniversary as a legally married couple. To celebrate, we are taking a road trip to New Mexico, Nevada and California. I feel blessed.

Tanner Williams, 19, is a junior double majoring in General Management and Nursing at the University of Oklahoma. He is also a pole vaulter on the track and field team. On June 19, 2014, he married his husband, Scott Williams, and the two live together in Norman, Oklahoma. Tanner can be reached via email at williamstanner21@gmail.com, on Facebook, Twitter (@jtannerwilliams), and Instagram (Will2Tan).

—————————————— ○ ——————————————

END OF CHAPTER QUESTIONS

1. How did homophobia affect Tanner growing up in Oklahoma? How does homophobia affect Tanner as an adult?
2. Why is it important to have non-discrimination laws to protect same-sex marriage?
3. What is your response to Tanner's statement, "I think that being gay doesn't make you any less of a man. If anything, it makes you a better man."?
4. What factors complicated Tanner's relationship between his religion and sexual identity? How can one reconcile their religion and sexuality?

PART IV

Identity, Construction, and Experience

CHAPTER 11

Sexual Orientation as Community Boundary

LGBT Americans

Marye Tharp

Lesbian, gay, bisexual, and transsexual (LGBT) consumers constitute one of the most interesting and challenging consumer subcultures in multicultural America. Unlike race, age, or even ethnic origin, sexual orientation is not a characteristic easily observed by other people. Sexual orientation is such a personal topic that only in the past thirty years have more than a few individuals publicly identified themselves or others as "gay." Persons of alternative sexual orientations share "outsider" status and experience discrimination, even persecution, by other Americans. This has provided the catalyst for organizing LGBT communities.

The success of these organizations in representing LGBT rights has, in turn, created a basis for LGBT pride. Open acknowledgment of being lesbian, gay, bisexual, or transsexual and community groups representing the interests of these Americans are the cornerstones of access to this market. In 2014 a mere 18 out of 50 states, plus the District of Columbia, recognized same-sex marriage, civil unions, or domestic partnerships, in effect granting equal rights to LGBT persons.[1]

The existence of a subculture, even a large one, does not necessarily make its members a viable market for partnerships with business and civic organizations. There is no doubt that LGBT persons comprise a difficult market to understand. There are no U.S. Census Bureau data to describe the size and growth of the gay population. Even people who are gay disagree about whether a same-sex orientation is a result of genetics or environment. Where do the people who are bisexual fit in? Can marketers reach closeted gay people or only those who are "out"? These are typical questions that firms have when considering a partnership with LGBT consumers.

This chapter first describes events central to the self-identity of homosexuals in contemporary American society. The emphasis is on how individuals integrate their homosexuality with other aspects of social identity and character. The next section describes the controversy over the size of the LGBT population and the difficulties that this creates for marketers. Next, the geography of the LGBT community is described—that is, where in the United States are clusters of gay men and lesbians and what are and are not part of gay-oriented lifestyles and politics. The chapter then turns to the two-way impact of gays on American popular culture and media and to media sources for reaching LGBT consumers. The chapter ends with a discussion of marketing cases in which firms have become identified as members of the extended lesbian and gay community. We also touch on experiences gay men and lesbians have reported that influence their product and brand preferences.

Note: LGBT stands for lesbian, gay, bisexual, and transsexual. For readability, in this chapter we occasionally use the terms "gay" or "gay and lesbian" to indicate all LGBT persons.

BEING HOMOSEXUAL IN A STRAIGHT WORLD

Most LGBT Americans see themselves as different—outside the American mainstream, whatever it might be.[2] This recognition is essential to finding and expressing social identity. For some homosexuals, a feeling of being outside the boundary of "typical" Americans is reinforced by real discrimination.[3] For some, it leads to alternative communities where homosexuals constitute a majority. And some gay persons believe that their sexual orientation must always be denied, at least in public.[4] The following quotation expresses the feelings that this experience can engender.

> Being gay may be more acceptable in today's America, but it is still considered a deviation from majority behavior. Consider the following quotation on being gay in American society: "Thus we come to American society, dominated by a white, male, heterosexual, Christian culture. The dominant group expresses its power in and through the control of critical aspects of business, government, home life, education, etc. In addition, the accompanying ideological system often serves to legitimate and support that control. The material and the ideological work in concert with one another, reinforcing the societal hierarchy and making it seem "natural," "right," both to those in the position of dominance and to many of those who are themselves dominated. The ideology is reinforced, the "correctness" of the inequity re-created, over and over again, through the machinations of culture. . . . One gender, one sexual orientation, one religious affiliation, and one color of skin are seen as mainstream, while all others fall outside this social category.[5]

Acknowledging a Gay Identity

A consequence of socialization with these values can be strong, negative beliefs about being a homosexual.[6] This identity crisis can be particularly difficult as an individual experiences the usual pitfalls of adolescence. Gay persons must ultimately decide on a personal strategy for how to relate to mainstream American culture—assimilate (remain "closeted") or separate (declare shared identity with other homosexuals). In between those two extremes are the 30 percent of men and 15 percent of women who "do not have an exclusive heterosexual history" but who do not consider themselves gay.[7] There is a large difference between these numbers and the much smaller group who identify as gay. Early adolescence is the time when most gay people feel their LGBT identity emerging, but not until late adolescence or early adulthood is this identity consolidated and reinforced. Table 11.1 shows scientific research on median ages in the development of LGBT identity. Newer research on this topic is absent, but according to anecdotal accounts the age has dropped for every step in the process of developing and integrating a LGBT identity shown in the table. *The New Gay Teenager* reports that lesbians have their first same-sex contact at age 16 while gay men have their first same-sex contact at age 14.[8] That individuals experience successive stages of LGBT self-awareness, self-labeling, and LGBT behaviors still serves as a template for understanding the process involved in "coming out."[9]

TABLE 11.1   **Identity Issues Among Gay Men and Lesbians**

	MEDIAN AGE OF EXPERIENCE FOR:	
STAGE OF GAY IDENTITY DEVELOPMENT	GAY MEN	LESBIANS
Initial awareness of same-sex attraction	12–13	14–16
Initial same-sex experience	14–15	20–22
Self-identification as lesbian or gay	19–21	21–23
Initial same-sex sexual relationship	21–24	20–24
Positive gay or lesbian identity	22–26	24–29

Source: L.D. Garnets and D.C. Kimmel, "Lesbian and Gay Male Dimensions in the Psychological Study of Human Diversity," in *Psychological Perspectives on Human Diversity*, ed. J.D. Goodchilds (Washington, DC: American Psychological Association, 1991), 160–180. Reproduced by permission of American Psychological Association.

Declaring a gay identity in mainstream society, or "coming out of the closet," has psychological and behavioral dimensions. While "coming out" may be key for integrating a homosexual's self-concept, it has unknown ramifications. Most stressful is not being able to predict the reactions of family and other significant persons. "Passing for straight" is a common coping strategy to deal with this stress, but there are many variations of behavior along a continuum from "straight" to "gay" identity. Some people are in touch with their same-sex orientation earlier or later in life than others, and some choose consciously to deny their sexual orientation at various points in life.[10] Furthermore, homosexuality can be expressed as an identity label, an expression of same-sex desire or same-sex behavior. These differences between how one behaves (homosexual or bisexual sex) and how one sees him- or herself (gender-identity issues for transsexuals) or who one desires create unclear boundaries for who is—and who is not—part of the LGBT community.[11] As example, transgender individuals may never use the "gay" label, engage in same-sex behavior, or have same-sex desires.

A significant risk of "coming out" is the homophobia of other people and not being able to trust the strength of family or friendship bonds to overcome a phobic reaction. Men are more homophobic than women, but all heterosexuals express more prejudice against same-sex orientations when it involves their own gender.[12] Some research suggests that "gaydar," the ability to discern another person's sexual orientation, may be scent-based.[13] The need to accommodate these feelings and behaviors results in great variation in how gay identity is expressed. While most conservative estimates of the LGBT population consider adults over age 18, the age for "coming out," the typical age for self-awareness about sexual orientation is as young as 13 or 14.[14] In late 2010, a series of high school and college student suicides occurred after gay persons were bullied or "outed." LGBT persons are frequent victims of hate crimes.[15]

Due to the hostility that homosexuals face in the mainstream world, acceptance by and support of family members is extremely important.[16] At the same time, many gay persons expect rejection of their homosexuality and fear family members' pressure to keep them from "coming out" to other family members. Some homosexuals find family warmth only via a "chosen" and constructed family of friends who accept the whole person. The "extended family" of gay-friendly organizations extends to churches, media, businesses, professionals, and civic and cultural causes as well as to arts organizations, a usually gay-friendly arena.

Being LGBT in a Straight World

A primary issue for LGBT persons is what labels they use for themselves and which ones are acceptable for others to use. For example, "lesbian" and "gay" are terms used for and by people who have a same-sex orientation. Due to the exclusively sexual connotations of the term "homosexual," many men prefer to be called "gay," and women choose "lesbian." "Gay" is acceptable to most men and women of same-sex orientation. "Bisexual" describes people attracted to both men and women. Outside these terms, most of the slang words for members of this subculture are derogative (queer, fag, faggot, pansy, dyke, butch, ad infinitum). Nevertheless, both LGBT and "straight" people sometimes use the more offensive terms; outsiders use them pejoratively, and insiders use them as affirmation of "gay pride." Symbols also serve as markers of gay identity, such as the rainbow, the color lavender, a pink triangle, the number 338, and the Greek sign for lambda. Such labels are also used at times to chastise anyone who does not conform to mainstream gender ideals, especially effeminate men.[17]

It is important to remember that we depend on self-identification in addressing the labeling issue. While some LGBT people wish to be *respected* as a homosexual, many remain afraid of being *labeled* as homosexual. The best solution for marketers may be to use gay-owned or gay-friendly media so that labels are irrelevant. A game played between advertisers and consumers is the use of phrases with meanings specific to insiders of LGBT culture, called "gayspeak." Examples from advertisements are: "Another one coming out"; "Show your pride"; "We are everywhere"; "From an early age, it knew it was different," and "Feeling outrageous?" Even visual images of a sunflower field with only one sunflower above the others or a plane with pink eyelashes and a rainbow below it are used for signaling that the audience includes gay consumers. This strategy, used by both mainstream and gay-oriented advertisers, is an example of how codes and double meanings are a way to show gay consumers that an advertised brand or firm understands LGBT culture.[18]

Kitzinger identified five specific behaviors that result from the experience of being LGBT in a straight world.[19] First is a sense of alienation and self-protection, with a tendency to distrust others. Second is a health consciousness and focus on satisfying needs independently. Third, homosexuals seek affiliation and want group identity, especially with others "out of the closet." This means seeking communications with and loyalty to those who are friendly to the gay community. Fourth, gays generally try new things and want to experience new feelings. Fifth, they try to reduce stress in their lives.[20]

These endless accommodations within a gay person's self-concept mean that there is no such thing as a single gay or lesbian lifestyle. The significance for marketers is that there is a community boundary perceived by many gay and lesbian consumers between themselves and the rest of Americans. Sexual orientation is the characteristic that many homosexuals believe best "defines" them, independent of age, gender, race, or other aspects of identity.[21] In sum, the importance of sexual orientation to personal identity and a perceived community outside mainstream American culture are the foundations of LGBT subculture.

DEMOGRAPHICS OF LGBT AMERICANS

To whom do the terms "gays and lesbians" or "LGBT Americans" refer? Certainly, they include men and women with same-sex orientations. The term "gay" customarily includes bisexuals (people attracted to both men and women) as well. People with other sexual orientations, such as the transgendered, sadomasochists, fetishists, or pedophiles, are included with homosexuals and bisexuals by mainstream society when referring to people who engage in any alternative (nonheterosexual) sexual practices. Within the LGBT community, however, other labels are used in accordance with the sexual behavior in which a person engages.

"Transgendered" is a term that refers to both transsexuals and cross-dressers. It has been estimated that over 25,000 Americans have had sex-reassignment surgery and at least 2 percent of children have "discomfort with their assigned gender and may experiment with gender roles."[22] Neither the transgendered nor other LGBT persons use the terms "gay" and "lesbian" for effeminate men, "butch" women, hermaphrodites (intersexed persons), or for people who engage in other, alternative sexual practices.

Size of the LGBT Population

There are conflicting estimates of the size of the American gay population. The 1948 Kinsey study estimated the homosexual population at 10 percent, and this proportion was accepted as the "standard" until the 1990s, when several research studies challenged it. In 1993 the Battelle study reported that only 1 percent of male respondents considered themselves exclusively homosexual.[23] Gay activists who claimed that face-to-face surveys inevitably underestimate the incidence of same-sex relations, which are illegal in many states, criticized the methods of the Battelle study. Studies in Europe point to a range of 1 to 4 percent. Lesbians alone were estimated to comprise about 3 million women in the United States in 1993 (about 1 percent of the total U.S. population).[24]

The Yankelovich study in 1994, the first "blue chip" firm to study consumer attitudes of homosexuals, placed the estimate at 6 percent of the U.S. adult population.[25] This figure is consistent with the 6.7 percent figure used by Witeck and Combs (2006), but larger than 2–3 percent estimate of *The Gay & Lesbian Atlas* (2004) published by the Urban Institute. Differences in methodology probably account for some of the different findings, depending on whether they ask a person to categorize him or herself or his or her behavior. Many people who have had homosexual experiences do not consider themselves gay; thus, self-reports tend to be conservative.[26]

The 2010 population of the United States was estimated at 235 million adults over age 18. Based on the discussion above, the LGBT population could vary from 9.4 million (4 percent) to 23.5 million (10 percent). Using the Witeck and Combs calculation of 6.7 percent of those over age 18, the LGBT population in 2010 was more than 15.7 million. Table 7.2 shows these estimates of the size of the LGBT population, at 4 percent, 6.7 percent, and 10 percent of persons age 18 and older. In addition, the table shows the size of the adult LGBT population for the top 25 American cities. It is a conservative estimate of the entire LGBT market's size, yet it is consistent with the Yankelovich finding that gays are concentrated in the top 25 metropolitan areas.[27]

LBGT Geography

The Yankelovich 1994 study estimated that 27 percent of the adult population in cities with a population over 3 million and 34 percent of the population in cities with a population from 1 million to 3 million, were gay.[28] *The Gay & Lesbian Atlas*, however, provides more current details about the LGBT population in specific states, counties, and neighborhoods. The top 10 states with the highest concentration of

TABLE 11.2   Estimate of Gay and Lesbian Population in Top 25 U.S. Metropolitan Areas, 2010

METROPOLITAN AREA	2010 ADULT POPULATION*	4% OF ADULTS	6.7% OF ADULTS**	10% OF ADULTS
Estimate of 2010 U.S. Adult Population	235,016,000	9,400,640	15,746,072	23,501,600
Top twenty-five				
New York, NY	12,258,867	245,177	735,532	1,225,887
Los Angeles, CA	10,276,271	205,525	616,576	1,027,627
Chicago, IL	7,377,275	147,546	442,637	737,728
San Francisco, CA	4,513,854	90,277	270,831	451,386
Philadelphia, PA	3,885,962	77,719	233,158	388,596
Detroit, MI	3,111,639	62,232	186,698	311,164
Dallas, TX	2,971,673	59,434	178,300	297,167
Washington, DC	2,943,591	58,872	176,616	294,359
Boston, MA	2,887,604	57,752	173,256	288,760
Houston, TX	2,826,974	56,540	169,619	282,697
Atlanta, GA	2,337,713	46,754	140,263	233,771
Miami, FL	2,217,565	44,351	133,054	221,757
Seattle, WA	1,918,978	38,380	115,139	191,898
Cleveland, OH	1,798,035	35,961	107,882	179,804
San Diego, CA	1,780,259	35,605	106,816	178,026
Minneapolis, MN	1,779,287	35,586	106,757	177,929
Phoenix, AZ	1,666,938	33,339	100,016	166,694
St. Louis, MO	1,589,804	31,796	95,388	158,980
Denver, CO	1,442,217	28,844	86,533	144,222
Pittsburgh, PA	1,409,356	28,187	84,561	140,936
Tampa, FL	1,324,678	26,494	79,481	132,468
Cincinnati, OH	1,184,752	23,695	71,085	118,475
Portland, OR	1,111,965	22,239	66,718	111,197
Kansas City, KA/MO	1,081,818	21,636	64,909	108,182
Milwaukee, WI	1,048,000	20,960	62,880	104,800
Range for size of gay population in 25 metro areas		1,534,901	4,604,705	7,674,510

Source: U.S. Census Bureau, *U.S. Census 2010,* www.census.gov/2010census/; U.S. Census Bureau, "Table 2. Annual Estimates of the Population of Combined Statistical Areas," March 27, 2008.

*Includes only adults 18 or more years old.

**6.7 percent is the conservative estimate of LGBT percentage of adult population used by R. Witeck and W. Combs, *Business Inside Out: Capturing Millions of Brand Loyal Gay Consumers* (Chicago: Kaplan, 2006).

same-sex couples were Vermont, California, Washington, Massachusetts, Oregon, New Mexico, Nevada, New York, Maine, and Arizona. California has about 15 percent of all LGBT Americans, and New York has 7.8 percent, Texas 7.2 percent, and Florida 6.9 percent.[29] The top 5 Metropolitan Statistical Areas (MSAs) for LGBT persons were San Francisco (16 to 25 percent of adult men), Oakland (CA), Seattle, Fort Lauderdale, and Austin–San Marcos. Among midsize MSAs, the top 5 were Santa Rosa and Santa Cruz, CA, Portland, ME, Madison, WI, and Asheville, NC. The smallest MSAs with significant LGBT populations were Santa Fe, NM, Burlington, VT, Bloomington, IN, Iowa City, IA, and Barnstable–Yarmouth, MA. The distinction for being the "gayest" town was given to Provincetown, MA, where over 1 in 8 households were gay or lesbian (compared to the American average of 1 in 100 households).[30]

Gay and lesbian couples share a preference for living in 5 of the top 10 states with a LGBT concentration: California, Massachusetts, Washington, Arizona, and Vermont. But gay males choose Nevada, Florida, Georgia, Delaware, and New York as their next most populous locations, while lesbians choose New Mexico, Maine, New Hampshire, Oregon, and Colorado. Counties and cities such as San Francisco, Monroe, Florida, the District of Columbia, New York, and Arlington, VA, have large gay male populations, while Hampshire and Franklin in Massachusetts, Tompkins in New York, Sonoma and San Francisco in California, are counties with higher-than-average percentages of lesbian households.[31] While these data are based on the 2000 U.S. Census counts of same-sex households, they exclude the 75 percent of gay men and 60 percent of lesbians who were not part of a couple at that point in time.

What is most interesting is that when children are included in gay or lesbian households, those couples are more likely to live in states and metropolitan areas with a relatively low concentration of gay and lesbian households. About one in four of all LGBT couples lives with children, and they are raising them in states such as Mississippi, South Dakota, Alaska, South Carolina, and Louisiana. Individuals over age 55 make up about 30 percent of each state's population of gay and lesbian couples. With this exception—the presence of children—the LGBT population is most likely to live in highly urban and diverse metropolitan areas of the United States and in neighborhoods with above-average housing values, home ownership, and house sizes.

LGBT Incomes: Myth and Reality

Estimates of the spending power of gays and lesbians vary as much as estimates of the size of the population. In 2005 estimates of the gay market's disposable income topped $610 million, up from $580 million in 2004, based on 15.5 million persons.[32] By 2011 the purchasing power of LGBT consumers was estimated at $835 billion[33] by one source, and closer to $780 billion by others.[34] One reason that the estimates of spending power for gays and lesbians are so unstable is that individual and household incomes of LGBTs are used interchangeably.

In the 1990s the gay press publicized its readers as having an average household income almost 70 percent higher than that of heterosexuals.[35] More recent studies have refuted these data. *The Gay & Lesbian Atlas* reports gay men as having less household income than straight men. However, relying again on the Yankelovich Monitor Survey, their reports estimated household income at $37,400 for gay men and $39,300 for straight men, and $34,800 for lesbians, compared to $34,400 for straight women. They also found a higher percentage of gay over heterosexual men with incomes under $25,000, and a higher percentage over heterosexuals for gay and lesbian consumers with incomes above $50,000. Such skewed income distribution suggests that gay consumers include a smaller middle-income group, with larger low- and high-income groups. Ultimately the Yankelovich study, whose sample reflected the total U.S. population, found no significant differences in the incomes of gays and heterosexuals. Myths die hard, and years later the hype about higher LGBT incomes is still around.[36]

One consistency among all studies of the American gay and lesbian population is a finding of higher than average education levels. Fourteen percent of LGBTs attended graduate school, compared to 7 percent of heterosexuals; 49 percent have had some college, compared to 37 percent of the "straight" population, according to the Yankelovich study. As for occupations, 56 percent of gays/lesbians were in professional/managerial jobs versus 16 percent of heterosexuals. They are also more likely to be self-employed and a source of entrepreneurial marketing to fellow members of the LGBT community.

Ethnic Diversity Among LGBT Persons

Very few sources of information exist regarding ethnic differences in the gay and lesbian population. Nevertheless, the work by Beverly Greene is a testimony to cultural diversity in same-sex orientation.[37] In a study of over 700 homosexual African-American couples, she found a significant amount of income, education, and employment diversity. Unlike heterosexual couples, gay couples tended to have more mixed ethnicity. She also found that the income of male same-sex couples was statistically higher than that for female couples.[38] In *The Gay & Lesbian Atlas*, the Southern states and metropolitan areas have higher proportions of African-American gay and lesbian households. The Atlas also found Southwestern states with high concentrations of LGBT-Hispanic population; in addition, LGBT-Hispanics are found in large cities and southern states.[39]

Some Native American tribes have a same-sex tradition of "berdache" ("two-spirit" people) couples. Some African cultures celebrate "woman marriages," and some Asian cultures recognize male pair bonding.[40] Nevertheless, Greene suggests that a larger percentage of homosexuals in American ethnic communities remain closeted. An example of why this may be true is the Latino and Asian importance placed on family and a definition of family that excludes homosexuality.[41] Gender roles in these cultures are tightly defined, and males and females have distinctive role expectations. Disapproval of homosexuality in the Latino community may be more intense than that of non-Latino Americans.[42] "Coming out" for Asian Americans can be seen as a threat to "the continuation of the family line and a rejection of appropriate roles within the culture as well."[43] African and Native American homosexuals do not suffer such strict role definitions and thus may experience fewer fears of the consequence of "coming out" in their respective communities.

The opportunities for marketers who can connect with consumers who prefer LGBT relationships are significant indeed. The demographic profile of the gay market indicates potentially higher average levels of education, disposable income, and more LGBTs in managerial and professional occupations. How much higher these levels are is in dispute, but it translates to heavy product usage of luxury items such as vacation homes, electronic audiovisual equipment, credit cards, liquor and wine, domestic and foreign travel, and sports and fitness activities. A large percentage of readers of gay publications report that they are "very likely" to buy the national products advertised there.[44] London and Paris openly appeal to LGBT travelers, an American segment that spends between $17 billion and $47 billion on travel.[45]

NOTES

1. National Conference of State Legislatures, "Civil Unions and Domestic Partnership Statues," June 26, 2013, www.ncsl.org/research/human-services/civil-unions-and-domestic-partnership-statutes. aspx (MA, CN, VT, NH, DC, IA, NJ, OR, NV, WA, HW, WI, ME, RI, DL, IL, NY).

2. D. Johnson and A. Piore, "At Home in Two Worlds," *Newsweek*, October 18, 2004, 52; G. Lukenbill, *Untold Millions: Positioning Your Business for the Gay and Lesbian Consumer Revolution* (New York: HarperBusiness, 1995), 103–110.

3. D.G. Embruck, C.S. Walther, and C.M. Wickens, "Working Class Masculinity: Keeping Gay Men and Lesbians out of the Workplace," *Sex Roles* 56 (2007): 757–766; J. Cloud, "The Pioneer: Harvey Milk," *Time,* June 14, 1999, 183–186.

4. T.A. Stewart, "Gay in Corporate America: What's It Like and How Business Attitudes Are Changing," *Fortune*, December 16, 1991, 42–46, 50, 54, 56.

5. J.A. Costa, "Foreword," in *Gays, Lesbians, and Consumer Behavior: Theory, Practice, and Research Issues in Marketing,* ed. D.L. Wardlow (New York: Harrington Park Press, 1996), xvii–xviii.

6. B. Greene, "Lesbian and Gay Sexual Orientations: Implications for Clinical Training, Practice, and Research," in *Lesbian and Gay Psychology: Theory, Research and Clinical Applications,* ed. B. Greene and G. Herek (Thousand Oaks, CA: Sage, 1994), 1–25.

7. F.E. Jandt, *Intercultural Communication: An Introduction* (Thousand Oaks, CA: Sage, 1995), 356.

8. J. Cloud, "The Battle Over Gay Teens," *Time*, October 10, 2005, 42–51.

9. R.T. LeBeau and W.A. Jellison, "Why Get Involved? Exploring Gay and Bisexual Men's Experiences of the Gay Community," *Journal of Homosexuality* 56, no. 1 (2008): 56–76.

10. A. D'Augelli, "Lesbian and Gay Male Development: Steps Toward an Analysis of Lesbians' and Gay Men's Lives," in *Lesbian and Gay Psychology*, 118–132.

11. R. Witeck and W. Combs, *Business Inside Out: Capturing Millions of Brand Loyal Gay Consumers* (New York: Kaplan, 2006), 39.

12. G. Herek, "Gender Gaps in Public Opinion About Lesbians and Gay Men," *Public Opinion Quarterly* 66, no. 1 (2002): 40–66; G. Herek, "Assessing Heterosexuals' Attitudes Toward Lesbians and Gay Men," in *Lesbian and Gay Psychology*, 206–228; "Tuaca Targets Lesbians," *Marketing News*, August 14, 1995.

13. E. Svoboda, "Solving the Mystery of Gaydar," *Psychology Today* (January/February 2008): 73.

14. Witeck and Combs, *Business Inside Out*, 56.

15. K. Webley, "A Separate Peace?" *Time*, October 24, 2011, 40–46; M. Burford, "The Surge in Gary Teen Suicide," AOL, October 12, 2010, www.aolhealth.com/2010/10/12/gay-teen-suicide-surge/; Cloud, "The Battle over Gay Teens"; "Hate Crime," in Wikipedia, http://en.wikipedia.org/wiki/Hate_crime/.

16. J.L. Borgerson, J.E. Schroeder, B. Blomber, and E. Thorssen, "The Gay Family in the Ad: Consumer Responses to Non-Traditional Families in Marketing Communications," *Journal of Marketing Management* 22, no. 9 (2006): 955–578; L. Cobo-Hanlon, "My Child Is Gay, Que Hago?" *Latina* (November 1999): 122–125.

17. T.G. Sandfort, R.M. Melendez, and R.M. Diaz, "Gender Nonconformity, Homophobia, and Mental Distress in Latino and Bisexual Men," *Journal of Sex Research* 44, no. 2 (2007): 181–189; Jandt, *Intercultural Communication*, 357; Greene, "Lesbian and Gay Sexual Orientations."

18. G. Oakenfull and T. Greenlee, "Queer Eye for a Gay Guy: Using Market-Specific Symbols in Adver-

tising to Attract Gay Consumers Without Alienating the Mainstream," *Psychology & Marketing* 22, no. 5 (2005): 421–439.

19. C. Kitzinger, "Social Constructionism: Implications for Lesbian and Gay Psychology," in *Lesbian, Gay, and Bisexual Identities over the Lifespan: Psychological Perspectives*, ed. A.R. D'Augelli and C.J. Patterson (New York: Oxford University Press, 1995).

20. Lukenbill, *Untold Millions*, 106–110.

21. MarketingCharts staff, "Most Gay-Friendly Brands: Bravo, Apple, Showtime, HBO, Absolut, Levi's," Marketing Charts, May 13, 2008, www.marketingcharts.com/wp/direct/most-gay-friendly-brands-bravo-apple-showtime-hbo-absolutlevis-4573/.

22. L. Fitzpatrick, "The Gender Conundrum," *Time*, November 19, 2007, 59; J. Cloud, "Trans Across America," *Time*, July 20, 1998, 48–49.

23. P. Painton, "The Shrinking Ten Percent," *Time*, April 26, 1993, 27–29.

24. E. Salholz and D. Glick, "The Power and the Pride," *Newsweek*, June 21, 1993, 54–60.

25. D. Tuller, "Gays, Lesbians Listed as 6 Percent of Population," *San Francisco Chronicle*, June 10, 1994, A3.

26. Lukenbill, *Untold Millions*, 51; Jandt, *Intercultural Communication*, 353; L. Peñaloza, "We're Here, We're Queer, and We're Going Shopping! A Critical Perspective on the Accommodation of Gays and Lesbians in the U.S. Marketplace," in *Gays, Lesbians, and Consumer Behavior*, 9–41.

27. S. Elliott, "A Sharper View of Gay Consumers," *New York Times*, June 9, 1994, D1, D19.

28. H. Kahan and D. Mulryan, "Out of the Closet," *American Demographics* (May 1995): 40–43, 46–47.

29. G.J. Gates and J. Ost, *The Gay and Lesbian Atlas* (Washington, DC: Urban Institute Press, 2004), 24–30.

30. Ibid., 27.

31. Ibid.

32. E. Duecy, "Attracting the Gay Consumer's Dollars: Lucrative Demographic Drives Marketing Push," *Nation's Restaurant News*, April 18, 2005; PRNewswire. "Buying Power of U.S. Gays and Lesbians to Exceed $835 Billion by 2011," January 25, 2007.

33. "Should You Be Marketing to Gay Consumers?" Electronic Retailer Blog.com, March 25, 2008.

34. Witeck and Combs, *Business Inside Out*, 58.

35. A. Keating and D. McLoughlin, "Understanding the Emergence of Markets: A Social Constructionist Perspective on Gay Economy," *Consumption Markets & Culture* 8, no. 2 (2005): 131–152; R. Alsop, "Are Gay People More Affluent Than Others?" *Wall Street Journal*, December 30, 1999, B1, B3.

36. M. O'Connell and S. Feliz, "Same-Sex Couple Household Statistics from the 2010 Census," SEHSD Working Paper Number 2011–26, U.S. Census Bureau, Washington, DC, September 27, 2011); Alsop, "Are Gay People More Affluent Than Others?"

37. B. Greene, ed., *Ethnic and Cultural Diversity Among Lesbians and Gay Men* (Thousand Oaks, CA: Sage, 1997).

38. L. Peplau, S. Cochran, and V. Mays, "A National Survey of the Intimate Relationships of African American Lesbians and Gay Men," in *Ethnic and Cultural Diversity Among Lesbians and Gay Men*, 11–38.

39. Gates and Ost, *The Gay and Lesbian Atlas*, 50–52.

40. C. Potgieter, "From Apartheid to Mandela's Constitution," in *Ethnic and Cultural Diversity Among Lesbians and Gay Men*, 88–116.

41. Cobo-Hanlon, "My Child Is Gay, Que Hago?"

42. B. Greene, "Ethnic Minority Lesbians and Gay Men: Mental Health and Treatment Issues," in *Ethnic and Cultural Diversity Among Lesbians and Gay Men*, 216–239.

43. Ibid.

44. Community Marketing Inc., Lesbian Consumer Index™ (San Francisco, 2007); Community Marketing Inc., Gay Consumer Index™ (San Francisco, 2007).

45. R. Alsop, "London, Paris Are Burning to Lure Gay Travelers in New Campaigns," *Wall Street Journal*, September 28, 1999, B10.

———————— ○ ————————

END OF CHAPTER QUESTIONS

1. Why is identity important?
2. How can identity be dangerous?
3. What risks are involved in being a LGBT+ person in the United States?

Transgender Identities and Experiences

Sally Hines

Transgender identities are cut through with multiple variables such as gender, sexuality, 'race' and ethnicity, class, age, transitional time span and geographical location. [...] this chapter explores how transgender identities are constructed and experienced in relation to a range of additional composites.

There is a wealth of autobiographical work on transgender identity formation and recently work that can be considered under the banner of 'transgender theory' offers a postmodern mix of critical analysis, political critique and autobiography to explore the experiences of gender transition. Nataf (1996) and Feinberg (1996), for example, articulate a range of female-to-male (FtM) gender and sexual identities. Although Nataf explores gender as a performative concept, he does so by drawing on a range of transgender lesbian subjective experiences of the expression and interpretation of gender. In Feinberg's work, the author is placed at the centre of the narrative as the analytical investigation of transgender histories links with Feinberg's gender trajectory. Feinberg's later work (1999) vocalises a diversity of (trans)gender and sexual identities, and calls for an inclusive trans politics that is able to dually celebrate and specify difference. Significantly Feinberg incorporates the structures of age, class and ethnicity, as well as gender and sexuality, into the discussion of transgender identities, thus paving the way for a material and social analysis of transgender.

There are a number of studies within sociology, social policy, anthropology and literature and cultural studies that adopt a micro analysis variously to explore transgender identity constructions, behaviour patterns and politics. Devor (1989), Lewins (1995), Nataf (1996) and Cromwell (1999) explore a range of FtM gender and sexual identities. Halberstam (1998) makes visible the historical and contemporary diversity of female masculinity. Kulick (1998) examines the identities and experiences of transgendered prostitutes in Brazil. Wilson (2002) looks at the formation of transgender identities in Western Australia. Monro (2005) explores collective identities and transgender politics. Ekins and King (1999) have developed a cartography of transgendering to take account of the ways in which transgender narratives are distinct. Hirschauer (1997), King (2003) and Ekins and King (2006) employ the concept of gender 'migration' to examine experiences of transition. King suggests that this concept be employed within sociological studies as it "enables sociology to get a grasp of the micro and macro social process involved in 'changing sex'" (2003: 187). Much of this body of work, however, is from the US and there is an absence of empirical work from the UK on transgender identity formation.[1] It is from this juncture that the chapter moves on substantively to explore a number of ways in which transgender experiences and identities are constructed.

First, the chapter considers understandings and experiences of gender identity prior to transition; second, it explores the formation of transgender identities. Next, the chapter draws upon recollections of 'significant moments' within the process of transgender identity formation. The chapter then addresses the notion of the 'wrong body' in relation to medical discourse and practice, and subjective understandings of embodiment. Here I consider the extent to which participants' narratives may be read as 'rehearsed narratives', which are constructed and reconstructed through repetition and retelling to particular audiences. The chapter then develops the theme of embodiment to consider the impact of bodily changes upon identity. The penultimate section considers the relevance of analysing transgender identity positions as gender performances and looks at discourses around gender authenticity. Finally, the chapter explores the ways in which transgender identities are linguistically articulated to produce distinct identity positions.

PRE-TRANSITION IDENTITIES

While recollections of childhood may be read as constructed narratives, they remain "materials from which individuals mold current identities and, therefore are valid and significant" (Gagne and Tewksbury, 1997: 486). In recollections of pre-transition identities, all but one of the people interviewed spoke of transgendered feelings or experiences during childhood or puberty. For some participants these feelings manifested themselves at a very young age. David (age 26), for example, says:

> I'd always just identified as being male, I'd never thought of myself as anything else. [. . .] I knew there was a difference at four years old between a boy and a girl, but I never thought of myself as a girl. I thought that one day I'd wake up and I'd be a boy and that would be the end of it. I didn't see it as a long-term thing. I remember having arguments with my parents and having tantrums as a child, saying 'I want to be a boy'. I remember on one occasion crying and my mum telling me 'you're not a boy and that's the end of it'. And I don't remember what led up to it. And so I felt there was nothing my parents could do about it so I didn't talk to them about it. I knew who I was but no one could see that.
>
> And in my teenage years I grew a chest and it was 'where has this come from?'

Dan (age 37) also recalls discomfort with the conventions of femininity as a child:

> [. . .] I had my hair very short. I hated wearing skirts. When I had to wear skirts for school uniform I'd make sure that I did things like wear my father's ties as a rebellious token, something that was my identity because I was different. So conforming in one direction, but not going the whole way. And I used to argue with the teachers at primary school because I wasn't allowed to do woodwork. My parents gave us no gender stereotypes

at all. There were three of us and we did everything, we all did the washing up, we basically had the choices we wanted and we played with each other's toys. There wasn't a problem in that direction. My father did a lot of DIY and I was always the one who helped him and so I couldn't understand why at school I couldn't do woodwork and I had numerous arguments and all they said was 'you can't do it, you're a girl'. [. . .] But the answer as to why I couldn't do these things was because I was girl, which didn't make any sense at all.

Both David and Dan present narratives in which their understandings of the relationships between gender identity and body parts and appearance is arrived at from a young age. While David locates tension between assumed gender identity and self-identity in the home, for Dan, this was worked out at school. In Dan's story, clothes are identified as a key signifier of gender identity and his discomfort with gender identity is linked to his hatred of wearing skirts. Moreover, in modifying his school uniform by wearing his father's ties, Dan used clothes as a means of gender rebellion.

Clothes also appear as a signifier of gender rebellion in the narratives of transgender women. A frequent theme to arise in the childhood recollections of transgender women is the wearing of female clothes as a child. Dionne (age 40), for example, says: "I know I've always had these feelings from when I was a kid. I used to dress up as a girl, all my life, but always in secret." In childhood, participants learnt that clothes are a key cultural indicator of gender. Moreover, dressing in female clothes as a boy can be seen as a form of gender resistance through which assumptions around the intrinsic relationship between biological sex and gendered appearance are challenged. Such a challenge, however, is not easy and, in articulating the secrecy of cross-dressing, participants show that they were aware of the cultural imperative to perform gender appropriately.

In addition to clothes, toys and activities are key signifiers of gender roles in childhood. Common to the narratives of both transgender men and women are childhood recollections of disassociating from perceived gender-appropriate toys or activities. Karen (age 31), for example, says:

As I was going through my younger years I used to identify with females a lot more, I used to have a lot of female friends. I didn't have many male friends, didn't want to play their games and so on. When I got to comprehensive school I tried to be more masculine and to do sports like football and rugby, which I didn't feel very comfortable with but I did them anyway.

Participants' recollections of childhood, then, illustrate how gender rules are learnt from a young age in the home and at school. These stories indicate a developing awareness that resistance to ascribed gender identity is socially unacceptable. Consequently, gender rebellion is largely experienced and practised individually and out of sight of family, friends and teachers. Alienation from culturally determined appropriate gender behaviour is not, however, an exclusive prerogative of transgender biographies. Thus common to both feminist and lesbian life-story narratives is a childhood rejection of stereotypically gendered appearance or activities. Within transgender narratives, however, puberty can be seen to be a particularly significant time for disassociation with assigned gender. Thus many participants speak of the occurrence of transgender feelings during puberty and early adulthood. Amanda (age 45), for example, says:

> Like the old clichés, I didn't feel like the other boys. But it was when puberty came when all the wrong signals came up on the screen so to speak. And then all your hormones are racing and that was a troublesome period that started off massive depressions, clinical depressions. Everyone else was having a great time and I was in and out of the hospital with clinical depression.

Although puberty may mark a subjective turning point in relation to an increased awareness of gender discomfort, the social and cultural pressure to live within the gender binary means that many participants worked hard at conforming to their ascribed gender role. Thus Gabrielle (age 45) speaks about how she worked to maintain her ascribed masculine identity: "I was successful at being a young man as far as other people were concerned and I maintained that externally for quite a long time." Gender management is also evident across the life course. As I will explore in the next section, gender appearance may be maintained, and appropriate gender behaviour practised, for many years through adulthood.

COMING OUT

The formation of a transgender identity came at different life-stages for participants in this research. While a small number of participants came out as transgendered in their teens or early 20s, for many others, transition took place later in life. Gender management is frequently evident across the life course as normative gender appearance and appropriate gender behaviour are practised into adulthood. For many participants, social and cultural pressures to conform to ascribed gender identity are experienced as problematic and, for some, can bring detrimental psychological and physical consequences. Although she had cross-dressed for many years, Lynne (age 67) was in her 50s when she began the process of gender transition:

> I got into a very secret cross-dressing situation, which was really dangerous when I think about it. I mean my livelihood was with the Air Force and by this time I'd got a wife and two kids. It was a stupid thing to do really, looking back on it. You only have to think about attitudes from the military to gay people. And so imagine what would have happened if I'd have said 'I want to be a woman.' So I just kept it to myself. Basically I became a workaholic and when that happens your family life suffers and my wife and I drifted apart.

Here career considerations and family commitments are presented as reasons for later transition. In the following quotation, Gabrielle (age 45) draws attention to the significance of transitional time span in impacting upon experiences and identities of transition:

> In those times, we're going back to late 1960s, early 1970s, that was when I was at school, there was nothing positive that you could ever read or find

about transsexual people or trans issues. It was all sort of drag cabaret type places, in England anyway, or dry medical text books that were basically saying trans people were crazy, or bad, and if they didn't want to be cured they were very bad.

Thus transgender identities and experiences are constructed within specific social and temporal contexts. Certainly, the medical advice given to Bernadette's parents to "[. . .] make a man of him [. . .]" (Bernadette, MtF, age 71) contrasts with the experiences of younger participants. David (age 26), for example, was in his early 20s when he transitioned and his narrative contrasts positively with those of older participants:

I made the decision that I was going to get in touch with a doctor. I was still living at home. I went to the doctor and got myself referred to a psychiatrist. I had a meeting with the psychiatrist who said 'right, we'll start you on treatment'. It was good when my voice started to break. There was no mental change. It was just the changes I had been waiting for a long time. It was just exciting.

For younger participants, social pressures may be less severe, leading to less troubled narratives of transition. In sharp contrast to older participants' recollections of childhood experiences of gender, William (age 25), who transitioned as a teenager, presents a narrative in which gender difference is viewed as a positive attribution: "I always knew something was different and I always liked being different even though maybe I wasn't sure what that was. And I don't know if that is different to some people, but that was quite nice. I've always liked being a bit different."

There are significant differences, then, in the narratives of older and younger participants. As well as benefiting from a medical system that, following pressure from transgender organisations has become more attentive to the demands of transgender people, shifts in cultural politics and social attitudes can be seen to have enabled a less hostile climate. In turn, this can enable people to transition at an earlier age. In addition to enabling greater levels of self-confidence, findings suggest that these moves have also impacted positively upon social worlds and affective communities that give shape to self-understanding. As I will explore in the next section, affective relationships and intimate networks are also positioned as important factors in the decision to begin the process of gender transition.

SIGNIFICANT MOMENTS

A shift in the established routine of work or family life is a significant theme in many participants' narratives of developing a transgender identity. Tony (age 39), for example, connects his decision to begin transition to the break-up of his relationship: "I had known for a long time and I think splitting up with her had a lot to do with it as well." For Dionne (age 40), the decision to begin transition came about after losing a long-standing job: "I had a big trauma in my life. I was in the motor trade and I lost my job. It was about 1988 and my life was in turmoil and I had time to think about everything and what I wanted. And it developed from then."

For these participants, ruptures to key structures brought gender issues to the fore. As well as acting as a significant factor in participants' decisions about when to transition, occupation also impacts upon life experiences through and beyond transition. Findings indicate a notable difference between the identity experiences of participants who are self-employed within cultural fields such as art and music, and those who are employed in more formal occupations. For those employed within manual trades, in particular, coming out to colleagues is often difficult. Cheryl (age 45), for example, who works in engineering, has yet to disclose her transgender identity to her work colleagues: "I sit there at work and this goes over and over in my mind, if we have a quiet day or night it just goes round and round in my head. I really don't know how some of them are going to take it." Cheryl's fears are borne out by the experiences of Amanda (age 45), who works as a security officer for a large urban police force. In the following quotation, Amanda discusses how a work colleague disclosed her transgender identity to the national press:

> They [the tabloid press] did a real number on me. I was betrayed from someone who got into my personnel file [...] The papers were everywhere, people were sitting outside my home, camera lenses everywhere, knocking up the neighbours, going to my dad's, to where my ex-wife works, they even went to the pharmacy where I get my hormones from. They went everywhere, they knocked on every door. It was horrendous.

These narratives contrast with those of participants who work in more progressive environments. For example, Del (age 44), who is an artist, says:

> D: I used to think 'if I can do it then anybody can do it', but the truth is that not anybody can do it. People aren't all, you know, wired up like me. I'm pretty fearless and you can't teach somebody to be fearless. So what works for me is not necessarily going to work for somebody else.
>
> S: So do you feel that you have more privilege?
>
> D: Yeah. I do. I absolutely do. Not privilege that I was born into, but privilege that I have developed through a sporadic education and privilege that comes with having [pause]. Yeah I am privileged. I can live my life as an artist, as a poor artist but I don't have to go out and work in the same kind of ways. I feel like I've paid my dues. I've done that, but I don't have to come into contact with bigoted people in general.

Gabrielle (age 45), who is a musician, also gives a positive account of transitioning at work:

> I officially changed my name and said to the people that were employing me 'I'm ready now, so please call me she' and they were really nice and I kept working in the places that I'd been working. But to be honest I was playing music in bars so it wasn't a big deal.

Significantly, Cheryl and Amanda use the term 'transsexual' to describe their identities, whereas Del and Gabrielle use the term 'queer'. Queer subjectivities, then, may be lived out more smoothly in less constraining work environments, which, in turn, can enable less problematic experiences of transition. Taken a step further, this suggests that social class impacts upon the access to, and the articulation of, queer transgender identities. Findings here contribute to and build upon critical commentary that shows how 'queer' is classed (Hennesy, 1995; Fraser, 1999; Binnie, 2004; Taylor, 2005). Moreover, findings from this research show that participants who are anxious about the reaction of work colleagues seek to adopt normatively feminine or masculine appearances. Participants who are concerned about discrimination at work place more stress on the importance of 'passing' and are more likely to present a medically approved narrative of 'gender dysphoria' to psychiatrists in order to obtain the hormone therapy and surgical procedures required to 'pass'. In contrast, Del (age 44) made his queer identity explicit when requesting hormones from a private psychiatrist:

> I was very clear. I did go to [name of psychiatrist] and I was very clear with
> him that I wasn't a transsexual. And I said I wanted hormones and I would get
> them one way or another, but I would prefer it if he prescribed them to me.

A further significant factor within transitional narratives is intimacy, and the formation of new intimate relationships is often linked to increased self-recognition. Rebecca (age 55), for example, discusses how meeting a new partner enabled her to explore her feelings around gender:

> It wasn't really until maybe eight or ten years ago when my last partner
> allowed me to explore this in a way in which I never had done before that
> I actually started looking closer at it and believing that I could move to a
> gender description that was more congruent with my own feelings.

Self-validation may also come from other sources. For Greg (age 44), leaving home represented a significant moment, which led to developing self-awareness: "I went to university and that was when I first broke away from parental control which had tried to stop me being who I was. [. . .] I was quite excited that there was a category that I did fit into. I wasn't unique. I wasn't on my own."

In these discussions, the emergence of new milieux through breaks with the past routines of work, home life and intimate relationships, enables a shift in gender identity. In discussing emerging self-validation, participants frequently relate to the importance of naming their feelings, which in turn brings the awareness that there are others with similar gender experiences. Cultural resources may also bring collective identification. Amanda (age 45), for example, connected with a song:

> My first contact with anything transgendered was 'Lola', you know, 'The
> Kinks', which was around the same time. And a spike came straight out
> of the radio every time I heard it. I thought 'God, wow'. It was a defining
> moment when I heard the record for the first time.

These discussions point to the significance of cultural representations in developing self-awareness. There is a link here to the role of community in identity formation (Taylor and Whittier, 1992). However, the power of gender normativity meant that for most participants self-validation of gender difference was not enough, leading a majority to seek legitimisation from professional authorities. From their US-based study of the coming-out experiences of transgender women, Gagne and Tewksbury argue that "those whose gender identity and gender presentations fall outside of the binary are stigmatized, ostracized, and socially delegitimized to the extent that they may fail to be socially recognized" (1997: 480). One way of gaining social recognition is through the sanction of the 'expert'. Thus the construction of a transgender identity frequently relies upon medical discourse and practice and access to medical intervention. Findings from this research largely support the argument of Gagne and Tewksbury that "while new identities are emergent, they are created within the constraints of current understandings" (1997: 490). [...] At the heart of medical understanding and practice is the notion of the 'wrong body'. The following section develops this theme to examine how trans-subjectivities are both constructed through, and practised in opposition to, medical discourse around the notion of the 'wrong body'.

NOTES

1. Ekins' work (1993) on the experiences of transitioning from male to female; King's (1993) work, which uses empirical case studies to distinguish between transvestite and transsexual identities, and Monro's work on transgender politics (2005) and the experiences of young trans people (2006b) are important exceptions here.

2. The 'real-life experience' is defined as the full adaptation of a new gender role. Clinicians assess a person's real-life experience by reviewing the following criteria:

    1   to maintain full or part-time employment;
    2   to function as a student;
    3   to function in community-based volunteer activity;
    4   to undertake some combination of items 1–3;
    5   to acquire a (legal) gender-identity-appropriate first name;
    6   to provide documentation that persons other than the therapist know that the patient functions in the desired gender role.

    (Harry Benjamin International Gender Dysphoria Association, 2001)

BIBLIOGRAPHY

Binnie, J. (2004) *The Globalisation of Sexuality*, London: Sage.

Cromwell, J. (1999) *Transmen and FTMs: Identities, Bodies, Genders and Sexualities*, Champaign, IL: University of Illinois Press.

Devor, H. (1989) *Gender Blending: Confronting the Limits of Duality*, Bloomington, IN: Indiana University Press.

Ekins, R. (1993) 'On Male Femaling: A Grounded Theory Approach to Cross-Dressing and Sex-Changing', *Sociological Review*, vol 41: 1–29.

Elkins, R. and King, D. (1999) 'Towards a Sociology of Trangendered Bodies', *Sociological Review*, vol 47: 580–602.

Ekins, R. and King, D. (2006) *The Transgender Phenomenon*, London: Sage.

Feinberg, L. (1996) *Transgender Warriors: Making History From Joan of Arc to Dennis Rodman*, Boston, MA: Beacon Press.

Feinberg, L. (1999) *Trans Liberation: Beyond Pink or Blue*, Boston, MA: Beacon Press.

Fraser, N. (1999) 'Classing Queer: Politics in Competition', *Theory, Culture and Society*, vol 16, no 2: 107–31.

Gagne, P. and Tewksbury, R. (1997) 'Coming Out and Crossing Over: Identity Formation and Proclamation in a Trans-gender Community', *Gender & Society*, vol 11, no 4: 478–508.

Halberstam, J. (1998) *Female Masculinity*, Durham, NC: Duke University Press.

Harry Benjamin International Gender Dysphoria Association (2001) 'Standards of Care for Gender Identity Disorders, Sixth Version', at www.pfc.org.uk/medical/soc2001.htm

Hennessy, R. (1995) 'Queer Visibility in Commodity Culture', in L. Nicholson and S. Seidman (eds) *Social Postmodernism: Beyond Identity Politics*, Cambridge: Cambridge University Press.

Hirschauer, S. (1997) 'The Medicalization of Gender Migration', *International Journal of Transgenderism*, vol 1, no 1, at www.symposion.com/ijt/ijtc0104.htm

King, D. (2003) 'Gender Migration: A Sociological Analysis (or the Leaving of Liverpool)', *Sexualities*, vol 6, no 2: 173–94.

Kulick, D. (1998) *Travesti: Sex, Gender and Culture among Brazilian Transgendered Prostitutes*, Chicago, IL: University of Chicago Press.

Lewins, F. (1995) *Transsexualism in Society: A Sociology of Male-To-Female Transsexuals*, South Melbourne: Macmillan Education.

Monro, S. (2005) *Gender Politics: Citizenship, Activism and Sexual Diversity*, London: Pluto Press.

Monro, S. (2006b) 'Transmuting Binaries: The Theoretical Challenge', *Sociological Research Online*, vol 12, no 1.

Nataf, Z. (1996) *Lesbians Talk Transgender*, London: Scarlet Press.

Taylor, V. and Whittier, N. (1992) 'Collective Identity in Social Movement Communities: Lesbian Feminist Mobilization', in A. Morris and C. Mueller (eds) *Feminist Frontiers*, New York, NY: McGraw Hill.

Taylor, Y. (2005) 'The Gap and How to Mind It: Intersections of Class and Sexuality', *Sociological Research Online*, vol 10, no 3.

Wilson, M. (2002) '"I am the Prince of Pain, for I am a Princess in the Brain": Liminal Transgender Identities, Narratives and the Elimination of Ambiguities', *Sexualities*, vol 5, no 4: 425–48.

———————————— ○ ————————————

END OF CHAPTER QUESTIONS

1. What is transphobia?
2. Why is community important to identity formation for a transgender person?
3. How are transgender identities and experiences constructed within social contexts?
4. What social pressures are placed on transgender people?

Good and Messy

Lesbian and Transgender Identities

Matt Richardson

Of the list of questions that we have collectively considered, the one that most animates me is this: how do we address the contentious borders between lesbian and transgender identities, between passing women and transmen, and between gender identity and sexual identity? It is an interesting question because it forces us to acknowledge that these borders are not only contentious, but also messy. And I think that is a good thing.

People are wonderfully creative in their gender expressions and sexual identities. For example, in working-class Black trans communities that I'm familiar with, some people who have been assigned female at birth are content to keep their bodies the same, but use male pronouns for themselves. Not everyone has the ability or the desire to change their birth-sex assignment physically, socially, and/or legally. However some people elect to be understood as men and identified as such, at least in some spaces and with selected people, as a possible way of inhabiting manhood. This kind of flexibility allows for trans people to gather multiple communities around them. One can be a (masculine) woman with certain family members, with employers, or during interactions with the state but also have a section of one's life where one's manhood is validated with male pronouns.

There is both an expansiveness and particularity to such locally created understandings of gender. The terms "dom," "stud," "aggressive," and "butch" refer to female masculinity. However, these terms have cultural and regional specificity and some inventiveness with respect to pushing the boundaries of masculinity. For example, in the New York area "aggressive" is a nuanced identity that is multi-dimensional. In addition to connoting masculinity, it can be used by people who embrace femininity a central component to their gender identity.[1] "Stem" (or the combination of "stud" and "femme") is a Southern African American term for someone who identifies as masculine and feminine.

The alternative to such messiness is the impossible demand that everyone claim a non-normative gender or sexuality identify in the same way and call themselves the same thing. The globalization of the terms "queer" and "LGBT" can be critiqued for precisely such a reason, because the normative use of these terms functions as a colonizing maneuver.[2] The implicit pressure to use these terms in order to access funding, especially from international granting agencies, contorts the variety and expanded possibilities of local understandings into an often ill-fitting consistency and stability. Within the United States, people imagine themselves in terms other than the limited available sense of transition and trans-identification. For example, I have heard some US Black women say, "When I am applying for funding, then I am transgender. Otherwise, I'm just a woman."

Matt Richardson, "Good and Messy: Lesbian and Transgender Identities," *Feminist Studies*, vol. 39, no. 2, pp. 371-374. Copyright © 2013 by Feminist Studies, Inc. Reprinted with permission. Provided by ProQuest LLC. All rights reserved.

The fixed imagined borders between sexual identity and gender identity are enlivened by the inability to recognize that transpeople can also be lesbians and gay men. The quote above about being "just a woman" requires us to expand our understanding of the categories that are familiar to us. Trans people identify with, and mingle within, sexually diverse networks. When we think in restricted terms, we forget the fact that transpeople have been part of lesbian and gay communities for a long time. To draw an example from my own life: about twenty years ago, before I started my own transition, I was part of a lesbian and gay organization in northern New England. This was (and still is) a predominantly rural part of the country. At that time, I was a part of small band of lesbian and gay adults who tried to start a youth group in a place where there was virtually nothing for queer youth except suspicion and sometimes outright hostility from educational institutions and local law enforcement. We had a debate (shortlived, but a debate nonetheless) about whether or not to include trans kids in our services. One argument was that this was an organization for young lesbians and gay men (we pretty much ignored bisexual people) and that according to the prevailing notions, transsexuals, as we called them, were straight people waiting to get surgery in order to join the majority in heterosexual privilege. I pointed out that one of the women who had been a major part of our lesbian community for almost thirty years was trans and that we were denying the longstanding presence of transpeople in our own circle when taking an exclusionary position. Of course, today, the inclusion of transgender youth would no longer be as controversial and would not be predicated on proving their gayness. However, this incident is relevant here because of the inability of some to contemplate how transpeople have participated, and continue to participate, in the creation and emergence of lesbian and gay culture and identity.

Another example I can draw on from oral histories I have conducted is of a Black transwoman who was kicked out of African Ancestral Lesbians United for Societal Change in the early 1990s. Until she was outed, she had been part of that community for some time, participating in dialogues and events and helping to sustain the organization. Members of the organization determined, however, that she was a "male infiltrator" who had to be extracted. Her assertion that she was a lesbian among lesbians was viewed as a hostile takeover in the eyes of the other members of the group. What would happen if, instead of being an object of fear and suspicion, there was recognition among lesbians that transwomen have helped shape lesbian politics and culture? How would that change the narrative of women's history?

On a related note, I think that there is a lot of potential for research on transmen who are in relationships with cisgender men.[3] I have been in conversation with Black men about their sexual encounters and relationships with cisgender gay men. Speaking about their attractions and relationships with other transmen and genderqueer people is something that white transmen and genderqueer men talk about fairly openly, but for Black men, such conversations are rare. When formal internal conversations do occur, they are well attended, perhaps because the opportunity occurs so infrequently. Transmen who are attracted to men repeatedly express a fear of not being considered a "real man" if they present as gay or bisexual, or of being found out by their women partners, who in turn are afraid that their transmen partners are HIV infected because they had sexual relationships with men (the "down low" discourse is very dangerous in this regard).[4] Cisgendered men, on the other hand, say their interest in transmen has a lot to do with wanting a particular gender presentation—specifically partners who are "straight looking" and "straight acting." Some gay men look to gay transmen for the hypermasculine gender and same-sex attraction they seek.

Finally, the fact that lesbians are sometimes attracted to and have long-term relationships with transmen also speaks to the messiness of these sexual and gender identity boundaries. How do we talk about the phenomenon of lesbian desire for (trans)men in our rendering of lesbian history? These are the kinds of complications and questions that confront us, and they remind us that categories are messy and continually changing—and with them, women's history.

NOTES

1. For the best examples of this, see the documentary *The Aggressives*, directed by Daniel Peddle (Los Angeles: Seventh Art, 2005), 75 mins.

2. For a discussion of disidentification with LGBT identities, see David Valentine, *Imagining Transgender: An Ethnography of a Category* (Durham, NC: Duke University Press, 2007); and Arnaldo Cruz-Malave and Martin Manalansan, eds,, *Queer Globalizations: Citizenship and the Afterlife of Colonialism* (New York: New York University Press, 2002).

3. "Cisgender" is a term that has emerged in queer scholarship to refer to someone who is not transgender. In other words, a person's gender "matches" with the sex assigned at birth according to dominant norms. See Julia Serano, "Whipping Girl FAQ on Cissexual, Cisgender, and Cis Privilege," *Live-Journal* (blog), May 14, 2009, http://juliaserano.livejournal.com/14700.html.

4. On February 1, 2000, *The Village Voice* ran an article by Guy Trebay entitled "Homo Thugz Blow Up the Spot: Gay Hip Hop Scene Rises in the Bronx," focusing on a group of Black men in New York who were not discernibly gay by mainstream gender standards, nor gay-identified, and some of whom maintained relationships with women. The article implied that these men who "keep it on the d.l.," as one informant noted, are partially responsible for the rise of HIV infection in Black communities. A series of articles, books, documentaries, films, Oprah episodes, and a general cultural fascination with the "d.l." have followed.

———————————— o ————————————

END OF CHAPTER QUESTIONS

1. How do we address the borders between lesbian and transgender identities?

The History of the Idea of the Lesbian as a Kind of Person

Nan Alamilla Boyd

I'm going to start with the observation that the term lesbian is contested. One of the reasons why lesbian is contested is that lesbian history, as a field, often confuses the identity, as a container, with the community or social form that engages that identity. Historians wonder: Does someone have to verbally identify as a lesbian to be part of a lesbian community? Can we call a community lesbian if people don't use that term?

I would argue that lesbian history is actually the history of an idea rather than a group of people. Lesbian history includes all those involved in the discursive production of the category; that is, it includes all of the actors and institutions that participate in the production of meanings that contribute to the articulation and rearticulation of the concept lesbian, as it changes over time and moves across space.

One way that lesbian as an idea moves across time and space is as part of the process of the globalization of Western culture and capital—as an aspect of neocolonialism. But the concept of the lesbian as a kind of person is also transported and consumed via transnational media, moving in many directions. It is also transported and consumed via the realignment of capital. Clearly, the possible meanings of the category lesbian change in a transnational context, and they may change in a way that's useful to those doing the importing or consuming. So I wouldn't necessarily argue that every time the idea of the lesbian as a kind of person is taken up in a non-Western context that it's a neocolonial cultural form. However, I would assume that when the term lesbian is taken up in a non-Western context, it probably means something different than it did in a Western colonial context. But even in a Western colonial context ideas are going to mutate or be transformed or utilized in new ways any time that global capital forces the movement of people and the rearticulation of ideas about family and sexuality. All these forces work together to produce transnational cultures that reframe the meanings of gender and sexuality for new purposes. So, while I don't think the term lesbian can be used as an umbrella term for female same-sex sexualities across time and place, I do think it's important to discuss how and why the term continues to be taken up and consumed.

Along these lines. I'd like to comment on the contentious borders between lesbian and transgender identities, something I've written about and continue to teach. Like the movement of the idea of the lesbian as a kind of person across time and place (an identity that some people claim but many people participate in the discursive production of), the content or meanings attached to that idea have changed over time and place so that sometimes lesbian also means gender transgression (as in the sexological phrase "sexual inversion"); or sometimes lesbian also means racial or national identity (for example, US colonial or white Western); or sometimes lesbian also means aesthetic or political values (anti-style, anti-war); or sometimes lesbian means specific sexual behaviors (for example, no penetration or sex with dildos). These are just some stereotypical examples. Similarly, the idea of the transsexual as a kind of person has a history that has changed over time, sometimes overlapping with ideas attached to sexual identity or sexual behavior.

How do we address this overlap? I think it's possible to do so in much the same way that feminist historians have addressed other intersecting and overlapping identities or cultural practices: by historicizing the production of meanings. It is important to consider how people use or claim identities, allowing for messy interactions between ideas and their utility. In this way, when looking at the history of the production of meanings, it would make sense for someone, for instance, participating in an oral history interview to claim, "I didn't always identify as a person of color," or "I didn't always identify as a lesbian," or "I didn't always identify as a woman or a transsexual, but I do now . . . or I do sometimes . . . and here's why."

On the other hand, I think it's interesting that the idea of the lesbian as a kind of person who has always been a lesbian and will always be a lesbian exists. It's important to note that this idea (of the lifelong or "gold star" lesbian) has a lot of ideological weight. It's important to investigate (that is, historicize) the reasons why this idea has, in certain times and places, taken on a timeless and transhistorical application—as if the history of the idea does not merit investigation. Foucault warns us that it is at these moments that power is functioning in an uncontested manner, and I think it's important to ask: To whom is this idea useful? Whom does it serve? And when asked this way, it makes sense to consider the role lesbian historians and lesbian history have played in reproducing or reiterating these ideas, that is, in reifying an uncontested category.

When writing history, constructing historical narrative, it makes sense to consider that the communities attached to essentialized identities are also changing all the time. They have a history and a political utility that has something to do with the deployment of the idea of identity, but the history of the identity is often subsumed by the history of the community. This is an issue I thought about a lot while researching and writing *Wide Open Town*. In *Wide Open Town*, I make the case for two political constituencies (although of course there were more): one based on homophile activism (individual rights and a politics of sameness) and the other based in the bars and fights for the right to public assembly (group rights and a politics of difference). Many people I interviewed expressed both values and participated in both movements. Still, it is possible, as a historian, to trace the history of each as if they were separate communities with separate constituencies. And to some people, it felt that way: they never went to bars, while others wouldn't be caught dead at a Daughters of Bilitis (homophile activist) meeting. Generally, in writing my book, I associated homophile activism with the identity "lesbian" and bar-based activists with the identity "gay women," but there were many homophile activists who didn't use the term lesbian to describe themselves, and there were many gay women in bars who sometimes called themselves lesbians, or started to later in life, so that by the time I interviewed them they were mixing up the terms, and it was not clear when lesbian as an identity (or shorthand for community) became useful to them. In the end, it was unclear under what conditions the term lesbian was deployed, but I do know that it was deployed. And I do know that a lot of people contributed to its deployment and thus played a role in lesbian history per se. And while I really wanted to be able to historicize the utility of the deployment of the identity-based category "lesbian" around a specific set of political ideas, I couldn't. But I tried. And I guess what I want to say is that I tried, I wanted to historicize the idea of the lesbian as a historical actor, especially in relation to gender-transgressive identities and behaviors, but what I got was the history of a community that engaged with these ideas in different ways.

Also, as I mentioned earlier, when ideas, such as the concept of the lesbian as a particular type of person, are deployed really effectively, they take on a kind of materiality and cultural weight. The idea of the lesbian as a kind of person becomes a common sense way of humanizing historical actors in a way that's very difficult to challenge or historicize, but I think it's worth it. I think it's important to keep the history of the idea in mind when researching and writing the history of the community.

———————————— ○ ————————————

END OF CHAPTER QUESTIONS

1. What is your reaction to the title of the essay?
2. What is your reaction to the essay?
3. Why is it important to understand the history of "lesbian"?

ABOUT THE AUTHOR

S age Mauldin is an Adjunct Professor of Human Relations in the Department of Human Relations, and an Affiliate Faculty Member in the Department of Women's, Gender, and Sexuality Studies at The University of Oklahoma. Additionally, he serves as a reviewer for the Critical, Social Justice, and Diversity Perspectives track for the Academy of Human Resource Development.

Mauldin teaches courses every semester, focusing on subjects such as LGBT+ Activism, Human Rights, and Political Activism.

In 2018, Mauldin was recommended by the Mayor of Norman, Lynne Miller, and elected by Norman's City Council to serve as a Human Rights Commissioner for the City of Norman. In this role, he assists in the enforcement of fair employment practices in city contracts, makes recommendations to Norman's City Council for actions deemed necessary to the furtherance of equality and human rights, and institutes and conducts educational programs to promote understanding among all persons and groups in Norman.

Also in 2018, Mauldin was elected to serve on the American Civil Liberties Union (ACLU) of Oklahoma Board of Directors. In this role, he helps establish the vision, mission, and values of the organization, sets strategy and structure for the organization, and ensures the organization's structure and capability are appropriate for implementing chosen strategies.

Throughout Mauldin's career, he has been a vocal advocate for the rights of vulnerable and protected populations. He is the author and editor of *LGBT+ Issues in the United States*.

Mauldin received his BA in Psychology and MA in Human Relations from The University of Oklahoma.

Lastly, in 2018, Mauldin was selected as a NextGen Under 30 winner in the Adult & Higher Education category.